Generation to Generation

Generation to Generation

Life Cycles of the Family Business

Kelin E. Gersick
John A. Davis
Marion McCollom Hampton
Ivan Lansberg

Harvard Business School Press
Boston, Massachusetts

Library of Congress Cataloging-in-Publication Data

Generation to generation : life cycles of the family business /
   Kelin E. Gersick . . . [et al.].
        p.   cm.
   Includes bibliographical references and index.
   ISBN 0-87584-555-X (alk. paper)
      1. Family-owned business enterprises—Management.
2. Family-owned   business   enterprises—Succession.
I. Gersick, Kelin E.
HD62.25.G46 1997
658'.041—dc20   96-12529
                                                        CIP

The paper used in this publication meets the requirements
of the American National Standard for Permanence of
Paper for Printed Library Materials Z39.49-1984

Contents

Preface

ONE OF KURT LEWIN'S most famous aphorisms is "There is nothing so practical as a good theory." But that was only half of his message, and our experience writing this book also supports the other part, that nothing contributes more to good theory than practice. The four authors of this book all came to their focus on family business from academic backgrounds. All of us had been university based, conducting research and teaching undergraduate and graduate students. But each of us had also been drawn to the applied aspects of social science, so we were also consultants and field researchers. In our work with family businesses we found a great opportunity. This was a field drawing on the richest traditions of all the social and management sciences, which presented unexplored conceptual and theoretical territory and still provided almost-unlimited opportunities to offer practical service to fascinating real-world clients.

The particular activity that brought us together and got us writing this book was a consultation. In the early 1980s, John Davis and Ivan Lansberg began a project with Caterpillar, Inc. That multinational giant, itself a $100 billion, publicly held company that began as a family firm, distributes its product in North America through a network of independent dealerships—95 percent of which are family businesses. The executive leadership of Caterpillar wanted to assist its dealership group in all aspects of business survival, including managing family operations and continuity. In 1983 the Owner Managed Business Institute began what became a decade of collaboration with Caterpillar on these issues. Kelin Gersick joined the project in 1984 and Marion McCollom, in 1989. For all of us, that team effort was a unique and invigorating experience.

It was our work with the seventy Caterpillar dealers that prompted us to formalize the model presented in this book. As we got to know the owner-managers, their families, and their companies, we began to appreciate the characteristics that they shared and those that differentiated them. Our frequent meetings to plan week-long seminars and to discuss visits to individual dealerships began to evolve into conceptual generalizations and model building.

At the same time, we all began to chronicle the general issues that came up in our work with other family firms, which by then numbered in the hundreds. Our experience was also becoming more international. We developed family business programs with the Institute for Management Development in Lausanne, Switzerland; with University de Adolfo Ibañez in Chile; with INCAE throughout Central and South America; and with the Young President's Organization (YPO) around the world. We were accumulating details and stories, and at the same time becoming frustrated with the limitations of individual cases in the absence of theory. Our histories as academics began to nudge us into thinking more conceptually. We were convinced there must be a useful underlying framework that would help us make sense of our experiences and do better work in the future.

So frustration, the excitement of discovery, and the stimulation of colleagues led us to create the developmental model of family business presented here. This book is a pause to get it down on paper, but it is not an end point. We continue to revise our thinking as we learn more about these complex, fascinating companies. We look forward to commentary and further collaboration with our professional colleagues, and especially to responses from business owners. This is a new field, with much unexplored territory. The best work will emerge from dialogue among consultants, researchers, and the participants in family businesses themselves.

For that dialogue to continue, one important set of rules must be about honoring the privacy of the companies discussed. Confidentiality is very important to all of the companies with which we work and from which we have accumulated our experience. When a company's real name is used in this book, it means that either the individuals have specifically consented to be included or the story was taken from a publication or public forum. Most of the cases and vignettes that we use are disguised in some way. Some are descriptions of a single case; others are combinations of more than one case, changing names, industries, or other nonessential characteristics to make the sources unrecognizable. All of the examples are "real," but most have been altered. This is our best effort to satisfy the requirements of both good evidence and professional ethics.

Acknowledgments

T HE FIRST PEOPLE we need to thank for making this book possible are the families who have taught us what we know about family business. We have met hundreds of families of all sizes from all over the world. They invited us into their businesses and their lives. In the process of working with us on their goals, each family added something—a new story about child-rearing, a unique estate planning dilemma, an illustration of cultural differences in Chile or Norway, an industry with unusual constraints on strategy—and it is those stories and the lessons we learned from them that created this book.

In particular we want to mention the executives at Caterpillar Inc., especially Dave Lewis, Bob Kinne, and Ron Bonati, who sponsored the original project that got us rolling as a team. The Caterpillar dealers were very generous in sharing their experiences with us over a period of more than a decade, and many of their dilemmas and solutions are embedded in our model.

The Harvard Business School Press has our sincere thanks for helping us turn our ideas into a publication. Carol Franco's initial enthusiasm for the book convinced us that it would be worthwhile to try to write it; Hollis Heimbouch's continuous prodding and enthusiasm are what got us over the hurdles. All of the other staff at the Press, in editing, design, and marketing, have been a pleasure to work with. We also want to thank By Barnes and Howard Stevenson of the Harvard Business School for their extremely helpful reviews of earlier drafts.

It is especially important to us as participants in this young and developing professional field to acknowledge the influence and contributions of our colleagues. In the text we have tried to note the work of others that has laid the foundation for our own thinking. Beyond that, we want to try to recognize the enormous debt we owe to those individuals who have been our mentors. They have been teachers, advisers, sponsors, guides—and, ultimately, dear and trusted friends. To Dan Levinson, Ron Tagiuri, Dick Beckhard, Barbara Hollander, and Mort Deutsch: In ways that neither you nor we can isolate, your wisdom and teaching are embedded in the heart of our work.

Finally, we dedicate this book, with love, to our families.

To our parents and siblings,
who were the first to teach us about families and enterprise

To our spouses,
Connie, Nancy, Tom, and Margarita—our true partners

To the children in our lives,
who are our best hopes and our fondest dreams

Generation to Generation

Introduction

A Developmental Model of Family Business

WAL-MART. CARGILL. McGraw-Hill. As well as Petralli and Sons Auto Repair, Ethel's Tree Service, and Goldman Furniture Co. This book is about families who own or manage businesses and about the businesses themselves—from the corner convenience store with a handful of employees to the multinational conglomerate with fifty thousand. They include some of the best-known companies in the United States, as well as the thousands of unknowns. The variety is enormous, but all these varied companies share one core characteristic: they are connected to a family, and that connection is what makes them a special kind of business.

Some of those companies proudly identify themselves as family businesses, like the third-generation furniture store with brothers and sisters and cousins in all of the management roles. Others are controlled by families but do not think of themselves primarily as family businesses, but rather as "private" companies, manufacturers, real estate brokers, or members of the construction industry. Either way, the people involved feel the difference. Family business owners are well aware of how different their role is from that played by shareholders in companies owned by many public investors. Employees in family businesses know the difference that family control makes in their work lives, the company culture, and their careers. Marketers appreciate the advantage that the image of a family business presents to customers. And families know that being in business together is a powerful part of their lives.

Who Are the Family Firms?

Family businesses are the predominant form of enterprise around the world. They are so much a part of our economic and social landscape that we completely take them for granted. In capitalist economies, most firms start with the ideas, commitment, and investment of entrepreneurial individuals and their relatives. Married couples pool their savings and run a store together. Brothers and sisters learn their parents' business as children, hanging around behind the counters or outside the loading dock after school. It is not just an American dream to make a business venture succeed and then to add "and Sons" (and recently "and Daughters") to the sign over the front door. The success and continuity of family businesses are the economic Emerald City for a large portion of the world's population.

Articles on family business make various guesses about the number of family-controlled companies, but even the most conservative estimates put the proportion of all worldwide business enterprises that are owned or managed by families between 65 and 80 percent.[1] It is true that many of these companies are small sole proprietorships, which will never grow or be passed down from generation to generation. But it is also true that many of them are among the largest and most successful businesses in the world. It is estimated that 40 percent of the Fortune 500 are family owned or controlled.[2] Family businesses generate half of the U.S. gross domestic product (GDP) and employ half the workforce. In Europe, family firms dominate the small and medium-sized firms and are the majority of larger firms in some countries.[3] In Asia, the form of family control varies across nations and cultures, but family firms hold dominant positions in all of the most developed economies except China.[4] In Latin America, *grupos* built and controlled by families are the primary form of private ownership in most industrial sectors.[5]

If family businesses are so common, how can they also be special? When Freud was asked what he considered to be the secret of a full life, he gave a three-word answer: "*Lieben und arbeiten* [to love and to work]." For most people, the two most important things in their lives are their families and their work. It is easy to understand the compelling power of organizations that combine both. Being in a family firm affects all the participants. The role of chairman of the board is different when the company was founded by your father and when your mother and siblings sit around the table at board meetings, just as they sat around the dinner table. The job of a CEO is different when the vice president in the next office is also a younger sister. The role of partner is different when the other partner is a spouse or a child. The role of sales representative is different when you cover the same territory that your parent did twenty-five years earlier, and your grandparent twenty-five years before that. Even walking through the door on your first day of work on an assembly line or in a billing office is different if the name over that door is your own.

This sense of difference is not just a feeling. It is rooted in the reality of the business. Companies owned and managed by families are a special organizational form whose "specialness" has both positive and negative consequences. Family businesses draw special strength from the shared history, identity, and common language of families. When key managers are relatives, their traditions, values, and priorities spring from a common source. Verbal and nonverbal communication can be greatly speeded up in families. Owner-managers can decide to solve a problem "like we did it with Uncle Harry." Spouses and siblings are more likely to understand each other's spoken preferences and hidden strengths and weaknesses. Most important, commitment, even to the point of self-sacrifice, can be asked for in the name of the general family welfare.

However, this same intimacy can also work against the professionalism of executive behavior. Lifelong histories and family dynamics can intrude in business relationships. Authority may be harder to exercise with relatives. Roles in the family and in the business can become confused. Business pressures can overload and burn out family relationships. When they are working poorly, families can create levels of tension, anger, confusion, and despair that can destroy good businesses and healthy families amazingly quickly. The public is well aware of family tragedies that can accompany business disasters. The Bingham family in Louisville, the Pulitzers, and the du Ponts make for compelling reading. For many years "Dallas" and "Dynasty" were the two most popular television programs in the world, portraying an America of wealthy business families tearing themselves apart.

It is unfortunate that the sensational failures sometimes overshadow the beauty of successful family enterprise. When they are working well, families can bring a level of commitment, long-range investment, rapid action, and love for the company that nonfamily businesses yearn for but seldom achieve. *Lieben* and *arbeiten* together are a powerful foundation for a satisfying life. Family businesses are tremendously complicated, and at the same time these firms are critical to the health of our economy and to the life satisfaction of millions of people.

However, professionals are not always prepared to deal with the special nature of family companies. The influence of families on the businesses they own and manage is often invisible to management theorists and business schools. The core topics of management education—organizational behavior, strategy, finance, marketing, production, and accounting—are taught without differentiating between family and nonfamily businesses. The economic models underlying most management science depend on interchangeability of decision makers, so that it does not make any difference "who" anybody is. Business newspapers and magazines usually treat family involvement in a firm as anecdotal information—colorful and interesting, but rarely important.

This book presents a model for understanding this extraordinary form of business. It is designed to help professionals from all disciplines—business consultants, lawyers, accountants, family counselors, psychologists, and other advisers—to work with the enormous complexity of these systems. It is also intended to help family business owners think more clearly about themselves.

Conceptual Models of Family Firms

The study of family business is still relatively new. The scholarly work began with consultants' case descriptions of family firms. In the last few decades, researchers from management and organizational sciences have begun to apply their models, from organizational behavior, strategy, human resource management, and finance, to smaller-sized or privately owned companies. At the same time, family therapists have begun to apply concepts such as differentiation, enmeshment/disengagement, and triangles to the subgroup of families who have businesses. The contributions of these scholars and practitioners, as well as the work of psychologists, sociologists, economists, lawyers, accountants, historians, and others, have begun to coalesce into conceptual models of family business.

Family Businesses as Systems

The study of family businesses as systems began with a few standalone articles in the 1960s and 1970s.[6] These early classics focused on typical problems that appeared to hinder family firms, such as nepotism, generational and sibling rivalry, and unprofessional management. The underlying conceptual model held that family businesses are actually made up of two overlapping subsystems: the family and the business.[7] Each of these two "circles" has its own norms, membership rules, value structures, and organizational structures. Problems arise because the same individuals have to fulfill obligations in both circles; for example, as parents and as professional managers. In addition, the business itself has to operate according to sound business practices and principles, while at the same time meeting family needs for employment, identity, and income. From the beginning, it was clear that finding strategies that satisfy both subsystems is the key challenge facing all family enterprise.[8]

This two-system concept is still very much in evidence today. Researchers and scholars use it as a basis for their analyses of complex organizational behavior, strategy, competitiveness, and family dynamics. Consultants and other practitioners find it useful in clarifying the sources of individuals' behavior and decisions. For example, an estate planning attorney may be puzzled by a client's reluctance to implement the most rational distribution plan, until she considers the client's conflict between his desires as a parent (to treat each offspring equally) and as a business owner (to consolidate control in one successor). Similarly, an apparently illogical expansion strategy for a growing company may make sense only when one understands the needs of coowner siblings to keep their divisions equal size, no matter what. The conflicting pressure that the family and business circles put on individuals in the middle was the first practical concept in this field of study.

Tagiuri and Davis elaborated the two-system model with their work at Harvard in the early 1980s.[9] They argued that a more accurate portrayal of the full range of family firms would need to make a critical distinction between the ownership and management subsystems within the business circle. That is, some individuals are owners but not involved in the operation of the business; others are managers but do not control shares. Our work with many different sizes of companies has supported their argument that many of the most important dilemmas faced by family businesses—for example, the dynamics of complex, cousin-controlled family businesses—have more to do with the distinction between owners and managers than between the family and the business as a whole. As a result, the *three-circle model* (figure I-1) emerged.

The three-circle model describes the family business system as three

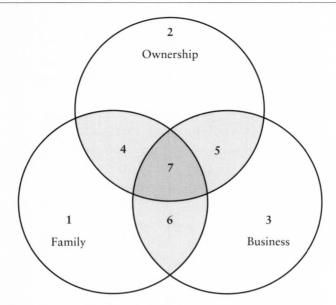

Figure I-1 ■ *The Three-Circle Model of Family Business*

independent but overlapping subsystems: business, ownership, and family. Any individual in a family business can be placed in one of the seven sectors that are formed by the overlapping circles of the subsystems. For example, all owners (partners or shareholders), and *only* owners, will be somewhere within the top circle. Similarly, all family members are somewhere in the bottom left circle and all employees, in the bottom right. A person who has only one connection to the firm will be in one of the outside sectors— 1, 2, or 3. For example, a shareholder who is not a family member and not an employee belongs in sector 2—inside the ownership circle, but outside the others. A family member who is neither an owner nor an employee will be in sector 1.

Individuals who have more than one connection to the business will be in one of the overlapping sectors, which fall in two or three of the circles at the same time. An owner who is also a family member but not an employee will be in sector 4, which is inside both the ownership and family circles. An owner who works in the company but is not a family member will be in sector 5. Finally, an owner who is also a family member and an employee would be in the center sector, 7, which is inside all three circles. Every individual who is a member of the family business system has one location, and only one location, in this model.

The reason that the three-circle model has met with such widespread acceptance is that it is both theoretically elegant and immediately applicable. It is a very useful tool for understanding the source of interpersonal conflicts, role dilemmas, priorities, and boundaries in family firms. Specifying different roles and subsystems helps to break down the complex interactions within a family business and makes it easier to see what is actually happening, and why. For example, family struggles over dividend policy or succession planning become understandable in a new way if each participant's position in the three-circle model is taken into account. An individual in sector 4 (a family member/owner/nonemployee) may want to increase dividends, feeling that it is a legitimate reward of family membership and a reasonable return on investment as an owner. On the other hand, a person in sector 6 (a family member/employee/nonowner) may want to suspend dividends in order to reinvest in expansion, which might create better career advancement opportunities. These two individuals may also be siblings—similar in personality and style, and with a close emotional bond—who do not understand why they cannot agree on this question. Another common example concerns the difficult decisions a family must make about offering jobs to family members. Which children should be employed in the business? How much should they be paid? Will they be promoted? Viewed through the three-circle lens, different individuals' opinions on questions like these become more understandable. A person in sector 1 (family circle only) might feel, "Give them all a chance. They're all our children." Sector 3 (business circle only), on the other hand, could say, "We only hire relatives if they are better than all other candidates, and their career movement is determined strictly by performance." The three-circle model helps everyone see how organizational role can color a person's point of view; personality conflicts are not the only explanation.

A further example can illustrate how messages from all three circles can be exchanged at the same time. The board of directors of Tru-Color, Inc., a family-owned paint manufacturer, is trying to decide how to respond to a buyout offer from a large competitor. The board is made up of six members of the Franklin family (figure I-2).[10] Mr. Franklin, Al, and Carol work in the company. Because they are simultaneously family members, employees, and owners, they are in sector 7 of the three-circle model. Mrs. Franklin, Bob, and David do not work in the firm. As family owners, they are in sector 4. David has never participated in the board and has given his proxy to his mother. As the board debates the offer, each person's

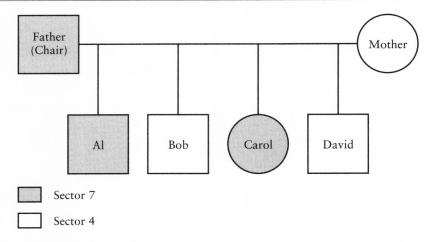

Figure I-2 ■ *The Franklin Family*

statements reflect his or her role in all three circles: the family, the business, and the ownership group. In table I-1, on page 9, excerpts from their conversation appear in the left-hand column. Columns 2, 3, and 4 present the "between the lines" points that each individual is trying to make, reflecting his or her three different roles.

Mr. Franklin is convinced that he is serving all his roles—chair, CEO, and father—by keeping the company. As a father, Mr. Franklin is most concerned with his responsibility to take care of his family financially. He describes the company as his "legacy" for his children. As CEO, he wants to protect his authority to run the company as he sees fit, and as chair of the board, he insists that shares in Tru-Color are still a wise investment. His most vocal challenger is his second son, Bob, who views the same decision from the point of view of a younger sibling, nonemployee, and minority investor. Bob is acting as a son who has always had a difficult relationship with his father, as a critical observer of the CEO's management style, and as a worried investor. The two men may be in conflict on many things, but their disagreement on this issue appears more rational and less arbitrary in light of their very different roles in each circle.

As the meeting progresses, other board members join the debate (see table I-2, page 10). Siblings may have grown up in the same family, but they also represent different combinations of roles. In the conversation captured in table I-2, Carol is not only guided by her personality and indi-

Table 1-1 ■ Tru-Color, Inc.: Bob's Opinions

Actual Conversation	Family Circle Perspective	Business Circle Perspective	Ownership Circle Perspective
Chair: I've resisted bringing this matter to a vote because I prefer us to reach consensus. But I'm beginning to see that may not be possible. As you know, I'm very opposed to this sale—especially at this time, when the company is on the brink of tremendous growth.	**Father:** I've always tried to involve each of you kids in decisions, but some of you are too stubborn to listen to reason. I founded this company, and I'm not about to give it away. It will be my legacy to each of you.	**CEO:** I believe in participative decision making, but only with my key managers—not passive owners. The company is running very well and is still profitable. We have many new initiatives, and our forecast is for significant growth.	**Chair (30 percent):** My position is very firm: we should not sell. The offer is totally inadequate, especially at this time, when we're anticipating tremendous growth.
Board member Bob: You've talked about growth for years, but is it realistic? The new solvent may never be patented. Perhaps we should take a bird in the hand.	**Second son Bob:** I know I should keep my mouth shut, but somehow I can't keep myself from disagreeing with Dad. He's a dreamer, and he's never appreciated my realistic opinions anyway.	**Nonemployee Bob:** Your leadership used to be great, but the business world has passed you by. The old, paternalistic style of dealing with employees just doesn't work anymore.	**Shareholder Bob (10 percent):** Our dividends have been dropping steadily. The patent on the new solvent may never be granted. I think it's time to cash out.
Chair: In my view, you've opposed every move I've made with this company since you joined the board. What do you really want?	**Father:** You've always complained but never really tried to be a success at anything except basketball. Your mother and I have given you every chance.	**CEO:** That's typical of you. You know nothing about this company or this industry.	**Chair:** Why can't you see that this company is your best opportunity for return on your investment?

Table I-2 ■ Tru-Color, Inc.: Carol's Opinions

Actual Conversation	Family Circle Perspective	Business Circle Perspective	Ownership Circle Perspective
Board member Carol: I think the board should let those of us who also work in the company make the decision. The chair has been running this company for almost thirty years, and his judgment has been pretty damn good so far. If he wants to turn down the offer, I don't see why we need a vote. It's his company, and that's that.	**Daughter Carol:** Dad has always taken care of us and provided everything that we own. He knows what's best. It's his decision, and that's that.	**Sales manager Carol:** The executives and managers should make the decision. You can't get any perspective on current operations from the outside. There were lots of reasons why sales were flat last quarter. New owners would almost certainly mean layoffs. A lot of us would be out of work.	**Shareholder Carol (10 percent):** Bob has always seen this as just an investment, looking only at short-term returns. If the chair wants to turn down the offer, I don't see why we need a vote. He and his wife's proxy control the company anyway.
Board member Bob: I absolutely disagree. That's not how this board should work. Ever since you became sales manager and received these shares, you've been nothing but a yes-woman.	**Second son Bob:** That's so typical of you. Whatever Dad says must be right. When are you going to grow up and stand on your own two feet?	**Nonemployee Bob:** Being inside the company makes you absolutely blind. Blind loyalty! If that's the kind of behavior that is rewarded by this CEO, how can we have confidence in the company?	**Shareholder Bob:** That's not responsible director behavior. You support the chair on every issue. Employee shareholders should not be on the board. We need a critical evaluation of shareholder interests here.

vidual style, she is also in the role of youngest child, only daughter, recently promoted employee, key manager, and new shareholder. It is easy to understand why she finds herself in conflict with her older, nonemployed brother.*

Later in the meeting, the oldest son, Al, who has been quiet until now, is asked for his point of view (see table I-3, page 12). Everyone assumes that he will give a ringing endorsement for keeping the company in the family. The dynamics between generations are always complicated, especially between the current and designated leaders. Each of them is responding to the anticipated transfer of leadership in each of the three circles. Both Mr. Franklin and Al express the ambivalence he feels about "letting go" and "taking over." The three-circle model helps us keep in mind that, not one, but three separate transitions are taking place, and they may occur at different times and involve different participants.

At the end of the board meeting, Mr. Franklin confidently announces that, even with Bob in opposition, the majority of shareholders clearly favor keeping the company. At that moment, Carol announces that she has a letter from Mrs. Franklin concerning the voting of her shares and those of the absent sibling, David. She has instructions to read it if the board was not unanimous (see table I-4, page 13).

The members of the Tru-Color family illustrate the complexity of family businesses that gives them such a special character. The major players are responding to more than one powerful agenda at a time. Each participant sees all the others as parents or children, coworkers, and coinvestors simultaneously. Messages often become confused when they originate in ambivalence. Even the individuals themselves do not understand what they are feeling, or where the tension and conflict originate. All of these dynamics complicate the tasks of any of the circles—family, business, or ownership.

The goals of theory, research, and intervention all converge on discovering frameworks to untangle the knots of such complex behavior. The three-circle model has been a powerful tool toward reaching that goal. By separating the domains, it clarifies the motivation and perspectives of individuals at various locations in the overall system. But an additional

---

*The most common terms used to differentiate shareholders who work in a company from those who do not are *active* and *passive*. That nomenclature is contrary to our emphasis on the critical role of ownership in the family firm, independent of the shareholder's employment status. We will therefore use *employed owner* and *nonemployed owner* to differentiate those groups.

Table 1-3 ■ *Tru-Color, Inc.: Al's Opinions*

Actual Conversation	Family Circle Perspective	Business Circle Perspective	Ownership Circle Perspective
Board member Al: You know that as president I have the most to lose by selling out, so I'll vote to reject the offer. However, it's not as easy a decision as you think. I don't relish continuing to try to run this company with this kind of a board, and a big part of me thinks it might be just as well to get out now and start over. This board has resisted every major change I've proposed, and it's wearing thin.	**Oldest son Al:** Being the oldest is really a pain. Dad has always been very generous with me, but very demanding, too. Nothing I've done has ever been quite good enough. Other men my age run their own companies. I'm still a "junior," and I always will be. The rest of you, except for Carol, have always been jealous and competitive.	**President Al:** I have the title of president, but nobody knows what that means. The CEO resists any changes from the way he always ran the company. The financial performance of the company is flattening out, but I can't put together enough authority to do much about it. I'm seriously thinking about my opportunities elsewhere.	**Shareholder Al (10 percent):** I hope to own this company someday; I'll vote to reject the offer. However, it isn't an easy decision. I might end up putting all my energy into making everyone else rich and taking continual criticism all along the way. As it is, I only have an equal share with my brothers and sisters, and I don't know if Dad and Mom intend to give me control. They don't bring it up, and I don't see how I can. It might be better to get my money out now and make my own start.
Chair: Just be a little patient. When I retire, you can do whatever you want.	**Father:** Some of you have been right by my side, and others feel almost like strangers. Either way, your mother and I want you all to benefit from what we've accomplished, if you can just be a little patient.	**CEO:** I'll get out of the way as soon as you've shown me that you have what it takes to run this company. Your performance since I made you president has been pretty uneven.	**Chair:** This is a proven business you'll be getting. But you can't blame me for being cautious— it's my financial security you'll be playing with when I retire, not just yours.

Table 1-4 ■ *Tru-Color, Inc.: Mother's Opinions*

Actual Conversation	Family Circle Perspective	Business Circle Perspective	Ownership Circle Perspective
Board member Mother's letter: As all of you know, I have rarely attended board meetings and have always voted with the chair. If you are reading this letter, it means that you are not able to reach consensus and are all still disagreeing on what to do with the company. Here is what I think. Al has done an excellent job as president. He has worked hard for almost twenty years in the company, and he knows every part of it. He also has new ideas. Our current chair is almost sixty-five years old. There are other things that he should do with his life, and this may be his last chance to leave while he is still young enough and healthy enough to enjoy himself. Therefore, here is how I vote my shares. If the chair will step down and turn control of the company over to the president, I will vote to reject the offer. If he will not, then I vote to sell.	**Mother's letter:** Our oldest son is a grown man with a big family of his own to support. He has always been in his father's shadow. My husband is almost sixty-five. There are other things that we want to do together, and this may be his last chance to leave while he is still young and healthy enough to enjoy himself. Most important, this constant fighting is tearing our family apart. I may be wrong, but I think we may get along better if some of you, or all of you, were out of the business. Therefore, I vote like this: if my husband will retire and we can live the rest of our lives away from the business, I will vote to reject the offer. If he will not, then I vote to sell.	**Nonemployee Mother's letter:** I have always supported the CEO, and we talk more about the business than you think. The president has worked hard for almost twenty years in the company. He is not the charismatic leader the CEO is, but the company may not need that now. His new ideas can be a real benefit in the complex business that we have become. The tension between the CEO and the president is weakening the morale of key employees. Therefore, I vote like this. If the CEO will step down and turn real control of the company over to the president, I will vote to reject the offer. If not, then I vote to sell.	**Shareholder Mother's letter (30 percent):** The buyout offer is generous enough that each shareholder will come away with a comfortable sum. It would be enough to support the chair and myself in retirement, and to offer new investment or entrepreneurial opportunities for the other shareholders. I believe the president can safeguard your investment and support our retirement equally well. Therefore I vote like this. If the chair will join me in redeeming our shares so as to turn ownership of the company over to the other shareholders, I will vote to reject the offer. If he will not, then I vote to sell.

dimension is needed to bring this framework to life, and to make it more applicable to the reality of family and business organizations. That dimension is time.

Time and the Inevitability of Change

Psychological research is valuable in expanding our knowledge, but for most people, what we understand about human behavior comes from our personal experiences, often remembered in the form of stories. Consider the following four stories about family businesses:

Mr. A Jr. feels trapped in unending squabbles with his father. Mr. A Sr. founded the company twenty years ago, and just passed the role of CEO to Mr. A Jr. last summer. Managing his father's continuing interference is only one of Mr. A Jr.'s problems. Profits are flat, and there is a need for significant new product development, which was a low priority in his father's last years in the company. Mr. A Jr.'s wife feels that he has been working much too hard since taking over as CEO. He is so busy that he has almost no time for their daughter, and she is not sure about having more children soon if he will not be able to be more helpful.

Mr. B does not know how to respond to his brother Jim's request that he employ Jim's daughter in the company. Jim is one of the family shareholders and owns 25 percent of the company. Mr. B's own daughter joined the accounting department last year after graduating from college, and his son is trying to decide whether to join the company or take a job with somebody else. Two of the company's key nonfamily managers have expressed serious concern about too many family members in the business.

Mr. C's daughter, the company's vice president for marketing, wants to take the company in a new strategic direction. His son, who is the operations manager in the manufacturing plant, is opposed to any major changes. The board of directors and senior managers are split on the issue. Mr. C believes that some of the conflict is fueled by increasing competition between his children for the inside track as his successor. Both offspring have been with the company for ten years.

Mr. D and his wife intended to retire in three years, when Mr. D turns sixty-five, but now he is having second thoughts. He believes that his forty-year-old daughter, whom he named president two years ago, can successfully run the company, but he is not sure she comprehends how hard it will be. There is also troublesome conflict between his grandson, who works in the sales department, and his nephew, who is the new sales manager. In addition, a large corporation has recently approached Mr. D with a good offer to buy the company.

What do these stories have in common? They portray four typical dilemmas experienced by owner-managers in family businesses. They all illustrate examples of the complexity of managing differing norms, values, and expectations from various positions in the three circles. But, most surprisingly, they are all drawn from the *same* family business, at different points in time. Mr. A is Ben Smith at thirty, Mr. B is the same man at forty-five, Mr. C is Ben at fifty-five, and Mr. D is Ben at sixty-three.

To be alive is to be constantly changing. The A, B, C, and D stories about Ben Smith may all be about the same person in the sense that they are all about one human life, but in another sense Mr. Smith is never the same, from week to week or from year to year. Each experience and decision affects all those that follow. The course of any person's unique development is the product of both the individual's own maturation and his or her experiences in the world.

Systems and organizations also age and change. The family made up of a young couple and their six-month-old baby is not the same as the family with teenagers, or the family with elderly grandparents, adult offspring, and a new generation starting school. Similarly, entrepreneurial startups are not the same as businesses that have secured a place in the market but are concerned about growing. And both of these are different from older businesses, losing their edge and trying to generate the new ventures that will keep them competitive in the future. Because of the critical roles played by key individuals over long time spans, family businesses are especially affected by the inevitable aging of people in each of the sectors. The most important lesson we have learned in the past fifteen years of work with family companies is that our models must take time and change into account if they are to reflect the real world accurately.

Building a Developmental Model

The business, ownership, and family circles can create a snapshot of any family business system at a particular time. This can be a very valuable first step in understanding the firm. However, many of the most important dilemmas that family businesses encounter are caused by the passage of time. They involve changes in the organization, in the family, and in the distribution of ownership. For example, in the Tru-Color case, how different would the entire meeting have been a few years earlier, before the minority shares had been distributed to the four children? How different will it be a few years later, when Mr. Franklin has retired from the CEO position, and the balance of ownership has shifted to the younger generation?

It is easy to see how each of the circles changes when people enter and leave it over time. Families are an endless series of entries through marriage and birth, and departures through divorce and death. All of us have an intuitive understanding, based on our experience in our own families, that each of these additions and subtractions changes the family in some fundamental way. It is the same with businesses, as key managers come and go, and with shareholder groups, as new owners take on the responsibility of ownership and old ones relinquish it.

It is also important to see how the whole family business changes as individuals move across boundaries *inside* the system. In other words, a person's movement from one sector to another, such as from "family member" to "family member/employee," or from "employee" to "employee/owner," can also stimulate a general reaction in the entire system. The full-time employment of the first member of a new generation in the business—as that individual crosses the boundary from family member only to family member/employee—is an important marker event. The first time that ownership shares are passed to new individuals, family members or nonfamily, is also a critical moment. Many of these transitions may be invisible—embedded in a tax-minimizing estate plan or an annual gift— but nevertheless have far-reaching consequences. So does the retirement of a senior family member executive, or the cashing out of shares by a family member or branch. The system's adjustments to these boundary-crossing journeys of its members, and the meaning of those journeys in the lives of the individuals, are at the core of the entire family business phenomenon.

The result of adding development over time to the three circles is a *three-dimensional developmental model* of family business (see figure I-3). For each of the three subsystems—ownership, family, and business—there is a separate developmental dimension. The ownership subsystem goes through its sequence of stages, the family subsystem has its own sequence, and the business also progresses through a sequence of stages. These devel-

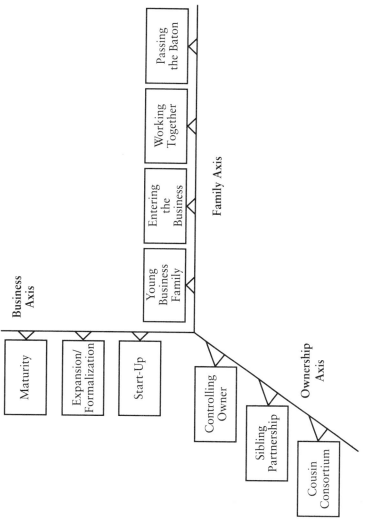

Figure 1-3 ■ *The Three-Dimensional Developmental Model*

opmental progressions influence each other, but they are also independent. Each part changes at its own pace and according to its own sequence.

Taken together as three axes of ownership, family, and business development, the model depicts a three-dimensional space. Every family business has progressed to some point on the ownership developmental axis, some point on the family developmental axis, and some point on the business developmental axis. The enterprise takes on a particular character defined by these three developmental points. As the family business moves to a new stage on any of the dimensions, it takes on a new shape, with new characteristics. We will discuss the way the three dimensions work together after first presenting each dimension in more detail.

The Ownership Developmental Dimension

The first dimension describes the development of *ownership* over time (figure I-4). Our description of this dimension draws heavily on the work of John Ward.[11] It recognizes that the different forms of family ownership result in fundamental differences in every aspect of the family business. There is, of course, an almost-limitless array of ownership structures in family firms. Some companies are owned by one individual, or by a couple, or by two unrelated partners. At the other end of the complexity scale are companies owned by combinations of family members (sometimes numbering in the hundreds), public shareholders, trusts, and other companies. For this dimension, as for the other two, the model strives for useful simplicity. No model of such a complex phenomenon can present categories that are completely exhaustive and nonoverlapping. However, we have found that the core issues of ownership development are well captured in three stages: Controlling Owner companies, Sibling Partnerships, and Cousin Consortium companies. These three categories help the professionals who are working with family businesses to make some critical distinctions between companies of different types, and help families themselves to understand how their current ownership structure affects all the other aspects of business and family operation. The ownership developmental dimension is discussed in chapter 1.

This dimension is not just three categories; it also assumes an underlying developmental direction. It suggests that most businesses begin with the single owner.[12] Many family businesses then move, over time, through the Sibling Partnership to the Cousin Consortium. This is not to say that family companies always follow this sequence. In fact, many companies

Figure I-4 ■ *The Ownership Axis*

are founded and owned by combinations of more than one family generation and may transition from any combination to any other. For example,
replacing an individual owner-manager with a single successor from the
next generation is one type of succession, which in this model would be
represented by a Controlling Owner company remaining at that stage. But
that is not the only possibility. Some controlling owners distribute their
holdings to two or more of their offspring, creating a Sibling Partnership.
Some Sibling Partnerships, in turn, distribute ownership to a Cousin Consortium, or restrict it to a next-generation Sibling Partnership. And both
of the later forms can recycle to the Controlling Owner stage if a single
individual buys out all the others and reconsolidates ownership. The addition of multiple-family ownership groups, nonfamily shareholders,
classes of stock, trusts, and annuities adds spice to individual cases. However, these three developmental stages still explain most of the variance
across the widest range of companies. At any point in time, most family
companies can be located primarily in one of the three stages, and there
is an underlying developmental dynamic that pulls them through the generational sequence from Controlling Owners toward Sibling Partnerships
and then Cousin Consortiums. That is why the ownership developmental
dimension is the first in this model of family business.

The Family Developmental Dimension

The model's second dimension describes the development of the *family*
over time. This dimension captures the structural and interpersonal development of the family, through such issues as marriage, parenthood, adult
sibling relationships, in-laws, communication patterns, and family roles.
To conceptualize individual and family development, we looked to the
pioneering work on normal adult development by Daniel Levinson and his
colleagues and to the many fine theorists studying family life cycles.[13]
Dividing business families into developmental subgroups helps sort out the
enormous variety of business-owning families. Although there is variability
in and overlap between stages, we saw that families within a stage had

much in common. We also saw that the transition from one stage to another was a recognizable, meaningful moment in a family's developmental history. The families that we work with respond immediately to the concept of change over time. They recognize themselves in the descriptions of the various stages. The sense of similarity with other family firms in the same stage is at once enlightening and reassuring. They find it particularly useful to learn about the challenges that likely await them in later developmental stages, so that they can anticipate and prepare for the future.

After considering the life histories of hundreds of business-owning families of all sizes and types in light of these developmental theories, we found that business families could be usefully divided into four stages, defined by the ages of the members of each generation active in the business. We call these stages Young Business Family, Entering the Business, Working Together, and Passing the Baton (figure I-5).

The first stage, Young Business Family, is a period of intense activity, including defining a marital partnership that can support the owner-manager role; deciding whether or not to have children and raising them; and forming a new relationship with aging parents. Returning to the four-part example that began this section, Ben Smith A is concerned primarily with resolving his continuing conflict with his father and becoming the business leader in fact as well as in name. His wife is troubled by the demands of the business. She needs his involvement in the family circle as well, in order to cover the tasks of home building and child rearing, and perhaps to allow her to pursue her own career dreams. The YBF stage presents parents with all the dilemmas of early adulthood as defined by Levinson's adult development model: creating a dream of the future, exploring alternative lifestyles, establishing credibility, committing to a career and, most often, to a family role, and finally "becoming one's own person" in the late thirties.[14]

At one stage farther up the axis, in Entering the Business, each generation is ten to fifteen years older than in the Young Business Family stage. This is the stage when families have to nurture the movement of the younger generation out of childhood and into productive lives as adults.

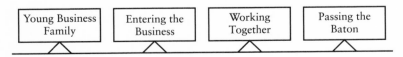

Figure I-5 ■ *The Family Axis*

EB families are concerned with creating entry criteria and career paths for the young adult generation, which include deciding whether or not to join the firm; with working on midlife transition issues as a couple and as siblings; and with defining a role as the middle of three adult generations, between elderly surviving parents and children who are getting ready to form families of their own.

As is common in business families, Ben Smith B has to manage not only his own children's entry into the company, but that of his siblings' children as well. As the owner-manager moves through his or her forties, this is often the time of learning the first lessons of "letting go"; that is, letting go of children as they become adults, letting go of direct control over all aspects of a more complex business, and letting go of some of the options for alternative lives. These are the challenges of the midlife transition.

As the parental generation moves through the decade of its fifties and the younger generation is in its twenties and thirties, the family is in the Working Together stage. In the Working Together stage, families are attempting to manage complex relations of parents, siblings, in-laws, cousins, and children of widely ranging ages. The capacity of the business system to support a rapidly expanding family is tested during these years, especially in two ways: can the company's profitability keep up with the income and lifestyle needs of the whole family, and can the size of the business provide meaningful career opportunities for qualified family members?

Ben Smith C is in the enviable position of having a thriving business and two competent offspring in the company at this stage. Even so, the complexity of so many different career plans and personal agendas is putting a strain on his business. This is the stage that puts a premium on family communication and clear operating procedures. It is also the stage when many families become dramatically more complex themselves. There is now a whole new adult generation adding to the mix of marriage, divorce and remarriage, stepchildren and half-siblings, and grandparenthood. Working together is the goal, but it requires the skill of an orchestra conductor.

Finally, in the Passing the Baton stage, everyone is preoccupied with transition. Although succession is often thought of as a business issue, we have been impressed with its enormous importance in the family circle as well. There are choices to be made about the sharing or passing of leadership from senior to middle generations in all aspects of family life. Business families have the symbolic issue of management and ownership control in the business to help them focus on the basic developmental questions of aging and intergenerational relationships. If the family prepares well and has the strength to overcome the many resistances to these powerful changes, then the work of Passing the Baton can be completed successfully. In any event, ready or not—too early, too late, or at just the right time—transitions inevitably occur, and the cycles begin again.

Ben Smith D thought he had a sound transition plan, but it proves harder to separate from his business than he had expected. Thinking about retirement causes him to take a good look at how he is relating in general to his son and daughter, both of whom are entering middle age themselves. The buyout offer also causes him to reconsider his own financial security. Looking forward to his senior adulthood, which could easily stretch for twenty or more years beyond his retirement from the presidency of his company, makes him realize that this stage is truly a transition, not an ending, and that it requires more "strategic planning" than he had thought.

The family developmental axis traces the developmental cycle of one nuclear family. However, as will be discussed in depth in chapter 2, as business families become more complex, there will be more than one family life cycle going on at the same time. In fact, within businesses that have reached the Sibling Partnership and Cousin Consortium stages on the ownership axis, there may be family groups that are in two, three, or even all four of the family stages. The interplay of different family groups, all dealing with their own developmental issues, creates some of the most interesting dynamics in family businesses and is one of the areas where this kind of model can be the most helpful.

The Business Developmental Dimension

The final dimension describes the development of the *business* over time. Our description of this dimension is built on the work of a number of business life cycle theorists, including Neil Churchill, Eric Flamholtz, Larry Greiner, and John Kimberly.[15] The maturity of the business enterprise has been overlooked in most writing about family firms. However, there is important variation in growth, product maturity, capitalization and indebtedness, nonfamily manager development, and internationalization, which arises from the stage of the business. In fact, we found that the business's developmental stage often has a powerful but hidden impact on such decisions as sales of family shares to outsiders or the succession of family leadership.

Models of business life cycles generally make fine distinctions between the stages, marked off by specific changes in the organization's structure and operations. This level of differentiation is too specific for the purposes of this three-dimensional model. Once again, a simple three-stage progression captures the essential, useful differentiation of business stages (figure I-6); the variations within each stage will be discussed more fully in chapter 3. The first stage, Start-Up, covers the founding of the company and the early years when survival is in question. Whether for the business as a whole or for new business units as they are created in complex family conglomerates, it is undeniable that there is always a startup period with powerful, unique characteristics. Businesses in their first few years are different in important ways from the way they will be at any other point in their life cycles.

The second stage, Expansion/Formalization, covers a broad spectrum of companies. It includes all family companies from the point when they have established themselves in the market and have stabilized operations into an initial predictable routine, through expansion and increasing organizational complexity, to the period when growth and organizational change slow dramatically. This stage may last a few years or many years, even beyond a generation. It is the time when family companies try to shape the growth curve and emerging structure of the business to serve the needs of the evolving ownership group and the developing family. Family businesses at this stage experience both positive and negative consequences of growth: increased opportunities and sense of possibility, and the concurrent stresses and strains as the expanding company outgrows its infrastructure (sometimes over and over again). If the business is succeeding, new opportunities are created for owners to realize acceptable returns on their investment and for family and nonfamily managers to build careers with attractive levels of compensation, authority, and status. When the business stalls or declines during the Expansion/Formalization stage, the

Figure I-6 ■ *The Business Axis*

consequences are felt beyond the business circle. The ownership group and the family must reassess their commitment to the business.

The final stage on the business developmental axis is Maturity. This stage has its roots in market assessment, describing the point when a product has stopped evolving and the competitive dynamics shift to increasingly unprofitable battles over market share. We are using it to describe a stage of stasis in a family company, when operations are routinized to the point of automatic behavior and expectations about growth are very modest. We do not present this as an indefinitely sustainable end state, however. Even when a company operates with extraordinary efficiency and has a controlling position in the market, the forces of developmental change cannot be held at bay indefinitely. There are two ways out of the Maturity stage for a family company: renewal and recycling, or the death of the firm.

There are limits on the usefulness of a typology of anything as complex as family enterprise. This model does allow businesses to be categorized into types. However, too much emphasis on categorizing can lead to oversimplification. Family businesses are constantly in motion, and distinctions between stages blur. There are many "hybrid" conditions, as when ownership is shared across generations, or in a complex business that is comfortably in maturity with its original product, while it starts some new ventures and grows others. We are not interested primarily in reducing family businesses to rigidly defined types; that moves us away from true understanding of their special nature. The model's best use is to provide a predictable framework for the development of family businesses over time in each dimension, and to suggest how a recognition of the current stage— and the combination of stages across ownership, family, and businesses— helps us to analyze the dynamics of any family firm.[16]

The chapters that follow explore the complex variety of individual companies, while focusing on the common elements that make a model possible. Part I (chapters 1 to 3) presents each of the three developmental dimensions in more detail. Part II (chapters 4 to 7) presents four classic types of family business and shows how their characteristics and key challenges are shaped by their stage in each of the developmental dimensions. Part III (chapters 8 to 9) distills some of the specific lessons we have learned from intervention with family businesses as guided by the model. These ideas are intended for the various professionals who are advisers to family firms and for the owning families themselves.

NOTES

1. Dreux 1990, 1992. A truly reliable data base that will give specific demographic information about the number and type of family firms has yet to be developed. This is in part because the major sources of such data, such as the census bureau and business directories, do not classify companies according to the family status of owners or senior management. In two excellent new efforts, Massachusetts Mutual Insurance and Andersen Consulting have begun to gather broad sample survey data (Massachusetts Mutual Life Insurance Company 1994; Arthur Andersen & Co. 1995). When the facts are ambiguous, we prefer to use very conservative estimates.

2. Zeitlin 1976.

3. Collin and Bengtsson 1991; Donckles and Fröhlich 1991; Lank 1991.

4. Chau 1991.

5. Lansberg and Perrow 1990.

6. Some of the earliest publications include Calder 1961; Donnelley 1964; Levinson 1971; Barry 1975; Danco 1975; and Barnes and Hershon 1976.

7. Beckhard and Dyer 1983; Lansberg 1983.

8. There has been some very interesting discussion in the literature about the relative balance between sub-system and whole-system analysis. See Kepner 1983; Hollander and Elman 1988; Benson, Crego, and Drucker 1990; and Whiteside and Brown 1991).

9. Tagiuri and Davis 1982.

10. This form of family diagram is called a "genogram." It depicts the organizational structure of a family, indicating the age, gender, and family relationships of each individual. For more information on genograms, see McGoldrick and Gerson 1985.

11. Ward 1987, 1991.

12. As with all the stages in all three of the developmental dimensions, the titles given do not reflect all the variations in that stage. For example, although the stage is called "Controlling Owner," in some cases a couple may own a business together, or there may be one dominant owner with a small number of other investors. The determinant of this stage is that one voice, usually one person, controls and speaks for ownership interests.

13. Levinson 1978, 1986, 1996. See also Erickson 1963; Vaillant 1977; Gould 1978; Gilligan 1982; and Levinson and Gooden 1985.

14. Levinson 1978, 144–165; 1996, 143–148.

15. Greiner 1972; Kimberly 1979; Kimberly, Miles, and Assoc. 1980; Churchill and Lewis 1983; Flamholtz 1986.

16. O'Rand and Krecker provide an elegant analysis of the utility and limitations of such "heuristic uses of the life-cycle idea" in the social sciences (1990, 259).

PART I

The Three-Dimensional Developmental Model

THE FIRST THREE chapters of this book present the three developmental dimensions that make up our model: ownership, family, and business. Each chapter explores the stages of one dimension in detail, providing the theoretical and conceptual foundation for our generalizations and conclusions about family business. In particular, we focus on the key challenges of each stage, which must be met as the system continues to develop.

1

The Ownership Developmental Dimension

EVEN MORE THAN the family name on the door or the number of relatives in top management, it is family ownership that defines the family business. Just as for family and business structure, there are many forms that ownership may take in the family business. The structure and distribution of ownership—who owns how much of what kind of stock—can have profound effects on other business and family decisions (who will be CEO or a family leader, for instance) and on many aspects of operations and strategy. In fact, we have observed that even minor structural changes in ownership, whether triggered by the aging of family members or by strategic decisions, can have powerful ripple effects through each of the three circles for generations. These different patterns of ownership, evolving over time, make up the first developmental dimension of this model.

Private ownership of enterprise has been a hot topic for many centuries. Aristotle's *Politics* and Plato's *Laws* and *Republic* had much to say about the role of private ownership in the creation of the ideal state.[1] Debates over inheritance laws and customs have been well documented in the cultural history of societies as varied as medieval Europe, ancient China, and the colonial Americas.[2] One central premise of the *Communist Manifesto* was the abolition of private ownership and inheritance (especially of work enterprises).[3] At the same time, capitalist economies were witnessing the dramatic expansion of the business-owning middle class and the introduction of public shareholding. Even theology has addressed private enterprise, as in the Papal Encyclical of 1891, which found divine justification for the family's right to "the ownership of profitable property" and its "transmission to children by inheritance."[4]

Even so, early work in the family business field gave less attention to ownership than to either management or family dynamics. Recently, however, some of the best research on family firms has been on their governance and ownership dynamics. The three-circle model explicitly identified the ownership group in the family business system, replacing the two-circle concept that did not differentiate between ownership and management.[5] Then the insightful work of John Ward first called attention to different categories of ownership for family companies.[6] Ward proposed a typical progression of ownership from founder to sibling partnership, and finally to the family dynasty. Our own thinking about how the ownership structure develops in a family company, and how ownership influences the dynamics of the entire system, has been strongly influenced by Ward's work.

There has been a tendency to see ownership as simply passed from one generation to another as a by-product of management control. Actually, an accurate and detailed portrayal of the range of family businesses reveals a much broader and more interesting variety of ownership structures. Ownership can be held through different classes of stock, in an infinite variety of trusts, and by elaborate multigenerational combinations of large and small distributions. Furthermore, these shareholding configurations are typically the prime determining characteristic of the stage of development of the family company.

Thinking Developmentally about Ownership

The structure of ownership in a family business can remain static for generations, even as the individual owners change. For example, a winery outside Lausanne, Switzerland, has placed majority control in the hands of one family member in each generation for fourteen generations—a sequence of single dominant owners for over 300 years. Typically, however, after the first generation, the form of ownership, not just the individual owners, changes between generations. Most often, ownership becomes increasingly diluted from a single majority owner, to a few or several owners, and then on to a much broader distribution. With each change in the ownership structure, there are corresponding changes in the dynamics of the business and the family, the level of power held by employed and

Figure 1-1 ■ *The Ownership Developmental Dimension*

nonemployed shareholders, and the financial demands placed on the business.

Although the specific ownership structure in any family company reflects its unique history and family membership, most cases fall into one of three types (figure 1-1): companies controlled by single owners (Controlling Owner), by siblings (Sibling Partnership), and by a group of cousins (Cousin Consortium).[7] We think of the progression of ownership from one form to another as developmental because it follows a predictable sequence and is at least partially driven by the aging and expansion of the owning family. However, this is a loose interpretation of the concept of development. The sequence of stages is not inalterably determined along a fixed path, as is much of biological development. And companies may be founded with any of the three ownership forms. As in the Swiss winery, ownership of the family business may remain concentrated in one or a few persons for many generations. Alternatively, the distribution of shares can move back and forth among individual, sibling, and cousin control, following periods of consolidation, expansion, and transfer of ownership both within and between generations.

The Ownership Stages of the Family Business

In the United States and most other Western economies, we estimate that about 75 percent of all family companies are majority owned by one person or by a married couple; we categorize them as Controlling Owner family companies. Around 20 percent of all U.S. family companies are ownership controlled by Sibling Partnerships. Finally, we estimate that around 5 percent of family companies are Cousin Consortiums.[8]

Many family companies have hybrid ownership forms;[9] for instance, majority controlled by one group of siblings but with some cousin shareholders as well, and perhaps even managed by the minority cousin owners. These hybrids normally represent transitions from one stage to another. Especially in later generations, the range of siblings' and cousins' ages can be broad and the generations can become mixed. Therefore it is very common for ownership to change from one stage to another in a series of intermediate steps that may last from a few months to many years.

The Controlling Owner Stage

Characteristics

Most, but not all, family businesses are founded as Controlling Owner companies, in which ownership is controlled by one owner or, less typically, a married couple.[10] It is tempting to label these companies "entrepreneurial" family businesses, because most founder businesses are of this form, but that would be somewhat inaccurate. Not all Controlling Owner family businesses are entrepreneurial (in the sense of being innovative or risk taking), and not all entrepreneurial businesses have one controlling owner.

The Controlling Owner Stage of Ownership Development

Characteristics
- Ownership control consolidated in one individual or couple
- Other owners, if any, have only token holdings and do not exercise significant ownership authority

Key Challenges
- Capitalization
- Balancing unitary control with input from key stakeholders
- Choosing an ownership structure for the next generation

Controlling Owner family businesses vary enormously in size. Although most remain modest in scale, some achieve revenues of many millions of dollars, sometimes even within the first generation. Family employees are most often limited to the nuclear family of the owner. The board of directors, especially in the first generation of an owner-manager family business, is typically a "paper board," which exists only to meet incorporation requirements but performs no real advisory role, or a "rubber stamp board," which meets only to endorse what the owner-manager has already decided to do. In both cases, these boards tend to be composed entirely or primarily of family members. Because of the owner-manager's dominant position in the company and often in the family, board meetings are generally not forums for business or family debate.

Cragston Employment Services

A powerful illustration of the importance of ownership factors at the Controlling Owner stage is provided by Cragston, an impressive service business that has grown to over $100 million in sales in its first generation. In 1978 Arthur Cragston, the charismatic and visionary founder, bought a small firm that processed workers' compensation claims. Arthur had just earned a degree from a local law school. Since he was already thirty-six, with a family to support, he was pessimistic about his chances to rise quickly enough in the hierarchy of a major law firm. When he learned that the father of a law school acquaintance was trying to sell a small company that processed workers' compensation claims, he put together his modest savings and went to a local bank to borrow the rest of the purchase price. The bank turned him down, citing his lack of business experience. But Arthur was determined. He remortgaged his home and convinced the company's seller to finance the rest of the purchase with a 10-year note. The office came with two full-time and two part-time employees. Arthur's second wife, Carolyn, helped him run the office for a few years, then returned to her vocation as a novelist.

The firm was modestly successful for two years, until Arthur began to read about a new trend toward contract employees. Craig, a longtime friend who was a CPA, came to Arthur with an idea to transform Arthur's company. They would serve medium-sized companies by "hiring" all their employees for them, handling all benefit and tax matters, and leasing the staff back to the employer. Craig proposed a partnership, but Arthur offered a generous salary and profit share instead. Craig contributed a small amount of investment capital from his savings in return for a 10 percent share of the stock, and the deal was made. Arthur and Craig put together a packet of sales materials and began to make the rounds of Arthur's current workers' compensation clients, pitching the new arrangement. Only two were interested, but it gave the new company, Cragston Employment Services, the experience it needed. Just after the first six months with these first two clients, two very favorable rulings came down from the IRS, in support of the employee leasing concept. Suddenly, demand exploded; Cragston was riding a huge new wave and began to grow rapidly.

To save on initial operating costs, Arthur continued to run Cragston out of the tiny office that he had used for his workers' compensation employees. He hired new staff one by one as he needed them, stretching current staff near the breaking point with long hours and overtime until it was essential to add a new person. His personal style with each employee and his stories about the great company they were building worked amazingly well to motivate the staff.

One day, at a business lunch, Arthur met Frank Hampton, who was also developing an employee leasing program for a large employment services company. Arthur decided he needed Frank's expertise at Cragston and offered him a 50 percent raise over his current salary and generous performance incentives to come to work for him. When Craig heard about the offer, he was furious. After a bitter and near-violent fight, Arthur fired Craig. Craig filed suit and, with Arthur refusing to settle out of court, the battle dragged on for almost three years, eventually costing the company thousands of dollars.

Frank took over management of the individual client plans, while Arthur handled marketing. The office was in constant turmoil because of the frantic level of activity in the cramped space. Arthur was a gifted salesman, and he was rapidly generating business. Frank often complained that he could not keep up without new staff, better computers, and more room. Arthur's first response was always, "If the customers don't see it, we can't afford to spend money on it." The real problem was that Arthur still insisted on knowing every part of each customer's package. Each new proposal required Arthur's approval at every step. Since he was also out in the field selling new accounts, paperwork piled up on his desk. Frank finally convinced Arthur to hire a new accountant to get the books in order and take a look at their cash flow. As a result of this work, it became clear that the business could afford higher rent and more staff out of current operating revenues, avoiding the kind of debt that Arthur feared. Following the move to a larger, better equipped office, things calmed down, and Arthur took a week's vacation with his family—his first time away from the company in three years.

Key Challenges

Three key challenges characterize the Controlling Owner stage: securing adequate capital, dealing with the consequences of ownership concentration, and devising an ownership structure for continuity. Arthur Cragston succeeded because he responded well to the first of these challenges and survived his problems with the second one. However, as shown later, his avoidance of the continuity issue may mean that the business never moves beyond the Controlling Owner stage.

Capitalization. In first-generation firms, where the owner-manager is the founder, the principal sources of capital are usually the savings and "sweat equity" invested by the majority owner, family, and friends. Unless the individual owner-manager has considerable investment capital, first-generation firms usually pool assets from family members. Although there may be important psychological strings attached, these are still the most unencumbered sources: the spouse (investing either his or her own funds or assets inherited from the in-law family), parents, siblings, or even children of the owner-manager. Relatives are more likely than outsiders to loan money to the founder with only the promise of dividends and asset appreciation if the business succeeds, and without any intention to help run the company. Sometimes there is a family norm of putting excess cash into relatives' new ventures. Sometimes new spouses have savings, in the family business version of a modern dowry. Arthur Cragston was lucky in that he could buy an already operating business from the seller at favorable debt terms. He had just enough equity in his home and savings to make the purchase. It meant that he and his wife were risking all their assets, including the small fund they had started for their children's college education, but they had no other family members who were in a position to help.

Nonfamily shareholding is rare in smaller family companies. True venture capital investors usually require significant control over the company, which makes them relatively unattractive to founders who are interested in controlling their creations. However, outside ownership sometimes happens at the start of the business, when the founder is helped financially by a partner (either active in the business or "silent") with whom he or she has a personal relationship. In some cases, these partners are bought out by the end of the first generation or the beginning of the second. In other cases, ownership is passed down into the families of each founder, creating a multifamily business. These companies are a fascinating subset of family firms, which have the potential to remain stable for several generations. The forces for disentanglement, however, are very strong, and if the company survives, it is more typical for the families to split or sell the business and disengage in the second or third generation.

The most common nonfamily source of capital for Controlling Owner firms is banks. Banks may have relatively stringent credit requirements and be conservative in their assessment of risk, but they rarely seek to interfere in business operations once they have made a loan. Arthur Cragston tried the bank first, but to no avail. After his company got started, he did everything he could to avoid significant bank debt, even when it would have speeded up the growth of the business.

If family investors receive shares of stock in return for their investment, then the business begins to move away from the classic Controlling Owner form. This is one of those common hybrid situations, in which the line between Controlling Owner and Sibling Partnership companies is not always sharply drawn. When one individual acts like a controlling owner, with individual discretion to run the company as he or she sees fit, then we would call it a Controlling Owner company even if other family members have minority interests and some legal rights. To the degree that the owner takes into consideration the opinions of other family shareholders, the company begins to operate more like a Sibling Partnership.

Balancing Unitary Control with Input from Key Stakeholders. The second key challenge is to find the right balance between the controlling owner's autonomous control of the business and responsiveness to input from constructive stakeholders. No business has authority more concentrated than one that is wholly owned and managed by one person. Controlling Owner businesses can exploit the advantages of clarity and efficiency that come from having a clearly identified single leader. Internal stakeholders (managers and employees) appreciate the lack of confusion about the owner's directives, and there is less risk of missing an opportunity while disagreeing owners struggle for dominance. A single leader can also make life easier for the organizational environment (banks and other creditors, customers, suppliers, accountants, and attorneys), who prefer "looking into one pair of eyes" when they need a decision.

But there are also risks at this stage. Controlling Owner companies often succeed or fail on the competence, energy, versatility, and luck of a single individual. Many controlling owners feel they have to be present every moment and be part of every decision. The business can be paralyzed if the controlling owner experiences illness, depression, distractions, or fatigue. The owner of a ten-year-old printing company in California said, "I hadn't taken a vacation in many years, so we took off to go skiing.

I couldn't stand it—I was getting ten phone messages a day—so we came home two days early." The time demands are often extreme, but sometimes controlling owners, particularly founders, become trapped in a style of overintense involvement. They convince themselves of their indispensability. They may remain reluctant to seek the advice and assistance of family members and others for fear of losing their independence. This can become a serious problem if the company did rely on the owner for everything in achieving its initial success, but now rapid growth and development demand insights and skills that are beyond the leader's capacity.

Arthur Cragston was a classic controlling owner who was at the center of every activity, significant or trivial, in his company. He was willing to hire some key managers, but he limited their autonomy. Every day began with a "coffee meeting" in his office, where he was brought up to date on everything that had happened the previous day while he was out selling new customers. Frank Hampton was the kind of manager who flourished under Arthur's leadership; Frank loved being "number two." The frustrations of a few of the other managers were muted because the company was growing so fast, salaries were kept high, and Arthur responded with personal encouragement (and sometimes gifts) if anyone's feathers got too ruffled. Still, some of the staff could not tolerate being constantly second-guessed, and left. His handling of Craig cost Arthur a friend and the company a bundle of money. But when you left the company, like Craig had done, you left the planet as far as Arthur was concerned; he never looked back.

The good and bad aspects of leadership concentration can be reinforced in the family circle as well. Especially in the founder generation, controlling owners are often also a pivotal psychological force in their families. If the business succeeds and grows, the anticipated employment, wealth, and status opportunity it provides for the family can lead to great influence for the controlling owner. The controlling owner's voice carries special weight in family discussions. His or her decisions regarding the business have great importance for the family, both for purely financial reasons and, in many cases, because the family's identity or reputation is linked to the company. There is often substantial competition among offspring for the owner-manager's attention, approval, and favor. Arthur's family did not (yet) own shares in the company, but he was generous with his growing income. He settled an old dispute with his first wife over alimony and child support, and his relationship with his son from that marriage improved greatly. His two brothers and his sister began to look to him for occasional advice, particularly on financial matters. He was able to help his parents relocate to Arizona, and moved into the large family home where he had grown up. After that, it was only natural for Arthur to host the family Thanksgiving and Christmas dinners as his parents had done. Arthur became the clear leader in the Cragston family.

Choosing an Ownership Structure for the Next Generation. As a controlling owner anticipates the end of his or her tenure, if he or she decides to keep the business in the family, then a decision must be made about whether to continue to invest ownership control in one individual or to divide it among a group of heirs. (The complexities of this decision process are discussed more fully in chapter 7.) In forming an estate plan, the controlling owner has to weigh many financial considerations regarding ownership shares: tax minimization, financial needs for retirement, responsibilities to provide for the spouse and other dependents, indebtedness, and so forth. Some estate planning instruments, particularly trusts, which are established for tax reasons, can also strongly influence the development of the family firm. Trusts may require decisions that restrict options on the distribution or liquidation of ownership shares for many years.[11] Although they have undeniable tax benefits, they also may have the effect (intended or unintended) of perpetuating the controlling owner's control indefinitely—even after death.

The controlling owner's core decision about ownership structure rests on a value judgment about what form makes the most sense for the business and the family. There are many influences on these judgments.[12] Cultural traditions, reflected in inheritance laws, social norms, and religious doctrine, may play a part.[13] For example, some controlling owners fear that anything short of an equal distribution of shares will stir up jealousies and encourage rival offspring to vie for power. Interestingly, equal distributions rarely quell longstanding rivalries, but the desire to contain family conflict often motivates parents to hold on tight to strict equality and not consider other alternatives.[14]

Eight years after the founding of Cragston Employment Services, the company had grown to annual sales of $20 million. Arthur decided to pass some of his shares down to his son, who worked as a salesman for Cragston, and to his daughter, whose husband also had joined the company after completing an MBA. Arthur's plan was to eventually give ownership control to his son, preserving the Controlling Owner form. But Arthur is vague whenever he is asked about the timetable for the transition, and his relationship with his son has always been strained and low on mutual trust. Ownership had been Arthur's chief lever in being able to control his company and family and to design a life that kept him in the center. It is unlikely that he will relinquish ownership control of the company until he dies, and equally unlikely that his son will still be involved in the company when that happens.

When families have a tradition of identifying one business leader in each generation, most members of the younger generation know from an early age that their careers will lie outside the business. If the current controlling owner is most concerned about autonomy and clarity in the business circle, and believes that smooth business operation requires one unencumbered leader, then he or she may seek out a new controlling owner. If, on the other hand, the current leader values equity, family harmony, and fair asset distribution as more fundamentally important to the future of the family, then the likelihood increases that he or she will prefer a Sibling Partnership form. This introduces the next stage of ownership development.

The Sibling Partnership Stage

Characteristics

Because nearly all Sibling Partnerships are in their second or later family generation, they have, on average, survived longer and grown larger than firms in the Controlling Owner stage. Ownership control at the Sibling Partnership stage is shared by two or more brothers and sisters, who may or may not be active in the business. There may be additional owners, either from the parents' generation or among the sibling's children, but they do not exercise significant ownership influence in the Sibling Partnership. If the parent does retain an active role but the ownership control has passed to the sibling group, then the firm is a hybrid of the two stages (Controlling Owner and Sibling Partnership). The more the parent is still seen as the ultimate authority, the more the company will behave like a Controlling Owner firm.

Fashion Imports

Fashion Imports, founded in 1962 by Maria and Joseph Giulanni, imports infants' and childrens' knitwear. In the early years, the focus was on Italian and French designs for the middle market of small retailers and specialty shops. Gradually the percentage of imports from Taiwan, Korea, and most recently Indonesia grew, and now the primary customers are large discount chains and department stores. Maria and Joseph ran the company together in the early years. Joseph was the buyer, making several trips each year to Europe to find suppliers who were not well known in the American market. Maria was in charge of sales. As the company grew, they were very comfortable bringing on professional managers, beginning with a warehouse supervisor and later including a growing and more complex sales and marketing operation. By 1990 annual sales had reached $22 million.

The Giulannis had five children—three sons, followed by two daughters. All five children worked in the company off and on during their school years, but only the two oldest sons and the youngest daughter considered the business a career. The oldest, Joseph Jr., was a natural leader. He came to work full time right out of college. Over the years that followed, Joe Jr. was moved around through all the divisions of the company, gaining experience and a very good reputation among the managers and employees. In 1991, at the age of thirty-eight, he was vice president of sales. His younger brother and youngest sister were also working in the company at the time. Franco was a buyer, who spent much of his time in Asia. Sophie was a designer. Their other brother operated a small restaurant in town, and their other sister was an attorney in a local law firm.

Prompted by a mild heart attack in 1991, Joseph Sr. began some long-delayed work on his and Maria's wills and estate plans. Joseph worked for a few months with their attorney and accountant to fashion a plan that would give the bulk of the company stock to Joe Jr., with smaller shareholdings for Franco and Sophie, and other assets going to the other siblings. Joseph Sr. felt strongly that the business needed a strong leader who had ownership control and that family harmony would be served by making that clear in advance.

When Maria saw the draft of the plan, she turned to her husband and said, "This is not possible." She was adamant in her belief that all five children should inherit equal portions of the company and benefit equally as coowners, even if only some of them worked in the company. "We have spent our whole lives building this company for one reason—to have something of substance to leave to all of our children. They have been wonderful together all of their lives. I will not separate them out now and give some more than others." She was absolutely unmovable in her beliefs.

Unsure what to do, Joseph called in a family business consultant for assistance. After a series of meetings and interviews, the second generation began to meet as a group without the parents present. In a relatively short time, three principles were agreed on: (1) that all the siblings had confidence in Joe Jr. as the future leader of the business; (2) that each of them wanted to remain as an owner of the company, to honor their connection to the family; and (3) that they would find other ways, through salary and other benefits, to reward siblings, who work in the company, for their efforts. With Joseph Sr.'s and Maria's blessing, they began to address the creation of a board of directors and the drafting of policies to guide participation and compensation.

Key Challenges

Developing a Process for Shared Control among Owners. The Sibling Partnership stage includes a range of structures, reflecting different distributions of shares and control among the sibling group. The first key challenge is to design a Sibling Partnership that fits the individuals in a particular family. In one form, one of the siblings adopts the role of quasi-parental leader. This form, which most closely resembles the Controlling Owner stage, is more likely when that sibling has been given ownership control (more than 50 percent of the voting stock). It is also

The Sibling Partnership Stage of Ownership Development

Characteristics
- Two or more siblings with ownership control
- Effective control in the hands of one sibling generation

Key Challenges
- Developing a process for shared control among owners
- Defining the role of nonemployed owners
- Retaining capital
- Controlling the factional orientation of family branches

more common when one or both parents have died at relatively young ages, or when there is a significant age gap between oldest and younger siblings. In theory, when one individual has ownership control, an alliance among the sibling shareholders will not be required to make strategic decisions for the company. That individual has the legal right to have the final word, and all the other siblings know it. This can liberate the new owner-manager from needing to reach consensus with brothers and sisters and help streamline decision making. However, even in the most harmonious situations, the controlling sibling is naive if he or she feels that the deciding 1 percent majority allows the same unquestioned autonomy as was exercised by the sole owner. Without the support of the sibling minority shareholders, life can be miserable for the quasi-parental sibling—and all of the brothers and sisters know that.[15]

The quasi-parental form of Sibling Partnership usually occurs when there is a history of a very close relationship between the parents (or at least the surviving parent) and the selected offspring, which began long before the leadership transition. If that sibling has always been the informal leader of his or her generation in the family, the gradual adoption of quasi-parental responsibility for brothers and sisters can be a natural outcome. Sometimes he or she adopts some of the symbolic representations of the parental role, such as living in the family home or hosting family celebrations. It may be understood that this individual will gradually consolidate ownership and buy out the minority siblings over time, to avoid conflict in the next generation. If the new leader is competent and responsibly consultative with minority shareholders, and the other siblings believe the distribution is fair, this solution may be workable. However, this form can become unstable as the other siblings get older and begin to challenge the legitimacy of the identified sibling's paternalism. Even in the best cases, it is hard to sustain this form for many years, because the rising cousin generation is even less likely to feel comfortable with such a disparity in power among the various subfamilies. There is a Greek myth about a revolt on Mount Olympus in which Zeus led a group of his siblings in overthrowing their father, Cronos, as chief of the gods. After the rebellion, Zeus was accepted as the leader of the sibling group, but when he started adopting the "quasi-parent" role—demanding, for example, that they address him as "Father Zeus"—they tied him up in a hundred knots to teach him a lesson in humility.[16]

A more contemporary story of such a revolt, although it did not occur during the quasi-parent's lifetime, involves Steinberg, Inc., one of Canada's largest conglomerates. Sam Steinberg, the most dynamic of four brothers in the second generation, dominated the business for many years. Sam was clearly the entrepreneurial genius behind the growth of Steinberg, Inc., from a small grocery store founded by their mother into a multimillion-dollar supermarket and real estate empire. He was also one of the best examples of the risks of abuse of power by a lead sibling. As described in the book *Steinberg: The Breakup of a Family Empire*, Sam far surpassed his brothers in talent and business acumen and, according to his daughter Mitzi, dictated their every move. ("When he said sit, they sat down; lie down, they lay down.") In the end, this quasi-parental system was ill equipped for continuity. Family resentment over Sam's dictatorial style no doubt contributed to the downfall and sale of a very successful enterprise at Sam's death.[17]

A second form of Sibling Partnership is the "first among equals."[18] In this case, one individual acts as the lead sibling but stops short of the quasi-parental role. This form is more likely when minority shareholders intend to exercise some rights but do not want the responsibility of equal involvement. The first-among-equals role is a delicate one to manage. Too much leadership, and the siblings will revolt against the parental presumptions of the leader; too little, and the system can break down in bickering and factionalism. When the leader is skilled and the family has a good history of collaboration, however, this system can effectively balance the sibling owners' desire for respect and involvement with good ownership decision making.

The success of the first-among-equals arrangement depends quite a bit on how the leader was chosen. In the best cases, the leader has well-established credentials as the strongest visionary for the company, coupled with a style that conveys respect and openness to the other siblings. A parental designation as the "first among equals" is usually helpful, but so is voluntary endorsement by all the brothers and sisters. This was the fortunate situation in the Giulanni family. Joseph had envisioned a quasi-parental arrangement, but Maria insisted on equal division of ownership and a more collaborative system. They had all the ingredients for a first-among-equals solution: the right leader, the right family environment, and the right sibling relationships. Even so, they have considerable work ahead of them in forging the specific arrangements of authority, input, and rewards that all the siblings will continue to regard as fair.

In some families it does not go so smoothly. The other siblings, whether they work in the business or are nonemployed shareholders, may not appreciate this arrangement. They may feel the parent has made the wrong choice, or that the controlling sibling should be more constrained by majority rule. As in the quasi-parental form, disaffected relatives who are minority shareholders may not be able to steer the company, but they can still stir up family and business trouble for the new boss (as the explosion of minority shareholder lawsuits demonstrates).

Finally, some sibling partnerships operate as truly egalitarian arrangements. This is, of course, most common when ownership is very evenly divided. In the absence of strong individual leadership, ownership authority is exercised through the sibling team, often via their roles on the board of directors. These companies find creative ways for each of the partners to share the power and the glory. For example, Jerry Scolari and his brother Louis, who are equal owners of Scolari's Warehouse Markets, a chain of grocery stores based in Sparks, Nevada, rotate the presidency every May when their fiscal year begins. Jerry Scolari says the shared presidency has mainly symbolic importance, emphasizing to employees and store managers that the brothers "make our business decisions together."[19] The Houghton family of the Corning Company decided some time ago on an entirely different approach. Mrs. Houghton decided that both of her sons should have an opportunity to lead the company for a number of years. By prearrangement, Amory Houghton, Jr., the oldest son, served as CEO for twenty years, then resigned and pursued a career in Congress after turning over the top position to his younger brother, Jaime.[20] Other families have experimented with cochairs or with having one of the nonfamily members of the board fill the chair role.

Once again, egalitarian Sibling Partnerships are a delicate dance. As with the other two forms, the key is the fit between the overall family style and sibling history and the ownership structure that is chosen. If the siblings have always operated as a leaderless group or have rotated leadership according to different tasks and special skills, the egalitarian team can be very satisfying and productive. (This is one of those cases where classic organization theory fails in the face of family business. Lansberg likens this to the scientists who determined that, according to the laws of physics, the bumblebee cannot fly.[21] Most experts on organizational governance would argue against shared ownership power. And yet, in some family businesses it works.)

Defining the Role of Nonemployed Owners. A second key challenge in the Sibling Partnership stage is creating a workable relationship between those sibling owners who work in the company and those who do not. Parents worry a great deal about the impact of shared ownership on the relationships among their adult children. Some controlling owners try to minimize conflict by leaving company shares only to those offspring who work in the business, reflecting a family value that those who earn the profits should benefit from them. It also usually means that there are other assets that allow the parents to provide for all offspring while limiting stock to those who work in the company. For families fortunate enough to be in this situation, passing ownership only to employed offspring can simplify fairness issues, but it is unlikely to resolve them completely. There are often disparities in the degree to which siblings felt invited to join the firm and thereby to benefit from its financial rewards and future growth.

Other families distribute ownership to all offspring. This reflects a family value that the business is a legacy asset, created by the parents for the benefit of all their children. In these cases, finding a process that responds to the needs of both the employed and the nonemployed siblings is probably the most difficult challenge of the Sibling Partnership stage of ownership. We have found that employed owners are most concerned with achieving their career goals and receiving the status and financial rewards that they feel they deserve for their service to the family company. They vary in their awareness of their obligations to nonemployed siblings, although most are comfortable with the general idea of sharing the proceeds of a successful company in return for their siblings' support, both emotional and financial. The nonemployed siblings are typically seeking a way to have responsible input. Some prefer to be completely passive and actively resist any expectations of participation of any kind. Others want to be heard. Successful Sibling Partnerships pay attention to these dynamics and do the work necessary to learn and try to respond to the varying needs of individuals. They use a variety of techniques to meet this challenge: internal markets and opportunities for selling shares, good communication, family councils, and well-constructed governance structures, including boards of directors. As difficult as this issue can be, the rewards can also be great. Those Sibling Partnerships that resolve communication and role issues between employed and nonemployed sibling owners are among the most satisfying and impressive business families that we have seen.

Retaining Capital. A third key challenge of the Sibling Partnership stage is attracting and retaining capital. Older companies tend to be more reliable debtors for banks and other lending institutions. Sibling Partnerships in our experience tend to have an easier time funding growth through debt than do first-generation Controlling Owner companies. However, because the Sibling Partnership stage usually brings an increase in the number of people who are owners but not employees, the balance of priorities between reinvestment and dividends may shift. In their quest to continue to live comfortably (which sometimes becomes competitive, or at least comparative, in the sibling group), or to fund outside business ventures, siblings may exert pressure for significant dividends. The employed siblings may feel obligated to respond to the needs of their siblings who are not employed in the company, especially if some of the outsiders were excluded from the opportunity to make a career in the business. Sometimes this leads Sibling Partnerships to draw excessive funds out of the company, unwittingly dampening its growth prospects. When banks see such behavior, they are less likely to extend their own funds. Educating all the stakeholders about the company's capital needs is one of the most important responsibilities of the leaders of the Sibling Partnership.

Controlling the Factional Orientation of Family Branches. Finally, as the Sibling Partnership ages and the next generation approaches adulthood, a new challenge arises. While sibling coowners are acting primarily as brothers and sisters (and concurrently as sons and daughters), they may be held together by their common history and their close personal ties. As their children grow, however, they also begin to interact as mothers and fathers themselves, and as heads of family branches. Siblings may begin to act as if their responsibility is to represent their own family branch, as opposed to the company or the shareholder group as a whole. This constituent orientation can distract shareholders and board members from the needs of the business and foster competitiveness and mistrust. Siblings who have senior management roles in the company may want to protect special access to careers in the business for their children. Those who are more junior or who do not work in the business may want to level the playing field and guarantee equal opportunity for their children. Even sibling partners who have been collaborative and generous with each other over the years feel the pressure to protect the interests of their own children as those offspring approach adulthood. These parental concerns can suddenly and significantly increase conflict in the sibling group, although the cause often goes unrecognized because the arguments may occur around routine business or shareholder issues.

In-laws bring their own strengths and issues to the family and can serve to either strengthen or weaken the shareholder group. Because in-laws do not naturally perceive family dynamics through the lens of the family's history, they can import objectivity and a spirit of cooperation into a sibling culture. On the other hand, because in-laws tend to focus on their own spouse and children, and because they have their own needs and styles, they can contribute to a factional approach to the business. Although they rarely sit on boards, the behavior of in-laws is an important factor influencing whether sibling shareholder groups will be effective and reasonably harmonious.

All of these challenges continue right up until the time when the Sibling Partnership readies itself for the next generational transition. As the sibling leaders approach retirement, the ownership group must decide what the structure will be in the future. Occasionally a Sibling Partnership resolves itself by returning to the Controlling Owner stage, either through misfortune (the death of other siblings in small families) or buyout. Somewhat more often, a new Sibling Partnership will be formed in the next generation by concentrating ownership in only one branch of the family. However, the most common transition is for offspring in more than one branch to receive ownership, creating the most complex ownership stage: the Cousin Consortium.

The Cousin Consortium Stage

Characteristics

At this stage, ownership control is exercised by many cousins from different sibling branches; no single branch has enough voting shares to control decisions. Again, there are mixed models. Cousin ownership groups in small families with only a limited number of shareholders share some of the characteristics of Sibling Partnerships. However, the classic business family at this stage in our model includes at least ten or more owners (we have seen Cousin Consortiums with several hundred family shareholders). It usually takes at least three generations for a company to reach this ownership stage; hence, Cousin Consortiums tend to be larger and more

The Cousin Consortium Stage of Ownership Development

Characteristics
- Many cousin shareholders
- Mixture of employed and nonemployed owners

Key Challenges
- Managing the complexity of the family and the shareholder group
- Creating a family business capital market

complex businesses than the other two types. Still, we see a wide variety of sizes and shapes of Cousin Consortium family companies.

Holiday Hotels, Inc.

Members of the third and fourth generations of the Sanderson family currently own 70 percent of this diversified recreational facility corporation. The remainder is divided between an Employee Stock Ownership Plan (ESOP) and a few outside investors. The company owns and manages six hotels and vacation resorts in the Caribbean and along the U.S. Gulf Coast, as well as a vacation planning service and tour packaging company. It was founded by August Sanderson, a professional gambler who parlayed a lucky streak into ownership of a small residential hotel in Miami Beach in the 1940s. August died in 1969. Through the seventies and eighties, the company was owned by five members of the second generation—four of August's children and a niece. August's second son, the designated successor, died in a boating accident the following year. His widow, who inherited his shares in the growing company, remarried a real estate developer, Mike Ransomme. Because none of the other siblings was very committed to business operations, Mike gradually took over management control of Holiday Hotels. Mike was an aggressive deal maker and heavily leveraged the company to acquire more hotels and expand services. When he died in 1987, the company had tripled in size to $80 million in annual revenues, but it was still carrying significant debt and was vulnerable to a downturn in the tourist economy.

At that time there were twenty-eight individual shareholders in the Sanderson family, as well as a number of trusts. The Ransomme family and another sibling branch sold out their interests after Mike's death. The battle over valuation of the shares was a difficult one, fueled by old family resentments stemming from August's tendency to encourage competition among his children "to see who's the champ in the litter." The chair of the board at that time was the oldest sibling, Sam Sanderson, but the company was actually in the hands of a nonfamily manager who had been COO under Mike for many years. When the dust settled in 1992, the 70 percent family holdings were divided approximately equally among the remaining three family branches: Sam and his three children, a younger sister (Elizabeth) and their five children, and their cousin (Susan Connelly) and her four children from two marriages. The sibling generation had never recovered from their childhood conflicts; they were not close and talked mainly through their attorneys. The nonfamily COO had developed a good cadre of professional managers, but he was sixty-three years old, and no succession plan was in place. Three of the cousins, one from each branch, worked in the company, although there had never been much talk about career planning or the ultimate role of the family in senior management.

In 1993 Susan Connelly died, and her shares were divided among her four children. Her second husband had been a very wealthy businessman, and her family was well recognized among the elite of Alabama, where they lived. During her lifetime she had always kept her distance from Holiday Hotels, although her oldest daughter had come to work for the company as a chef after completing her degree at the Culinary Institute. Her children wondered what to do with their significant ownership in this company.

Key Challenges

Most of the distinctive characteristics of the Cousin Consortium stem from the complexity of these amazing business enterprises. This complexity is most evident in two ways: (1) the increasing *complexity of the family*, as it grows through marriages and childbirth to a network of siblings, spouses, and children; and (2) the *complexity of ownership*, as the estate plans of different siblings and branches create a range of shareholder situations.

Managing the Complexity of the Family and the Shareholder Group. In Cousin Consortiums, there is often a broad range of ages, family relationships, wealth, and places of residence. Shareholders may be a mix of first cousins, aunts and uncles, second cousins, and even more distant relatives, some of whom may never have met. The personal connections that have been so powerful in the first two ownership stages are almost certainly diluted here. In fact, one of the most troublesome aspects of the transition between the Sibling Partnership and Cousin Consortium is siblings' difficulty realizing that the familial bond among their children cannot be the same as it has been in their sibling group. Regardless of how closely knit an extended family has been, cousins do not share the same parents or the same childhood. In addition, cousins are usually at least one generation further removed from the founding of a company. In many cases this is the first generation that includes shareholders who did not know the founder personally and did not witness the early years of the company. Family stories and legends can substitute in part, but not completely. Thus loyalty to the company cannot rest as firmly on personal loyalty to its founders and their vision.

As a result of these two dynamics, cousin relationships tend to be less intense and more politically motivated than those among siblings. Although we have seen Cousin Consortiums demonstrate high levels of commitment to the company across the whole cousin group, this tends to be a difficult state to achieve. Typically, different career paths in the sibling generation have led to a concentration of cousin managers from one branch. As that branch becomes dominant in the management of the business in the second generation, the other branches begin to withdraw from involvement in the company. If some siblings and their families now live far away, many cousins' attachment to the original family home, and the status that the company holds in its home city, are diminished. Furthermore, previous family conflicts can be transmitted to current generations of cousins, polarizing them into camps. It is not surprising, then, that many cousin shareholder groups act as if they have little in common besides their financial interests in the enterprise.

Families who manage this complexity best are those that clarify the distinction between membership in the ownership group and membership in the family. They work to create a shared family identity outside of the business, through activities and communication that emphasize family, not business. Successful cousin companies do not require family members to hold onto their stock if they would rather sell and use the money for other purposes. (The issue of creating a market for family shares in the firm will be discussed below.) Family members who choose not to be owners are not restricted from "first-class" status, even leadership, in the family.

In the Sanderson family, it was Susan Connelly's death in 1993, followed closely by Sam's death in 1994, that caused the cousin group to take stock of the family's current status and relationship to the company. At that time, ownership control was clearly in the cousin generation, with only one member of the sibling group still alive. The family gathered only at funerals. Although the cousins had been raised in close proximity as young children, most never saw each other as adults. Sam's oldest son, who was a vice president of the company, suggested that the cousin shareholders get together for a weekend at one of the properties to discuss their plans for the future. He expected a lukewarm response, but to his surprise all but three of the cousins decided to attend, and most wanted to bring their spouses and families. That was the first of what has become an annual family retreat.

Since the family is bigger at this stage, the percentage of adult family members who have made their careers in the firm is generally much lower in the cousin generation. It is rare to see more than a few of the cousins active in the business. The political dynamics that emerged in the Sibling Partnership stage became magnified in the Cousin Consortium. Even in the best of situations, the needs and interests of cousin owners who work in the company and those who do not tend to diverge over time. Employed owners feel that their entire work lives, and their egos as well, are tied up in the company; nonemployed owners see the company as only one commitment among many, all of which must compete for their attention and investment. Employed owners receive their financial returns from the company in many ways, including salary, benefits, "perks," and access to facilities and services. Even if the nonemployee cousins support those rewards as completely justified, they sometimes resent the lifestyle that they see the employed cousins enjoying if the company is also giving the message that profits do not warrant significant distributions. Nonemployed owners tend to focus on dividends, on which they may depend. They often feel "paper rich and cash poor" and question the value of their continued investment in the company. Employed owners feel that they should have control of decisions about risk and strategy, because they both have the knowledge and are more vulnerable to the consequences. Nonemployed owners may worry that the "insiders" are too ready to take risks with family investments, and that they suffer from self-protecting tunnel vision about the company's operations and its future. Finally, employed owners know that they have much information that their nonemployed cousins do not, but they cannot take the time to educate everyone fully. Nonemployed owners usually feel handicapped or shut out of the decision-making process and feel they are being asked to give blank-check endorsements of the judgment and fairness of those involved.

One arena where these differences can be played out is the board of directors. Active boards are rare in family businesses of any size, but they are more common in Cousin Consortiums—although they are still likely to be heavily dominated by family members. Most Cousin Consortium boards are constituent in nature, with some formula for representation of family branches. Although family constituent boards can be quite professional and effective, they tend to focus too much on the personal interests of branches, rather than confronting tough strategic issues facing the company. Often they can become stalemated and ineffective at resolving decisions about the direction, future leadership, and financing of the company. Their membership structure can be solely determined by rules about equalized family representation, without regard for qualifications or potential contribution. One key challenge facing Cousin Consortium families is to reach agreement on the requirements of responsible ownership. Those requirements most often include a public posture of loyalty and support, a willingness to think broadly about the common financial needs of the enterprise along with individual needs, and a willingness to contribute in some appropriate way one's talent, effort, and opinions.

In the Sanderson family, the main agenda at the first cousins' retreat was talking about a board of directors. The discussion probably would have degenerated into the bickering that characterized most interaction in the prior generation, were it not for the inspired leadership of the nonfamily COO, who had been invited to make a presentation on the company and its needs for the future. He had prepared a compelling discussion of new management initiatives and the advantages that would come from a restructured board that included strong nonfamily directors. As a result of his guidance, a system was designed that included both outside and family representation, chosen not only by branch but also according to preparation and willingness to remain informed about company operations. Over two years, a new board, with four outside directors, was built. The board and the COO were able to implement a procedure for family employment and promotion, which was in place in time for the COO to retire at age sixty-six in 1996. Sam's son Albert remained as chair, and a new nonfamily manager was recruited to head the company as president.

It is easy to understand why so few companies, especially in the United States, thrive under family control into the Cousin Consortium stage. There are many forces that chip away at the connections integrating all the parts of the family business system: interpersonal conflict; distance and lack of common experiences; normal family disruptions caused by death and divorce; and the increasing variability among family members in the financial costs and benefits of staying involved. Stronger family traditions and limited competing career opportunities have made Europe and Latin America a more fertile ground for Cousin Consortium companies. In the United States, with its strong emphasis on entrepreneurship, independence, mobility, and focus on the nuclear rather than the extended family, the bulk of family firms that survive past the first generation are more likely to subdivide and recycle to Controlling Owner and Sibling Partnership stages.

Creating a Family Business Capital Market. What happens when some members of the Cousin Consortium want out? Unplanned demands to be cashed out can be costly to the owner-management of a family company. Family companies have been sold out from under family management because some shareholders did not feel respectfully treated. But captive cousin owners are not the answer either. Owners who want to withdraw their investment for other purposes but cannot, or who do not agree with the actions of management but do not have enough shares to influence policy, can lead to very high costs in management time and family conflict and, ultimately, legal fees. Therefore the third key challenge of the Cousin Consortium stage is the creation of a workable internal market for family shareholders, so that family members have options to sell their interests, but the process is managed to minimize negative consequences for the company.

The keys to successfully creating the internal market are objectivity and fairness in the valuation of shareholdings, as well as patience. It is almost always necessary to use outside professionals to help value the holdings of individuals and branches. Sometimes more than one expert is needed, to increase the family's confidence in the result by confirmation, and to take into account all of the tax and legal ramifications of the valuation process. In addition, patience is required so that transactions can be accomplished without serious negative impact on the company's cash flow and viability. In this arena, as in most policies for Cousin Consortium enterprises, it is important and ultimately easier to create the rules before they are needed, so that policies are generated in an atmosphere of the general best interest instead of in response to the particular immediate needs of one sector of the family.

A related issue, which is not limited to the Cousin Consortium stage but arises most frequently in these later-generation family businesses, is the option of going public and opening the company to nonfamily investors. In some cases, the company's capital needs at the Cousin Consortium stage go beyond what can be generated by retained earnings and debt. Then a sale or some form of limited or public offering is considered.[22] Family companies that are large enough, with strong enough growth prospects to attract outside investors, need to weigh the attractiveness of new capital sources against the costs involved in giving up closely held ownership. In companies that lean toward public offering, ownership control is often extremely diluted, so that some family members may feel remote from the business and less interested in the family's maintaining its control. A professional board with a strong contingent of outsiders may direct the company, and the business may be in an industry or a point in its life cycle where a large influx of cash is required. The ones who resist are motivated primarily by their appreciation of a private company's ability to operate more secretively with respect to its competition, to flexibly compensate management without oversight by a public board, to make decisions more quickly, and ultimately, to control the direction, culture, and systems of the organization. (James Cargill, senior member of the board of Cargill, Inc., says: "When you go public you get two things, money and trouble, and Cargill has enough of both, thank you."[23]) In the end, fewer than 2 percent of all U.S. corporations ever sell their shares on the public market. When they do, most will sell just 20 to 40 percent of their shares, becoming a publicly traded but still family-controlled business.

The aftermath of public offerings is mixed. Some family businesses are delighted with the move, and others are disappointed. Those that are delighted generally cite the benefits of having more capital for growth, the excitement of being able to compete more aggressively, the increased professionalism demanded by the public market, and the greater career opportunities for talented managers. The disappointments include loss of decision-making privacy, the time and money costs of greater public reporting requirements, and the pressure to meet short-term (quarterly) financial goals, which can distract a company from meaningful long-term objectives. In fact, there are family companies, like Levi Strauss, that have gone to considerable lengths to buy back publicly held shares to regain the benefits of being privately held.

Finally, there comes a point in the Cousin Consortium stage when it becomes financially and politically difficult to reverse the developmental progression and return to a simpler form. Once ownership has become extremely diluted, no individual or branch has much ownership power, and the business comes to resemble a publicly held structure with many shareholders of roughly equal strength. Unless one branch of the family, through marriage or outside business interests, is able to generate sizable capital reserves, it is unlikely that any of the sibling groups or individuals will be able to buy out all the others and reconsolidate ownership. At this end state, further development is most often stimulated by changes in the family and business dimensions. Portions of the Cousin Consortium will withdraw investment or use other capital to create new ventures and entrepreneurial opportunities. If the original firm is still viable and the return on the investment to the cousins remains competitive generation after generation, the confederation may continue indefinitely as the "parent" in a network of enterprises. If these conditions are not met, then the Cousin Consortium business may dissolve and its resources become scattered into many new ventures, which begin their own cycles.

NOTES

1. Aristotle 1992 ed., 112–119; Plato (Saunders, ed.) 1970; Plato (Lee, ed.) 1987.
2. Marcus 1980; Cates and Sussman 1982; Chau 1991.
3. Engels and Marx, 1848; Engels, 1884 (in Engels, 1942).
4. Pope Leo XIII 1891 (in Husslein 1940, 173–4).
5. Tagiuri and Davis 1982.
6. Ward 1987, 1991; Ward and Aronoff 1994.

7. Because this is by definition a dimension of the development of *family* ownership over time, we have decided to include in the names of the stages the family relationships (siblings and cousins) that most often accompany the stage of ownership dispersal. The terms are not meant to be exclusive; we are using *Controlling Owner* to include a couple acting as an individual owner, as well as the case in which there are other minority shareholders who act as completely silent investors and do not seek a role in governance. "Sibling" Partnerships and "Cousin" Consortiums can include some nonfamily members or relatives from other parts of the family; the group interaction will be more or less characteristic of its stage depending on the concentration of the specified family relationship in the ownership group.

8. These statistics seem to hold for most Western cultures but probably vary

slightly internationally; for example, in Chinese Asia. Chinese families are more apt to share ownership among siblings when starting a family company, sometimes bypassing the Controlling Owner stage altogether. In addition, Chinese family companies practice a *coparcenary* (joint heirship) approach to ownership succession which divides ownership among each generation relatively equally (Hsu 1984; Chau 1991).

9. Lansberg, forthcoming.

10. When a couple rather than an individual fills the Controlling Owner role at this stage, they may be true "copreneurs," each owning half of the company and having active roles in its management. In other cases, the spouse is not active in the business and is only an owner on paper, or a potential owner because of community property provisions.

11. Cohn 1990; McCollom 1992.

12. Menchik 1980; Ward 1987; Ayers 1990; Swartz 1996.

13. Clignet 1995; Judge 1995. For example, primogeniture (preference for the firstborn son, common in many parts of the world, including England and Japan), coparcenary systems (where an estate is divided equally among the heirs, as in the traditional Chinese system), and the Benjamin rule (the Swiss system in which the youngest son inherits the farm) helped stabilize ownership transitions and maintain order within families and societies where they were dominant. In the American economy, the influence of many cultural inheritance systems, which arrived with each group of emigrating entrepreneurs since colonial days, has created a complicated mix of laws and norms. In some states, individual discretion is very broad; in others it is not; for example, remnants of the Napoleonic Code constrain the rights of the senior generation to exclude offspring from inheritance.

14. Gersick 1996.

15. Murdock and Murdock 1991.

16. Lansberg 1994.

17. Gibbon and Hadekel 1990; also Mintzberg and Waters 1982.

18. Lansberg 1994; forthcoming.

19. Hollander 1990, 40.

20. Vancil 1987; Sonnenfeld 1988, 247–251. The concept of shared executive authority, such as an "office of the president," is also beginning to achieve acceptance in public companies. For example, see Vance 1983, 193–251.

21. Lansberg, forthcoming.

22. Employee ownership is a controversial version of a restricted expansion of ownership in family businesses. An exploration of the pros and cons of ESOPs in family firms is beginning to appear in the professional literature. (For example, see Weiser, Brody, and Quarry 1988; Hoffmire, Willis, and Gilbert 1992.)

23. Carlock 1994, 300; see also Johnson 1990.

2

The Family Developmental Dimension

FAMILIES ARE the most compelling social institutions. For better or worse, our families make us who we are; they are the source of both the "nature" and the "nurture" of individual development. Psychologists, sociologists, historians, and economists all consider the family to be one of the critical building blocks of the systems they study.

The family dimension in our three-dimensional model is the easiest to conceptualize developmentally, because we are used to seeing our own families change year after year. Families follow the natural rhythms of human life. Each new nuclear family forms in its members' early adult years, grows and functions in increasingly diverse ways during their middle years, launches a new generation, and gradually dissolves as individuals grow old and die. Experiences and events, such as divorce and other reconfigurations, may add complexity, but the sequence of basic family tasks is fundamental. The continuity of human existence is carried out by children maturing into parents of their own children, over and over.

Thinking Developmentally about Families

When we consider how families continuously change, it is clear why a developmental approach to understanding family businesses is necessary. Many of the key issues that business families face—the entry of a new generation, the passing of authority from parents to children, the relationships between siblings and cousins, the effects of marriage and retirement—can be described only over time.

Among all the models that social scientists have applied to family development, we have found two perspectives most helpful in illuminating the key issues for business families. The first is the concept of normal adult development, particularly as investigated by Daniel Levinson and his colleagues at Yale University over the past three decades. Levinson's research on typical life experiences of men and women led him to develop a comprehensive theory of adult development. In this theory, normal adult life is not static after adolescence. Instead, it is made up of eras and periods in much the same way that childhood is divided into stages of development. Levinson found that these periods for adults form an alternating pattern of dramatic transitions and relative stability. The transitions are times when individuals reconsider the structure of their lives—the priorities, activities, goals, and values that guide everyday behavior. As transitions come to a close, individuals make decisions and choices about what will be most important in their lives (their "life structure") through the next period. The stable periods are times when people use that life structure to get along, day by day. People are tenacious during a stable period in hanging onto the life structure they have created (after all, it would be too exhausting to keep constantly changing your basic behaviors). They experience its strengths and its inadequacies. What is learned about the usefulness of a life structure can be used during the next transition period to make changes for the future.[1]

Our understanding of this concept of life structures moving through periods of stability and transition is captured in the metaphor of a person building a house he or she can live in. As individuals transition from the teenage years to young adulthood, around the age of twenty, they build a first structure that reflects the priorities of their new lives. The first structure is sometimes far from their parents' home, and sometimes right next door. It may be a simple A-frame, with a large bed, an entertainment center, a big microwave oven, a freezer for pizzas, and little else. "Stability" does not mean that nothing changes; as this person experiences the twenties, the house is adapted and redecorated as specific needs change—a garage may be added for a first car, a jacuzzi installed as the second or third job finally begins to generate some disposable income—but the basic structure is maintained until the next transition period, usually around age thirty. In the transition, life changes are significant enough to require not just redecorating, but rebuilding. The initial structure is torn down, and a new one is built that reflects new, different priorities. Now it has two bedrooms, to reflect marriage and the possibility of a child. Several bathrooms are added, and a full kitchen. The garage is expanded to accommodate two cars—the station wagon and the going-to-work car. The new structure reflects the current life situation of the person, shaped by the experience of the prior period and anticipating, as best one can, the needs of the dimly seen future. Once again, through the decade of the thirties, adjustments are made as circumstances require, but the basic structure is maintained until the next major transition—this time at midlife, between thirty-eight and forty-four. This pattern continues throughout life. During transition periods, new structures are built on the foundation of previous structures that are no longer adequate. The new structures are defended and tinkered with as long as possible through the next stable period, until they become unmanageably inappropriate for the persons' life as it has evolved, and a new transition is needed.

We use this model of adult development to understand a wide range of developmental issues in business families. It is a guide to the senior generation's behavior as business owners and managers, helping to explain the periods of full-speed-ahead ambition and of self-reflective changes in course that are a part of most owner-managers' careers. It also provides a framework for understanding the ups and downs of the younger generation's development in their own careers. In particular, as we will discuss more fully in the Working Together stage, it helps to explain some of the patterns in the quality of the work relationship between the generations, as each family member reaches out to the other from his or her own individual developmental stage.

The second perspective that we have found useful in understanding business family development is the concept of family life cycles.[2] The basic idea that a family also goes through predictable stages of development as a unit is widely accepted. Most models describe a cycle as beginning with the formation of a new family: marriage. Beyond that, however, theorists and researchers have focused on a variety of different definitions of stages in their models.[3] Some use the ages of parents and children.[4] Others look at events or the accomplishment of critical tasks, such as establishing a home, raising and socializing young children, launching children into independent lives, and managing senior adulthood after the offspring have begun families of their own. Still others have emphasized the cyclical aspects of family development, or the interaction of individual and family system development.[5]

The various models of family life cycles also vary as to how carefully they take into account contemporary definitions of what a "family" is.[6] The family is a remarkably durable social structure,[7] but that is not to say that the structure of the family is not changing dramatically. Population studies estimate that nearly half of all first marriages in the United States will end in divorce. Less than one-third of American children born in this decade will live through their childhood and adolescence in a "traditional nuclear family"; that is, a married couple with their shared offspring. Less than 10 percent of African-American children will do so.[8] In fact, "the 1950s model of the White middle-class nuclear family headed by a breadwinner-father and supported by a full-time homemaker-mother is currently found in only eight percent of U.S. households."[9] Single parenting and blended families, with three or four generations, step-relationships, and remarried spouses, have become the norm rather than the exception.

Therefore we have adapted and integrated these concepts of individual adult development and family life cycles—ages of parents and children, key events, and critical development tasks—to apply to business families, using the broadest general definition of the term *family*. The stages we use on the family developmental axis are based on the common developmental tasks that arise regardless of family size or structure. We are well aware that divorce and remarriage create nearly infinite variations, which require some tailoring to make the generic descriptions fit. But our experience has taught us that the core issues are remarkably consistent across many different definitions of *family*. Therefore, for example, we use the word *marriage* to refer to any intimate, two-person relationship that acts like a marriage in the family business system. The same is true for words like *parent, sibling, cousin,* and so forth. Being realistic about common variation, we have found that the stories of individual business families can be clustered into stages in a normal developmental cycle. We have also found that those stages of development help significantly in understanding the special challenges facing family relationships in business-owning families.

The Family Developmental Stages

The family developmental axis includes four sequential stages, illustrated in figure 2-1: the Young Business Family, the Entering the Business Family,

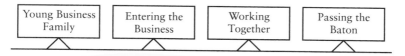

Figure 2-1 ■ *The Family Developmental Dimension*

the Working Together Family, and the Passing the Baton Family. The family axis is different from the other two axes (ownership and business) in this model. Because it is driven by the biological aging of family members, it is more of a one-way street than the others. Although it is possible to arrest development in a business, or to go forward or backward from any ownership form, you cannot do so as easily with families. It is certainly true that, in a particular family, a stage may be relatively shorter or longer, and the events in each stage may differ dramatically across families. Many adults recycle through stages as they move from first to second or later marriages. Some families have no children or a few; others have many. Some families have long periods of two or three generations working together; others have no time like that at all. Still, because none of us can stop time or grow younger, the progression of families through the stages as parents and children mature moves fundamentally in one direction.

This dimension is also different from depictions of other family life cycle theories because it is specifically about *business* families. Most important, this means that its stages cover the entire adult lifespan in approximately equal blocks. Nearly all other family life cycle models concentrate on the early years of the family, before the children reach adulthood. Late adolescents are described as "leaving" the family; and the remaining years of the senior generation are labeled "postparental." This is understandable, because for most families the amount of direct contact between the generations falls off dramatically after the offspring pass their early twenties.[10] In business families, however, the level of contact for at least some family members remains high throughout life and may actually be higher in adulthood than it was in late childhood. Along with the intensity of contact, the issues of importance are also lifelong. Therefore our model places special emphasis, and half of its stages, on the portion of family development during which there are at least two adult generations.

The Young Business Family

Characteristics

In Young Business Families, the parental generation is usually under forty years old, and if there are children, they are under eighteen. This stage can cover a long period for the family, from the early adult years of young entrepreneurs or successors through the teen years of their children. That includes, in one stage, many of the stages from traditional family development theories: courtship, marriage, settling down, birth of the first child, birth of other children, and the children's early school years.

The Young Business Family Stage of Family Development

Characteristics

- Adult generation under forty
- Children, if any, under eighteen

Key Challenges

- Creating a workable marriage enterprise
- Making initial decisions about the relationship between work and family
- Working out relationships with the extended family
- Raising children

Rockman Equipment Company: Part 1

Rockman Equipment Company was founded in 1926 by Micah ("Big Mike") Rockman. Micah had been working in an automobile repair shop and had foreseen the potential in the repair equipment business. Over the next seventy years, Rockman expanded to distribute and service all kinds of automobile maintenance and repair equipment. Micah ran Rockman Equipment his own way and developed a reputation as a shrewd businessman and a demanding employer. Micah's only son, Wyatt, began working at the company after school when he was eleven years old; it was the only job he ever had. Micah made sure that Wyatt learned everything there was to know about Rockman Equipment, starting on the shop floor, picking parts, and cleaning up around the repair bays. Wyatt was always a good student, and as he neared graduation he thought about going away to college. But when the boy graduated from high school, Micah made it clear that it would be preferable if Wyatt would enroll part time at the local junior college. Wyatt never considered disagreeing.

Wyatt met Margaret Sullivan on a blind date. Margaret had returned to their home town of Knowland after college and a few years of working in Texas. They got along well from the start. Margaret was more sophisticated than most of the girls Wyatt had dated. He liked her blend of calmness and self-confidence. She saw Wyatt as a diamond in the rough: lots of thoughtfulness and dependability, wrapped up in a surprising shyness. Given Wyatt's travel schedule, they saw each other only sporadically during the year and a half of their courtship. Finally Wyatt made a formal proposal. Margaret accepted without hesitation. They were married on Wyatt's twenty-fifth birthday; Margaret was only twenty-three. Over the eight years that followed, they had three children: Joe, Marcy, and David. With Micah's financial help, they bought a beautiful home on the outskirts of town. Wyatt was Micah's general manager and designated successor. The great American dream seemed well within their reach.

In 1968, when Micah died, Wyatt (age thirty-seven) was surprised at the depth of his own grief. He replayed scenes with his father over and over in his mind. He wondered what his father would have said to a customer or how he would have priced a deal. His greatest fear was that each person was saying to himself, "Wyatt's okay, but he's no Big Mike." Part of Wyatt's uncertainty came from the terms of Micah's will. Wyatt was given only 50 percent of the voting shares in the company. The other half was divided between his two sisters. Wyatt was not sure how he was going to make the sibling partnership work; he and his sisters had not been that close while growing up.

As the new president, Wyatt suddenly found himself working seven long days a week. He and Margaret had less and less time to talk. They rarely fought, but they also had less time for evenings out, or to be with friends. When Wyatt was invited by the mayor to chair the Businessmen's Committee for a major civic event, Margaret had been thrilled, but Wyatt had to turn down the appointment, saying that he couldn't possibly be out of the office that much at that time. Margaret argued, "You've been buried in that office for three years since your father died. This is supposed to be a business, not your whole life." But Wyatt could only respond, "Pretty soon we'll have more time together, and with the kids. But I can't take on something like this now."

Despite Margaret's desire for more of Wyatt's time, she was committed to keeping the family in the business. When Wyatt asked her if she thought he should consider selling out, she replied that the name of the company was Rockman Equipment, built by Micah for Wyatt and, in turn, for their children. Wyatt thought a great deal about her confidence and determination. He decided that it was time for their oldest son, Joe (age thirteen), to begin to spend some time at the company. Wyatt explained to Joe that he had a job for him at Rockman Equipment, so that he could earn some spending money and get used to the place. Joe was very excited about the idea. He agreed to spend all day Saturday helping out in the parts department. He was a little reluctant to give up his Saturday afternoon football game with his friends, but Wyatt was firm, and Joe wanted to please his father.

Wyatt was reminded of his own start in the company at about the same age. The difference was that he had spent every afternoon there, dropped off by the school bus. Big Mike would show up at the end of the day, usually to find some fault with his work before giving him a ride home. Thinking about his own son, Wyatt realized that his father had not done everything right—maybe there was some room for him to do better.

Key Challenges

Creating a Workable Marriage Enterprise. The first key challenge of the Young Business Family stage is establishing a relationship with a spouse or intimate partner, and the early years in the children's lives. With so much emphasis today on the difficulties of marriage and the anachronistic quality of the traditional family, it may be surprising that marriage remains so popular. In 1890 only 63 percent of the U.S. population ever married; in the 1970s the figure climbed to about 95 percent.[11]

Given the drawbacks and risks of marriage, why does it still appeal to so many people? The romantic view of marriage does not say much about how a couple goes about the business of daily living after the wedding is over. A more useful concept for our analysis is the "marriage enterprise":[12] the system that the couple builds to accomplish its dream of partnership and, in many cases, family. Contemporary marriages are complex psychological and social arrangements. In creating their psychological marriage, the couple develops implicit and explicit agreements and habits about money, work, affection, sex, children, social behavior, relationships with in-laws, and goals for the future. Violations of these agreements are the source of most marital conflict. But as the individuals grow and change, the marriage enterprise must change with them, while not abandoning its basic premises. Some people believe that allowing the marital enterprise to mature and develop as the individuals change is the most important task of marriage and the best predictor of marital longevity.

In families with businesses, the marital enterprise has special significance, but it can take very different forms. In the Rockman family, for example, Wyatt sees running the family business as his full-time job. He leaves home to go to the office early in the morning, works hard, and returns late. His implicit arrangement with his wife, Margaret, is that he will be the primary breadwinner and she will be the primary home manager and child rearer. Wyatt spent as much time as he could with his children on weekends, before Micah died and he had to go to the office most Saturdays and Sundays. Margaret worked outside the home before the children were born and thinks about returning to part-time work or starting a small business of her own when they are grown. In their marriage enterprise, Wyatt works on his dream of becoming a leader, matching his father and gaining the respect of his siblings, and reaching financial security. The marriage enterprise also supports Margaret's dream: to create a stable and enviable home, to raise successful children, and later to have a part of her life where she makes an important contribution outside of her family and spousal role.

Their friends the Huangs have formed a somewhat different enterprise. Ted and Elaine began a fast-food franchise together, with a loan from Elaine's father. Later they bought a restaurant and a small motel, and eventually another motel. Elaine still manages the restaurants; Ted is president of the motel company. They go to the office together every day. They bought their first motel when the youngest of their two children entered school. Since then, they have had a live-in housekeeper who takes care of the home, babysits, and cooks for the family. Neither Ted nor Elaine would make a significant business decision without consulting the other. Their work sometimes keeps one or both of them out of the house in the evening or on weekends, but they have made it a rule to have dinner at home as a family at least four nights each week, and to spend Saturdays together. Each is pursuing a dream that includes both business success and family identity. The business has created a great deal of conflict between the spouses over the years, but it has also made them a closely collaborative team.

In these two examples, many things look the same. The couples were married in the same year. They have the same number of children, and family members are the same ages. The businesses are comparable in size. Both marriages are happy. But the two marriage enterprises are very different. The spouses in the Rockman and Huang marriages expect different things from their partners and from being married. They have probably never articulated these expectations to each other, but each spouse has a good sense of what those expectations are. And neither wife or husband would likely be very satisfied with a spouse from the other couple.

The type of marriage enterprise that the couple forms in the Young Business Family stage has implications not only for their one-to-one relationship, but also for the family environment and its reflection in the business. For example, the couple will gradually evolve a style of interaction on the continuum that family theorists call *enmeshment-disengagement*.[13] In enmeshed families, anybody's business is everybody's business; there is a high level of intimacy and interdependence, and little privacy. In disengaged families, autonomy, self-reliance, and individuality are highly valued. Extremes in either direction can be dysfunctional. Most strong and healthy families demonstrate aspects of both styles.

Families with businesses tend to be at least a little on the enmeshed side. The family identification, close relationships, emphasis on trust, and comfort with group tasks in enmeshed families lead to many of the advantages of family businesses. But whichever style the family adopts at home, it has important implications for the structure of the business. If a family has a very enmeshed style, family members may look for opportunities to escape from the intense "togetherness" and create islands of independence. The business is an attractive opportunity to find such a refuge. As a result, some members from enmeshed families will be determined to enforce rigid boundaries protecting their space in the business. If taken to a dysfunctional extreme, their need for autonomy may come at the expense of good communication and integrated operations. Conversely, some individuals from strongly disengaged families will see the business as an opportunity to create a family bond. The business can be the prime integrating force in a disengaged family. Over the years we have encountered many families, particularly second- and third-generation disengaged families, in businesses that were founded by hard-driving, distant entrepreneurs, where family members have said clearly that if it were not for the business, their disengaged family would have spun apart long ago. But in this direction also, the extreme case can sometimes result in an overreliance on consensus models in management and in restrictive shareholding policies (prohibiting sales).

Another aspect of the marriage enterprise in the Young Business Family stage that is particularly important in business families is the distribution of power. All young business couples and families adopt a form of hierarchy as part of creating their marriage enterprise.[14] The traditional pattern of authority in families with businesses has been pictured as authoritarian: the husband/father in control, the wife/mother as a supportive partner (who may have authority in certain circumscribed areas at home), and children as apprentices. Although there are clearly families that demonstrate this style in its fullest sense, and although business families may be more traditional on average than the general population of families as a whole, this style is not as common as the popular culture believes. We have found that shared authority, spouse copreneurship, sibling partnerships, dominant children, and matriarchies are much more common in business families than was once thought. It may be that these more egalitarian forms are becoming more common because they are also more successful. Family systems where authority is more broadly shared may fit better with the varied and changing demands of running a business.[15] In addition, the increasing prevalence of second marriages may be encouraging more egalitarian patterns, especially among older adults. Second marriages in general have more balanced authority than first marriages, with less rigid sex-role differentiation.[16]

Some couples actually build the business together, and there are thousands of family businesses that were founded by copreneurial couples.[17] In some of these cases, the spouses work as equal partner-managers.[18] True partnership equalizes formal authority and facilitates communication. However, comanagement may also maximize conflict and make unconscious or covert power imbalances more obvious. More commonly, one spouse is more senior than the other. When a couple works together, their power relationship is part of all aspects of their lives—they cannot get away from it either by going to work or by going home.[19] This magnifies the satisfactions of an arrangement that both spouses like and equally magnifies the conflict and resentment in a relationship that is not comfortable for one or both of them. One encouraging finding is that, despite the intense demands in both the work setting and the home, most couples feel that developing a business together has strengthened their marriage.[20]

Making Initial Decisions about the Relationship between Work and Family. Whether or not both spouses work in the family business, it is a difficult challenge for the Young Business Family to nurture the domain of work and the domain of the family simultaneously. Time, energy, attention, and money are usually in short supply in any marriage at the young family stage. In business families, however, there are special pressures. First, there are the demands of the business itself. These often include late hours, seven-day work weeks, and the takeover of family social events by business discussions. There may be social obligations with customers and suppliers. The business may use up all of the Young Business Family's financial reserves and even require personally collateralized debt. It is sometimes hard for the partner on the outside to understand the level of involvement and identification experienced by the spouse in the business. For example, time pressure is the dominant feature of the Rockman family at this stage. Wyatt may be prone to be a hard worker, but his situation exaggerates that tendency. He is following a successful father with a strong personality and coping with all the posttransition demands of business, family, and ownership at the same time. Margaret tries to be supportive, but the nature of their marriage enterprise does not call for much sharing of information, so she cannot truly empathize with his situation.

Second, if the Young Business Family is part of a larger family business, then dynamics with the extended family may frequently intrude on the couple's private efforts to form their own marriage enterprise. Intense and shifting relationships with siblings, turf battles, and competition to perform conspicuously well in front of the parents can add enormous pressure to the young marriage enterprise, making the couple feel out of control of that part of their lives. Finally, when children are born, the Young Business Family has to cope with a new set of conflicts: work-parenting dilemmas and the expectations of the extended family, who are simultaneously employer/colleagues and grandparents/uncles/aunts/in-laws. To avoid conflict and confusion at this stage, the couple needs a strong sense of its own identity as a separate young family and a focus on its own concept of the marriage enterprise and the role of work in it.

Working out Relationships with the Extended Family. A third key challenge of the Young Business Family stage is finding a place for the new family in the extended families of both spouses. Keeping a balance between sides of the extended family is always a challenge for a young couple. It can be even harder if one spouse's family is involved in the business (on which the couple may be financially dependent) and the other spouse's family is not. The relatives of the spouse on the business side are then connected in all three circles—family, business, and ownership—whereas the relatives on the other side have only the family connection. The business-owning extended family may try to envelop the new marriage as if nothing had changed. This can create tension over the amount of time spent at quasi-business gatherings of the family of origin, such as Sunday barbecues, evening meetings, family vacations, or business trips. The young business couple then has to make a conscious effort to avoid spending all of its time with the business side of the extended family.

An opposite problem arises if the business-owning extended family does not approve of the marriage or like the new spouse, or if it is simply wary of all in-laws. This can be a special problem if the new family's style is very enmeshed. For example, in the Smith family, the parent-founders of the family printing company always expressed the value that whomever their four daughters married would be considered a full member of the family—just like a son. When the oldest daughter married, her husband was offered a job and a block of shares in the company. Two years later, the marriage ended in divorce, the son-in-law joined a competitor, and the family engaged in a lengthy legal battle to recover the outstanding shares. At that point, Mr. Smith approached his third daughter, who was planning to marry one of the company's accountants. Mr. Smith told her that not only would he not be giving any shares to the new husband, but he wanted the couple to sign a prenuptial agreement withholding her shares from community property, and he would prefer it if the new son-in-law gave up the company's account. This caused a major conflict in the family, the cancellation of a formal family wedding, and deeply hurt feelings. Mr. Smith was feeding a lifelong sibling rivalry between the two sisters. The younger daughter had been proud that her husband and marriage were going to succeed where her older sister's had failed, and that she would be proven more competent, loyal, and loving at last. Her father's action felt like advance punishment to her; she had lost something due to her sister's behavior. Her father, badly injured by the experience with his oldest daughter, could not understand how his younger daughter did not see the simple wisdom of his new policy.

Raising Children. Finally, Young Business Families face the formidable challenge of deciding whether or not to have children, when to have them, how many to have, and how to raise them. Most couples who do decide to become parents would agree that children change everything, *especially* the marital enterprise. Adding children to a marriage changes the vision of the future. It changes priorities, or at least brings priorities that have existed only in theory into the realm of here-and-now reality. And, perhaps most importantly, it adds an enormous new set of tasks to the marriage.[21]

In the Young Business Family stage, the impact on the business of becoming parents will depend to a large extent on the decisions that were made about work in the marriage enterprise. If one spouse has been working in the family business and the other has been a homemaker, as in the Rockman family, the marital contract may not need fundamental renegotiation when children are born. Having children may add many new responsibilities to the homemaker spouse, and new pressure for financial success to the business spouse, but the role differentiation can remain much the same.

On the other hand, if both spouses in the Young Business Family have been working in the business, as in the Huang family, becoming parents will have important consequences for both the marriage enterprise and the operation of the firm. There are limited options open to them to cover the responsibilities of child rearing. If both want to keep their positions in the company, they can enlist a family member or nonfamily employee to care for the children when they are young, supplemented by day care, nursery school, and school as they grow up. They can try to put strict limits on their hours in the business, covering for each other with staggered schedules (this solution often looks better on paper than in reality). However, the most common solution is for one spouse, traditionally the husband, to be a near-full-time owner-manager (perhaps helping at home as much as possible), while the other spouse, traditionally the wife, cuts back on her time in the business and covers the primary responsibility for the children. (This can lead to the situation of the "invisible woman" in the family business.[22]) Whatever solution is chosen, the key is for there to be an explicit renegotiation of the marriage enterprise—fully discussed until each spouse can support the new arrangement.

With the birth of children, the parents in the Young Business Family become the middle generation in the family business system. It is often the birth of children that causes a founder or founding copreneurial couple to consider for the very first time that their company might become a family business. Having children instantly pushes back the horizon of the future for most people. Their timetable for planning and dreaming stretches beyond the next year or the next milestone to include their children's growing up, becoming adults, and continuing the family in future generations. In business families, the company is a convenient vehicle for all those fantasies. It can serve as a context for the normal dreams of parents: providing for all the child's needs, teaching and guiding children as they develop skills, working together on increasingly mutual projects, even watching the children eventually carry on the family identity and legacy into the distant future, generation after generation.

In many business families, conveying the psychological legacy of the firm is an important part of child rearing from the beginning. Although the world of careers seems far in the future for the young children in the Young Business Family stage, this is a critical period for forming their impressions of the family business. Children will internalize their parents' attitudes and values about the firm, a sense of the quality of life it provides, and impressions of the business's impact on their parents' marriage and family relationships. Lessons learned at this stage, intentionally or unintentionally, will not be easily changed by the lectures that parents may give later in life, and they will determine in large part the potential for the business's continuity in the future. One second-generation CEO of a company that imported and manufactured women's knitwear expressed her dismay that none of her four children wanted to join her in the rapidly growing, profitable business. "It's a far better economic opportunity than any of them have anywhere else, but it looks like when I am ready to retire I'll have to sell it out." Interviews with her daughters and son made it clear that their decisions were actually predetermined many years earlier, in the Young Business Family stage. Their memories were all the same. "Every night, she would come home and be obsessed with how difficult it was, how miserable her coworkers and customers had been that day, how tough it was working with her brother. Now all of a sudden she wants us to see how much fun she was having, and how satisfying the business was all those years. It's too late; I have an idea about what family business is like, and it's not for me."

The Entering the Business Family

Characteristics

In the Entering the Business stage, the owner-manager and spouse are now typically between thirty-five and fifty-five, moving into and through middle age, and adjusting their business strategy and personal lifestyle accordingly. Most of the younger generation are now teenagers and young adults, just beginning their work lives, and making their initial decisions about entering the company. They need clarification on the opportunities the family

---

The Entering the Business Stage of Family Development

Characteristics
- Senior generation between thirty-five and fifty-five
- Junior generation in teens and twenties

Key Challenges
- Managing the midlife transition
- Separation and individuation of the younger generation
- Facilitating a good process for initial career decisions

---

business provides—both as future owners and as potential leaders. If the family is small or the business is demanding, the senior generation may face a recruitment task if it hopes to retain family management in the future. If the family is large and executive roles in the business are seen as very attractive, then the task is likely to be one of selection. In either case, the coming-of-age of a new generation forces the family business to redefine itself. Why are we a family business, and who will care about maintaining our identity in the future? How is "family" defined for us? Which offspring, or branch, or namesakes are entitled to access to employment and financial benefits from this business?

Although many family issues are important at this stage, three are most critical. The first is the midlife transition that the senior generation must transverse during this period. The second is the process of separation and individuation that moves the emerging adults out of the parental home. The third is the process by which the younger generation decides whether or not to join the business.

Rockman Equipment Company: Part 2

By 1984 the two oldest Rockman children, Joe (age twenty-five) and Marcy (age twenty-two), had finished college and were pursuing their first ventures into work careers. Dave, the youngest (age nineteen), had graduated from high school early and was also testing his abilities in the world of work.

Three years earlier, Joe had started working full time on the Monday after his Saturday graduation from college. He had never worked anywhere but at Rockman Equipment, except for one summer job in a construction company owned by a fraternity brother's father. Joe had always felt restless at college. He would have left college several times if it had not been for strong pressure from his mother, Margaret. She was relentlessly determined that he graduate.

Actually, Joe had been able to apply some of what he had learned as a business major and in his summer job to his work at Rockman. In his first job in a branch office, he had suggested to the sales manager that they have weekly staff meetings to inform each other about new developments with customers. Joe knew that, if he were not the owner's son, his ideas would have been ignored, but he didn't care why he was listened to as long as he got the results that he wanted. Then a few months later, Wyatt had suggested that he come back into the main office. Joe agreed and had been living at home ever since. He didn't mind his work, but he felt a little like he was still preparing to do a job, instead of doing it.

Marcy had graduated from the University of Colorado. Unlike Joe, Marcy had had a wonderful time in college. Besides the skiing, she had loved economics, psychology, Shakespeare, history of art, and, most of all, math. After graduation, her first plan had been to spend a year in Europe with her best friend. When that idea fell through, she returned to Knowland for the summer and naturally started helping out at the company. Soon she was going to the office every day, still on a "let's see what happens" basis, helping out in the finance office under the CFO.

Dave had graduated from Knowland High School a semester early and immediately began a six-month adventure sailing around the Pacific with the crew of an oceanographic research vessel. When the project ended, Dave decided to stay in California with one of the other crew members. Wyatt arranged a job for Dave with one of their suppliers in southern California. Dave wasn't thrilled about the prospect of spending his time in California working in a factory, but it was clear that his parents' approval for his staying, and their financial support, depended on his agreement. Things had worked out very well. The hours he was putting in at the factory were long, but Dave had to admit that he was enjoying it.

Margaret had reacted to the departure of her youngest child from home with some regret and a good deal of relief. After twenty-five years of taking care of children, it was now just Wyatt and her. Margaret was toying with the idea of becoming a kind of interior design consultant as a small business venture. She was reluctant to approach Wyatt about the idea; business was bad, and Wyatt was preoccupied with work. She was also a little worried about the constant bickering between Joe and Marcy. She had always felt that, if the two of them could spend some time together, they would overcome their childhood rivalries and learn to be good friends as adults.

Wyatt (age fifty-one) had begun to think that his anxiety was out of proportion to the business slump. He felt as if he was in a personal slump, dissatisfied with his accomplishments and eager to try something new. Wyatt's comfort came when he considered the family. He was very comfortable in his marriage, and he was also very grateful that the children had avoided most of the serious problems that plagued the young adult kids of so many of the people they knew. But he felt very uncertain about the future. Wyatt felt like he was running as fast as he could at the business, and just barely staying ahead of the wolves. Could he hang on and continue to build, so that his children would have a vibrant, healthy business to take over? And who was he building the business for? Did Joe really have what it takes? Was Marcy a realistic possibility, even in this new era? Could Dave ever live the life of a businessman in Knowland?

Key Challenges

Managing the Midlife Transition. Early in the Entering the Business stage, the parents are most likely to be going through the *midlife transition*. This term, one of the most significant contributions of Levinson's work on adult development, is a more complex elaboration of the "midlife crisis" that has become part of our popular culture. It refers to a period of several years, usually the early forties, when it is common for adults to experience a time of self-assessment. Wyatt Rockman is reflecting on the classic midlife transition—thinking about his accomplishments to date and wondering if he has enough time left to get closer to achieving his most important dreams.

The midlife transition is often a powerful experience, because it comes between two major sections of adult life: early adulthood, between the ages of twenty and forty, which is the exploratory, achievement-focused, and commitment-making era; and middle adulthood, between the ages of forty and sixty, which are the years of maximum authority, senior status, and control. It is during the early forties that most people stop and ask themselves if the path they have been on in early adulthood is compelling enough to continue in middle adulthood; that is, are their early choices still satisfying enough to be their life's work? All aspects of the life structure are brought under review: career, marriage or romance, parenting, extended family relationships, religion and spirituality, social role, physical and sexual activity, recreation, and whatever else occupies an important place in life. This time of life is experienced as "halftime." As has been demonstrated at many levels of analysis, the halfway point is a natural stimulus for stock taking, with a new sense that there is only limited time left.[23] There is still time, one feels, to make dramatic changes, to take a different path, and to do better—but that will not always be so.

There is so much going on in life during these years that it is difficult to separate internal developmental processes from responses to life events. The oldest children are leaving the parental home, and others are likely to be at various points in adolescence. In a business family, this may raise unconscious anxiety about the potential for continuity, even though the time of transition is only dimly imagined in the distant future. Parents may be troubled by their teenagers' normal separating behavior, concerned that once they leave home or jobs in the business, they will never return.

At the same time, the parents of midlife adults are aging more dramatically at this point, and some will die. In business families, this marks the completion of the prior generation's cycle of control. Now the mantle—and the burden—of leadership belong fully to the midlife generation, without the intrusion or the security of the parental guide. Both the parents and the offspring are departing; midlife adults can very quickly change from feeling that they are embedded in the middle of an active family to a sense that they are alone. For some this leads to a positive feeling of freedom. The burden of intense familial responsibility is finally reduced, they are released from the parental evaluative eye, and they are free to explore previously hidden sides of their personalities. For others, this freedom is accompanied by a sense of isolation, abandonment, and missed opportunities with both parents and children.[24]

There are other ways that the midlife transition has special meaning in business families at this Entering the Business stage. The initial career decisions of the younger generation stimulate self-questioning in the parental generation as well. While talking with their teenage and young adult children about whether or not to join the family firm, business owners are reminded of their own decisions. "How did I become a businessperson? Did I feel that I had a choice? Has working in this firm provided me with the rewards that I expected?" Most important, "If I had it to do over again, would I make the same decisions?" Two generations, asking themselves the same questions, are what set the dynamics of the Entering the Business stage into motion.[25]

Separation and Individuation of the Younger Generation. The parents' midlife transition coincides with the second key challenge of the Entering the Business stage: the departure of the offspring generation from the parental home. This separation goes far beyond a change of address for each child in turn. The family structure is changing. The marriage is changing. So is the meaning of the parental role, including what each generation needs from each other, expects from each other, and has to try to accept from each other.[26]

Many models of the family life cycle identify this stage with the concept of "launching." The idea is that the younger generation is ejected from the family one by one at about the time they graduate from high school. If the parents have done their job right, the preparation has been adequate, and the offspring are ready to relocate to college, or the armed services, or a job, or a marriage. The job of the nuclear family is mostly done; the responsibility for negotiating the world of adulthood now rests with the offspring.

It is clear that even in nonbusiness families it rarely works that way. Many young adults now continue to live in the parental home into their twenties.[27] Others leave and return, either at the breakup of an early marriage or just to save money. Even for those who move out, the transition from teenager to adult is a more gradual process in most families, covering a number of years. In addition, different families have very different visions of the optimal level of generational independence. In many neighborhoods, the course of the "launched capsule" is rarely more than a few blocks.[28] Ethnic groups differ in their models for appropriate relationships between the generations.[29] Still, there is a powerful norm in American culture that becoming an adult means leaving the parental world and forming an independent life, whether that entails moving across the country or only across the street.

The generational separation that is an inherent task of the Entering the Business stage is very difficult for many business-owning families. As a result, sometimes the family overfocuses on the single question of whether or not the offspring will join the family firm. In fact, families who negotiate this stage most successfully take a broader view, acknowledging that both generations have important transitions to accomplish. The older generation must begin to learn a new parenting role as parents of adults. And the younger generation must attend to all the components of moving into adulthood: career, self-reliance, financial responsibility, intimate partners, and social network.

Sibling dynamics are also critical to understanding family business systems in the Entering the Business stage. Siblings are life's longest relationships. For most people, there is no one who shares as much as a sibling—genetically, environmentally, and historically.[30] In the Entering the Business stage, the childhood relationships, largely shaped by parents, gradually evolve into adult sibling relationships, which are fashioned and sustained by the brothers and sisters themselves for the rest of their lives. This is the time when brothers and sisters make important decisions about how much their adult lives will remain intertwined. Choosing a career in the business usually means committing oneself to remaining intimate with siblings for a lifetime—interdependent not just on family matters, but on career and financial ones as well. The young adults in the Entering the Business stage have to decide whether that level of closeness seems workable for them.

In some business families, the company is always central to the sibling relationships, because the business dominates all aspects of family life. In these cases, the surest way for a child to get attention and rewards from the parents, even at an early age, is through the business. One, several, or all of the brothers and sisters may make it a point to learn about the business, spend free time at the office or in the factory, take a Saturday job at the front counter or cataloguing inventory, or work as a sales clerk in the summers during high school. By the Entering the Business stage, these children have absorbed the family priorities and understand their options. Staying in the business means keeping first-class status in the family; choosing another path means becoming peripheral to family interaction. The more successful you are in the company, the higher your value in your parents' eyes.

Other families create different sibling environments. The parents protect time away from the business to spend with the children individually and together. As a result, the sibling bond develops separately from work. This can be reinforced by family vacations that are not connected with business trips; dinners together where the topics of conversation are the children's day at school, not the parents' day at the office; and encouraging adolescent children to take part-time jobs somewhere else. When that is the pattern in early childhood, then siblings are more likely to view working in the business as a career option, not as a criterion for membership in the family. In addition, because each child has access to the parents in the personal family arena, competition for access to them through the business is reduced.

Among the many aspects of sibling relationships, three that are of special importance to business families are *birth order*, and the dynamics of *differentiation* and *identification*. Birth order is particularly important in business families because of the traditions of primogeniture (preference for firstborn males in inheritance).[31] Historically, strong traditions have supported primogeniture in business-owning families. First, the gender bias toward males as business leaders means that many families have traditionally looked to their sons as successor candidates. In addition, the natural family hierarchy of age, and the head start that older siblings have on education and experience, mean that preference often goes to first or early-born sibs. Finally, for some families primogeniture is less a choice than an avoidance of choice. Most families are uncomfortable with explicit competitive evaluation among siblings and will look for other decision rules, which protect the parents from the recrimination and guilt associated with favoritism. In choosing a next-generation leader, primogeniture is the most common automatic assumption—the way it will be unless and until some other solution replaces it.

An explicit or implicit assumption that the oldest son is the most likely heir to the business will have a strong effect on family dynamics in the Entering the Business stage. Depending on the style of the business and the family, the other siblings may react with intense envy or with relief. "Designated heir" status usually carries with it greater access to the parents and a wonderful sense of specialness. But it may also carry greater demands for performance. The chosen child may have little choice or, like Joe Rockman, may at least feel that way. For that child, early commitment to the firm may restrict options about school, extracurricular activities, weekend and vacation experiences, and friends. The parents may feel they are benefiting from primogeniture as a decision rule, because uncertainty is reduced and continuity is enhanced. But primogeniture is an arbitrary rule, based on family values about age and gender. Applying it to the business can leave the siblings with resentments that will influence their relationships for the rest of their lives.

Primogeniture is only one example of the way brothers and sisters divide up the psychological space of a family in order to achieve recognition as unique individuals.[32] Firstborns have an advantage in selecting a special role, because they enter an open field, but even in families that ignore primogeniture, this freedom is restricted by the conscious and unconscious desires of the parents. The firstborn may be highly motivated to try to become the person that the parents are hoping for. Or the firstborn may feel coerced into satisfying the parents' dreams and resent the perceived freedom of the other siblings to choose different paths. Later-born children are in a different situation; they can either compete with the same skills or look for distinctly different roles. Parents may encourage competition (wittingly or unwittingly) with an attitude of comparison, such as "I hope you will be as . . . as your sister," or, more negatively, "Why can't you be more like your brother?" This can be a complicated and tense dynamic in some families. Defeating or overtaking a sibling can be a Pyrrhic victory. A sibling's public failure can be an embarrassment for the whole family. And exaggerated competition at the Entering the Business stage can also make it very difficult to form a viable Sibling Partnership in later stages, when the parents are no longer around to referee.

Differentiation is the centrifugal force of sibling groups, acting to pull individuals apart. There is also an opposite, centripetal force, which holds them together: sibling identification. Intimacy with siblings has its own rewards, especially in coping with parents. When parents are preoccupied with the incessant demands of the business, sibling identification and interdependence can be enhanced—often evolving, during the Entering the

Business stage, into a powerful sibling alliance. The strength of this alliance may be an excellent predictor of the chances of success of a Sibling Partnership in the future.

All sibling groups demonstrate some balance of wanting to be together and wanting to be separate individuals. The differentiating pressure moves siblings to want to work in different parts of the company, or one to get an MBA while another disparages business education as irrelevant, or one to love being identified with the family business while another seems embarrassed by it. At the same time, the identification pressure encourages them to visit each other unexpectedly, to rally to one another's support when one is threatened or in trouble, to defend one another against parental criticism or attack, and sometimes to agree to comanagement of the business even if the individual would rather have unchallenged control. Both influences have to be taken into account in assessing the real collaborative potential of the sibling group in the Entering the Business stage.

Facilitating a Good Process for Initial Career Decisions. It is an oversimplification to portray this issue as it is most often presented in the succession literature: Do the parents try to coerce the offspring into joining the business, or are they given truly free choice? We have found that the actual process unfolds over a number of years and includes many interrelated questions, all of which must be resolved, such as:

- Will the business continue for another generation?

- Do the parents want their children to consider careers in management in the firm, or to participate only as owners?

- Will several members of the next generation run the firm together, or will only one individual be invited to join?

- Do the parents want to structure opportunity and experience so that they ultimately control who enters, or do they want the offspring to choose for themselves?

- Will offspring who want to be in the business start immediately after school and work straight through, or go away and then decide about coming back?

In finding answers to these questions, the senior generation must come to terms with its own dream for the future. Lansberg has explored in another volume the intricate power of the dream of continuity.[33] It is at this stage that parents are confronted with their own aspirations for their children. Many factors will undoubtedly contribute to the shape of those aspirations: their own history as offspring of prior generations of parents and grandparents; the pleasure or the struggle they have experienced in the business; their assessment of the firm's economic potential; their sense of each child's talents and potential. All parents confront the challenge of preparing their children to have the best opportunity for success as adults. What is different for parents in business families is that, in the midst of all the alternatives that young adults face, there is one specific opportunity that must be either accepted or rejected: the family firm.

Of course, the parental decision making is only one side of the generational separation issue. Perhaps the more important family processes in the Entering the Business stage are those occurring among the offspring. Some younger-generation members have been psychologically in the business since they were babies. They made plans to work in the company, had after-school and summer jobs, shaped their education around the demands of management roles in their industry, and consider their careers to be inevitable. Others never gave it a thought. Even if they did bookkeeping on Saturdays or drove the delivery truck all summer, it never occurred to them that their connection to the business would extend beyond their emancipation at the end of high school. And of course there are all kinds of combinations in between. For the vast majority of offspring, however, the question looms and must be confronted: Do I want to invest my work life in the family firm? Particularly at the Entering the Business stage, answering the underlying developmental dilemma is key: Can I become an independent adult, with a life of my own, and still stay embedded in the business (and therefore the world) of my parents? The younger generation's answers to these questions, as they work through the Entering the Business stage, will largely determine the future of the family business.

The Working Together Family

Characteristics

During the Working Together stage, two or more generations are fully involved in the family business together. The senior generation, most typically between fifty and sixty-five, is at the peak of its authority in the business circle. If the business is profitable, the owner-managers can use the income for expansion and new ventures, and to fund a comfortable lifestyle to which many adults aspire at this age—home, travel, social life, recreation, and place in the community.

The members of the junior generation are now in their twenties, thirties, and forties. They have made the decision, at least initially, about whether their work lives will be inside or outside the business. If in the

---

The Working Together Stage of Family Development

Characteristics
- Senior generation between fifty and sixty-five
- Junior generation between twenty and forty-five

Key Challenges
- Fostering cross-generational cooperation and communication
- Encouraging productive conflict management
- Managing the three-generation Working Together family

---

business, they are preoccupied with making space for themselves as independent, competent adults, in their parents' shop. How is it possible to be loyal but also distinctive; to show strong leadership potential, without being presumptive or condescending; to be authentic and genuine, but not act like the owner's kid; show your comparative value in relation to siblings without overtly competing with them?

For the senior generation, this is the time of the empty nest, as the youngest children leave home and the oldest move further into their own lives and their own new families. In fact, one of the hallmarks of the Working Together stage of development is that the family has become a network of families, as the younger generation marries and has children of its own. The parental marriage enterprise, formed in the Young Business Family stage and often tested in the midlife Entering the Business stage, now faces the challenge of commitment after the primary family task—raising children—has been completed. As Duvall put it in her landmark study of family life cycles, "The most important task of the middle years is that of finding each other as husband and wife again."[34]

Three of the family issues that are most critical in the Working Together stage are fostering good intergenerational cooperation, managing family communication and conflict in productive ways, and developing the family into an extended family network.

Rockman Equipment Company: Part 3

In 1982 Dave Rockman came back from California to begin college at the University of Texas, his mother's alma mater. When he graduated in 1986, he started working at Rockman Equipment as a salesman. For two years, between 1986 and 1988, all three of Wyatt and Margaret's children were working in the company. Joe was now general manager of the equipment division. Marcy had moved over to the Rapid Tune division, where she ran the accounting department. Dave took over the midwest sales territory.

In 1990, when Marcy returned after being away for two years getting an MBA, Wyatt began to think about planning for the future. He had joined a family business forum sponsored by a local business school, where a speaker on succession planning had really hammered home the point that you need to give successors real jobs with responsibility. After that, Wyatt decided to identify Joe, then age thirty-two, as the next president of Rockman Equipment. For now, he made Joe the vice president of operations, although he had a hard time specifying exactly which operations Joe would have managerial responsibility for.

One result of those decisions, unexpected by Wyatt, was that Dave and Marcy reconsidered their own careers. Both of them knew that, in the long run, they would have a very hard time working for their brother, Joe. Three months later, Marcy moved back to Denver to join a start-up software firm with a friend from business school. A month after that, Dave met a young attorney, Maria Schiavone, and soon after they were married. Maria's father offered Dave a job in his company in Chicago. Dave loved working with his father, but Wyatt had made his choice about Joe, and Dave needed to think of his and Maria's future, so he took the job.

In 1991 Joe also married. Wyatt and Margaret hoped that getting married would lighten Joe's moods and soften his style with people. In the business, moving Joe from middle manager to senior executive was a bumpy road. Wyatt had tried to pass significant responsibility to Joe and give him plenty of room to make his own mistakes. Making mistakes was something that Joe proved to be good at. When talking to "outsiders,"

Wyatt had a million good reasons for each of the problems and errors that Joe had made. Privately, he was very worried.

Joe began by making some changes in important positions in his department. Unfortunately, most of them did not work out, and Wyatt felt obliged to step in and correct the situations. Then Joe began a complete overhaul of the marketing department. Joe felt that the department had been doing little more than routine advertising; he wanted to implement a comprehensive market approach that he had learned at school. He spent a great deal of money on a glossy direct mail packet and hired a consultant who specialized in market segmentation and research. Wyatt was intrigued at first, but quickly grew alarmed at the expense of the plan that Joe was proposing, and at its lack of practical applicability. The idea died after a brief and heated discussion about the plan. Someone had left Wyatt a copy of the proposal, which Joe had not shared with him. He called Joe into his office for an angry meeting. Wyatt reprimanded Joe for his "secrecy," reminding him that Wyatt was still ultimately responsible for everything that happened in this company. Joe was very discouraged. He felt that this analysis was the best work he had done, and he was looking forward to showing it to his father. As usual, it had not worked out that way.

The tensions between Wyatt and Joe were very apparent to all the managers at Rockman. In private conversations, they would agree that, although some of Joe's new ideas were terrible, the company needed to try out some different approaches. One senior vice president told another, "Wyatt is open to new ideas. I just don't think he likes to hear them from Joe."

Joe found it easier to talk to his mother than to his father about his dissatisfaction at work. He complained that Wyatt did not give him the information he needed to do his job, and would chew him out one day and praise him to everyone else the next. Wyatt, on the other hand, was worried about Joe's poor "people skills." Ever since Joe had returned to Rockman Equipment from college, Wyatt had been getting complaints about Joe's arrogant manner. Even when Joe's ideas were good, Wyatt felt that his abrasive manner undermined his own best efforts. Still, he knew that he needed to do something to help Joe feel more ready to take over the company. Finally, he decided to create the position of president for Joe. Wyatt would change his title to chairman and CEO of the equipment company. Joe wondered what a president does when someone else is still CEO, but that was not the kind of question he could ask Wyatt.

Key Challenges

Fostering Cross-Generational Cooperation and Communication. The most common way that family members assess the quality of family life is by talking about communication. This is true throughout the family life cycle, but never more so than in the Working Together stage. Offspring are marrying, having children, establishing their own homes and social networks, and becoming more and more separate—even as they share management and ownership responsibilities in the company. The primary challenge of Working Together in the context of *family* development is creating the linking mechanisms that allow the family system to continue integrated operation in the face of dramatic decentralization and diversification. Communication is the most important of these linking mechanisms.

Families differ widely in the emotional tone of their typical interactions: warm or cold, intimate or distant, hostile or friendly, and so forth. In business families, however, it is also important to look at the quality of communication as a purposeful activity, a process essential to getting the business's work done. Working Together family communication needs to demonstrate certain characteristics:

1. *Honesty.* Honesty is simply the degree to which family members tell and expect the truth. In business families that value honest communication, a son or nephew who is a junior manager will expect that, when a parent-executive asks for an opinion or feedback, he can respond with the truth, without negative consequences.

2. *Openness.* All families have taboos against some topics, such as sex, money, teenagers' romances, problems at work, and death. In families that value openness, these restrictions are kept to a minimum. Across business families in general, the most common complaints about family communication concern frustration over limits on openness. For example, if talking about recent strategic decisions is considered a challenge to the authority structure, or if protecting individual turf means that no one can ask questions about someone else's division, the openness of communication is restricted.

3. *Consistency.* In some families, you can assume that one person's opinion today will be the same as his or her opinion tomorrow, and that

words and actions communicate the same thing (that is, a statement of affection is accompanied by a facial expression and a body posture that also communicate affection). In other families, that is often not the case. For example, a young manager may find that some days she has easy access to her father in his president's office, where he calls her "honey" and asks her to sit in on his senior staff meeting "just to see what it's like." The next day, when she comes into his office to deliver a market analysis, he informs her coldly that she is taking liberties as a family member and should *always* go through channels. Perfect consistency is neither desirable nor possible. However, in families where inconsistent communication is the norm, the members' confidence and sense of security may be low, and family relationships at work may be clouded by an atmosphere of perpetual anxiety.

Taken together, these three characteristics can give an accurate picture of the quality of communication in a business family. Individuals in a family may differ from each other in communication style. One parent may be very open and the other very closed, or one sister may always be a stickler for the truth, whereas the other tends to exaggerate. Overall, a Working Together family whose communication is high on honesty, openness, and consistency will be better able to manage conflicts productively than one that is low on several or all of the dimensions.

There are a few common communication bottlenecks in the Working Together family. Parents have a great deal of difficulty giving honest feedback to their children of any age. This can interfere with good management development of the younger generation if the parent is the only supervisor or mentor. Wyatt Rockman worried that he was constantly criticizing Joe, and he gradually became reluctant to provide any feedback at all. He did not realize that Joe was eager for good data about how he was doing, and that much of his anxiety came from having to read his father's mind and put together a sense of his reactions from small gestures and offhand comments. In fact, the relatively low level of both honesty and openness in their relationship made their work relationship a strain on both of them.

Also, parents often find it hard to add topics that were out of bounds when the offspring were children to the "permitted" list for their adult sons and daughters. For example, some parents in the Working Together stage find it hard to suddenly begin discussing financial issues in both the company and the family, especially in bad times. This reluctance is not just the parents' problem; the sons and daughters may also be ambivalent about "intruding on their parents' privacy," even if the information is necessary for them to fill their adult roles in the family and their management responsibilities in the company. These openness and honesty issues need to be resolved in the Working Together family.

If the family system has reached a high degree of complexity, especially in a Cousin Consortium, communication between branches may be particularly complicated. Different histories may have created different interpretations of the same material and different assumptions about communication rules. Asking for an opinion in one branch of the family might be a request for an honest appraisal; in another branch, a request for support and encouragement. Does the family strictly follow the organization chart or the family relationship network, or some combination, in sharing information? Should a sibling assume that sharing information with a brother also means sharing with his brother's wife? Do the employed siblings have a common understanding about what information is not to be passed on to those family shareholders who do not work in the company?

In-laws can be lightning rods for unexpressed family conflicts and repositories for old grievances that the family has difficulty resolving directly. For example, two brothers work together as managers in the company's corporate office. At the end of a difficult day, the older brother storms into his house and complains to his wife, "That younger brother of mine is a pain in the neck. He challenges everything I say just to give me a hard time. He came up with a harebrained idea today that I could tell was a waste of money just by glancing at it, but he expects me to jump on board everything he suggests. Having him around is taking all the fun out of working at the company." His wife is sympathetic, and angry with the brother for making life difficult for her husband and ruining their evening and his time with his children.

At the same time, on the other side of town, his brother is also steaming. "That older brother of mine is an arrogant SOB. He treats me like a child, just like he did when we were young. I tried to show him the project that I've been working on for a month, and he threw it away without even looking at it. I'm trying to support him, and he views everything as a challenge. Working for him is taking all the fun out of being at the company." His wife is also sympathetic, and remembers all the other times she felt her brother-in-law was slighting her husband.

The next day, the brothers meet in the hall and greet each other warmly. "I'm sorry about yesterday," says the older one. "I was frustrated about the Z account and took it out on you. I know you've put a lot of time in on that project, and I look forward to sitting down and going over it together." His brother responds, "Hey, the whole thing was my fault. I could see you were busy, but I pushed it on you anyway, and then I just blew up. Whenever you're ready to talk, just let me know."

The following Sunday, at the senior generation's house, the brothers are laughing in front of the barbecue, and their wives are staring at each other from opposite sides of the back yard. At one point in the afternoon, the older brother says to the younger, "It's really too bad that our wives don't get along better. I would have thought they'd be best friends."

In-laws are very prone to being drawn into the emotional dynamics of the business family, without benefit of the information or access to each other that their spouses who are in the business share. Because the process is invisible to the family members involved, conflict with in-laws can be misdiagnosed. Business families need to carefully examine the communication flow to all adult family members and take the steps necessary to reduce assumptions and increase the honesty, openness, and consistency of communication in the system as a whole.

Encouraging Productive Conflict Management. Once the two generations are working together, complex issues of authority and collaboration almost inevitably cause flare-ups. Application of the three-circle model makes it apparent that conflict is built into the structure of the family business system. Individuals, operating with the best of intentions, still have different agendas and perspectives on events because of their different roles. Sons or daughters, in trying to establish competence, may resent their parents' authority; parents may be hurt or angered by the disrespect they feel in the challenges of their children. Children who are not working in the business may feel that, in comparison with their working siblings, they are not receiving adequate benefits from the business or equal attention from their parents. There may be difficult role changes in the family, especially if the parents have health problems or other complications that begin to reverse the parent-child caretaking relationships that have characterized the family in the earlier stages of its life cycle.

This level of conflict is likely to increase as the family moves through the Working Together stage and begins to grapple with the succession process. The elevation of Joe Rockman to successor-designate caused

Marcy and David to reassess their futures. In the end, it was not a lack of appeal in the business itself that led them to seek other careers, but their lack of confidence in the future of their Sibling Partnership. They were lucky to recognize their feelings and to have other options; it would have been worse to have stayed in a situation that they found continually irritating.

Even when there is agreement and acceptance of the succession plan, conflict can result. For example, the Ackerman family, which owns a small printing company, had always been known for the harmonious atmosphere in the company and at home. As the parents neared sixty and began to think ahead to retirement, however, the level of anger seemed to increase. No one could explain what was causing the new friction among the three siblings and between each of them and their parents. The oldest son and his family suddenly decided not to join the rest of the family at the lake house in July, breaking a twenty-year tradition. The youngest daughter became more outspoken and derisive about her oldest sister's second husband, suggesting aloud that he only wanted to get in on the business. The nonfamily employees were also drawn into the conflicts, as management meetings became so hostile that important decisions could not be made. The family finally engaged a consultant, who began a series of meetings with family members. After only a few weeks, it became clear that the formal designation of the oldest daughter as the next general manager (though not a surprise to anyone) had released strong competitive feelings in the other family members. Brothers and sisters were responding to their experience (partly imagined and partly true) that other family members and key managers had begun to treat the "chosen one" differently from the others. Even though the siblings agreed with the choice, they could not control their unconscious resentment and fear about being treated as second-class family members.

Conflict is most productively treated as an inevitable aspect of family (and other group) life that cannot and should not be avoided. In fact, conflict can be valuable; it may clear the air, allow people to regain some distance in a relationship in which they feel temporarily overwhelmed, or help a group of family members work through a difficult decision. The Working Together task of transitioning from a unitary family, with one generational hierarchy, to a network of nuclear families requires a toleration of some level of conflict. It is the way the family and the business can grow and incorporate new norms and values. This is most important as the family makes room for new members (spouses and grandchildren). It is also critical to the beginning stages of a transfer of leadership from the senior generation to the junior one. Few families can make the changes that are necessary in the Working Together and Passing the Baton stages without some conflict.[35]

However, it is essential to manage the family conflict so that it is productive and not destructive, and so that it does not spill over, uncontrolled, into the business and ownership dimensions.[36] The costs of unmanaged conflict are higher in the Working Together stage than they were in earlier stages, because both generations have invested a great deal in the younger generation. Since avoiding conflict by separating is more difficult, the family needs to try to diagnose the sources of family conflict and change the process of conflict resolution, not just to battle through until there is a winner. Do people blame each other or take responsibility for the consequences of their behavior? Is conflict concentrated between two family members who fight on behalf of everyone else (a "conflict pair")? Do people vent their frustration by complaining endlessly about each other? Do arguments become abusive? Two reciprocal generational realizations are often called for: the senior generation's recognizing that the offspring generation is also made up of adults, whose points of view require respect; and the younger generation's accepting the fundamental realities of the authority hierarchy in the Working Together business. Often, a family council, as described in chapter 8, can be very helpful in providing a venue for conflict resolution outside the business structure.

Managing the Three-Generation Working Together Family. Because of increased average life expectancy, families in general are more vertically diverse than ever before. As the business family continues to grow, it may come to a point where there is a mix of three generations active in the business at the same time. It is difficult enough for the Working Together family to manage intergenerational dynamics between parents and their offspring. Adding a third generation brings in a whole new set of challenges. The senior generation may hold the CEO role, or be involved primarily through ownership and the board. If the former, it will carry ultimate responsibility for the company's performance. If the latter, it will be concerned with maintaining an appropriate level of input and authority within the bounds of this new role. The middle generation is probably dominant in most of the key family manager positions. The primary responsibility for running the company's operations will rest on its shoulders. The younger generation in the Working Together stage is likely to be new in the company, trying to find a foothold. Its members may be recently married, with young children, looking up the ladder from the bottom rung and wondering if they will be able to find a fulfilling and financially rewarding career in the business.

In the best of situations, this three-generation mix can create positive bonds that enhance the vitality of the extended family far beyond the norm in contemporary American culture.[37] Frequent cross-generational contact and true interdependence may enrich the lives of the children with a wide range of observable, meaningful, and varied role models. This is especially likely if the senior generation is sensitive to its offspring's legitimate need to be masters in their own homes and undisputed parents to their own children.

But often one consequence of this generational "sandwich" in the Working Together stage is that the clarity of the middle generation's authority is sometimes compromised. These midlife managers may feel subordinate and economically dependent on their parents long after their peers are financially in control of their own lives. It also has an impact on the third generation, which may see the grandparents as the truly powerful figures in the family. When the senior generation is unaware of that dynamic, the situation can lead to resentment and acting out by the middle generation. Whether the interference of the senior generation is intentional or not, the negative impact on the self-confidence and sense of control of the middle generation can be severe. Even if the work relationship between the generations in the Working Together stage is very good and the business is prospering, some middle-generation managers leave the firm. This can be a great loss to the business and may make continued family control of the business unlikely. It is an excellent example of how an unresolved dynamic in one dimension can have dramatic effects on another dimension.

One of the arenas in which the senior generation must be careful to play an appropriate role is in relation to the career choice decisions of the grandchildren. The senior generation is now heading a Working Together family, but the middle generation may be moving into the Entering the Business stage. This means that the youngest generation will be struggling with questions about whether or not to come into the business. Sometimes grandparents, especially if they are still active in the company, may be even more inclined to try to influence those decisions than the young person's parents are. Strong dynastic senior leaders may see the recruitment of the grandchildren's generation as the true test of the enduring power of their own legacy. Conversely, if the senior leader is experiencing regret or bitterness over the disappointments of his or her life career in the business, he or she may exert influence in the other direction, disparaging any statements of interest by the grandchildren. Either way, because the senior generation is unencumbered by the full parental role, it may be less inhibited about making its desires known to the grandchildren. It takes a strong response from the middle generation to prevent problems in these situations.

The Passing the Baton Family

Characteristics

Ironically, this is the most well researched stage in the life of business and ownership, and the least well understood stage of family development. The stage begins when the senior generation moves into late adulthood, usually around its sixties, and lasts until its death. In business families, many of the most important issues now are directly related to the actual change in ownership and management control in the firm. But it is a mistake to let the drama of transitions in the business obscure the equally powerful events that are occurring on the family axis. What began as a marriage many decades ago has developed along its own unique path into a complex clan of descendants. In most families, by this stage there will be at least two generations of offspring; in a few families there may be as many as four. It is now the second generation that is struggling with or has just moved through midlife. In almost all cases there will be a mixture of intact families, single-parent families, remarriage, and step-families—some close, enduring relationships and some disconnections.

The Passing the Baton Stage of Family Development

Characteristics
- Senior generation age sixty and above

Key Challenges
- Senior generation disengagement from the business
- Generational transfer of family leadership

As the American population ages, social scientists have become more interested in later life. Excellent work on gerontology has been done in recent years, although it has focused primarily on physiological aging and the individual experience of the elderly. Sociological and demographic studies have explored retirement, residential patterns, and intergenerational helping behavior. Still, we have only scratched the surface of what we need to know about family dynamics in the Passing the Baton stage of business families.

The key family issues of this stage are the elder generation's disengagement from the business, the generational shift in leadership, and the implied confrontation with death. The actual succession process will be discussed in depth in chapter 7. Here we focus on the family dynamics that are characteristic of this stage in the family's life course.

Rockman Equipment Company: Part 4

By 1996 Rockman Equipment had undergone a complete restructuring. A holding company, Rockman Industries, had been formed, with Wyatt as chairman and other family members on the board. There were now six operating companies. Then, as often happens, the most important family events came without planning or warning. In the middle of January 1996, Wyatt was stricken with a serious heart attack. In the early hours at the hospital, before the family could be reached, it was not clear he would survive. Margaret waited outside the emergency room until he was moved to intensive care, then contacted the rest of the family.

Joe's two years as president of Rockman Equipment had continued to be difficult. Rockman had been slow to respond to the recession and to changes in market opportunities. Joe could not seem to live down some of the early problems he had had in his new job. Joe and Carol had been married for five years and had two children. After getting the news of Wyatt's heart attack, all he could think was, "What do I do now? What do I do now?" over and over.

Dave's life over the same two years, in contrast, had seemed to move from one success to another. His work record in Chicago had been excellent. He was now thirty-five, married, a bit eager for a new challenge, but generally happy. He and Maria had reached the decision that things were finally settled enough to begin a family. Dave realized that he felt a sense of responsibility for his father's heart attack, because of his decision to leave Rockman. He wondered if he had grown up and left his family, or abandoned them.

Wyatt's triple-bypass went off smoothly, and he was given an excellent prognosis for recovery. The heart attack, terrifying as it had been, had also given Wyatt a new sense of freedom and determination. In the months after the surgery, Wyatt was preoccupied with plans for how he was going to take up the reins of the company again. Joe had done his best, Wyatt thought, but these difficult times required a more experienced leader. Day after day, Wyatt had thought about marketing, new ministores, a reorganized structure, and key managers who should be replaced.

An old friend helped Wyatt think more clearly by focusing on who he was and what he had accomplished, on his increased sense of pride and commitment to his family. He also talked about how he and Margaret had become closer than they had been in years. Gradually Wyatt realized that he had been protecting Joe for many years, waiting for him to grow into the kind of leader the company and the family needed. His health had jolted him out of the head-in-the-sand, reactive stance he had taken for years. Talking with Margaret, he came to the realization that Rockman Equipment's future and his were diverging.

Six months later, Wyatt was prepared to move Rockman Industries into a new stage. Margaret had been a partner in these decisions more than ever before in their lives, and they were both still a little uncertain about this new relationship. But the satisfaction that came from talking with her about everything was one of the most important, and surprising, things Wyatt had learned this year.

The culmination of all the planning was in January of 1997, almost one year to the day after Wyatt's heart attack, at the first meeting of the Rockman Family Council. Wyatt told the family that, in six months, he would be resigning as CEO of Rockman Equipment but remaining as chair of the board of Rockman Industries. He and Margaret had decided to spend about six months of every year in Costa Rica. Wyatt thanked Joe for the effort he had given as president, but told him that he had reached the conclusion that Joe could not be happy or successful running the company in the future. Marcy was entrenched and happy in her rapidly growing business in Colorado—newly married and working hard. Wyatt had decided to offer the CEO job to Dave. He set up a transitional year for Dave and Maria to see if they wanted to make the move back from Chicago. He hoped that Joe would stay in the company in some capacity.

Key Challenges

Succession is still the most discussed topic in the family business literature. We devote a full chapter (see chapter 7) to our view of this complex process. At this point we only want to highlight the most important family tasks at this stage of development. The most common story about succession is the clash of two opposing forces: the senior generation's difficulty leaving, and the junior generation's difficulty waiting. It seems that if there were a formula for determining precisely the optimal moment, the best meeting point of senior and junior readiness, a high percentage of family business dilemmas would be resolved.

Senior Generation Disengagement from the Business. In fact, the process is much more complicated than just timing. It is reflected in two words that are often used as synonyms: *succession* and *continuity.* Actually, these two concepts encompass two different yet complementary processes, and it is the dialectic between them that makes the process so complicated and dynamic. Succession reflects the sequential aspect of the transition, as one thing needs to end and be "succeeded" by something new. Continuity refers to the part of the present world that needs to be preserved in the new era. Both succession and continuity are essential, in proper balance, in order to minimize the disruptive consequences of a generational transition.

The transition of management leadership is a task of the business circle. The family task is to consider its own transition, and in so doing make possible the necessary changes in the business. In one sense, the first key task of the Passing the Baton stage is an acknowledgment that, in fact, the stage has been reached. Familial resistance to that step is formidable and widespread.[38] For the senior generation, leadership has provided status, meaning, power, and other rewards. As Jeffrey Sonnenfeld, the leading researcher on styles of patriarchal retirement in family firms puts it, the greatest impediments to peaceful transitions are the senior leader's fear of losing *heroic stature* and the *heroic mission.*[39] Heroic stature is the position of power and status that sets top leaders apart from everyone else. Heroic mission is the sense of "specialness" that comes with the leader's conviction that his or her cause is noble and important, and that he or she is uniquely qualified to accomplish it. The need to hang onto these two life-affirming rewards leads to a variety of coping styles, some of which work successfully to ease the transition and some of which undermine it.

The rest of the family often colludes in this resistance to acknowledging that the time for transition has arrived. There are cases where the successor generation is impatient, and cannot wait for the parents' departure from the business. However, we have found those cases to be less frequent than the situation where the younger generation is struggling with ambivalence and, as a result, joins fully in an avoidance of the topic. In his analysis of the "succession conspiracy" that delays attention to the inevitable transition, Lansberg identifies four classic family contributions: (1) the fear of differentiation among the siblings; (2) the offspring's fear of being perceived as greedy; (3) the spouse's fear of loss of identity and activities; and (4) the family's fear of the leader's death.[40] These factors lead all the other family members to collude in the senior generation's denial of the imperative of preparing to "let go." It has been one of our most interesting lessons to observe how often this general family resistance is stronger than the younger generation's impatience to "take over."

Another source of resistance to confronting the generational transfer is the poverty of our shared understanding of retirement.[41] The new literature on retirement is almost exclusively based on research on salaried workers; attitudes toward retirement among business owners rest on myths that are almost all negative. Many senior family members fear retirement as a certain precursor of failing health and a quick slide toward death. Others are preoccupied with "becoming less relevant, or even of being forgotten by those who follow."[42] Those friends who may be enjoying their retirement have often moved away or are no longer in the same social routine, so it is difficult to learn from their example. It is an uncomfortable, often undiscussable topic in our culture. As a result, this transition parallels the entry to adulthood described in the Entering the Business stage: A leap of faith into unchartered waters, where decisions must be made on the basis of too little data.

For all of these reasons, both generations may have difficulty thinking about and talking about the senior generation's disengagement from the firm. Even if all the ingredients are present, it often takes an external event to catalyze the process. Wyatt Rockman was jolted into action by his heart attack. Some dramatic physical crisis is probably the most common stimulus. Another is the retirement of an associate or friend. One of the most common triggers is a business milestone, in the form of a business anniversary or the completion of some long-term organizational project. Getting the issue of the seniors' withdrawal from active management on the table, with some shared sense of the appropriate timing and an emerging vision of the new roles that will follow the change, is the first task of this stage.

Generational Transfer of Family Leadership. The second hallmark of the Passing the Baton stage is the shift in responsibility for and control of family affairs from the most senior generation to the next in line. This may happen gradually or suddenly, but, like retirement, is very often precipitated by an unplanned event. There are a number of such "one-way" doors that the family can pass through. The most definitive is the death of one or both parents. But there are other events that can precipitate significant change in family leadership roles. The parents or the surviving parent may decide to sell the family home and move to a small condominium. They may move even farther, to a warmer climate or back to the community they were born or grew up in. As in the Rockman family, there are many physical events that can happen without warning, such as heart attack, stroke, or accident. There are also others that occur over time, such as debilitating illness, dementia, Alzheimer's, or slow recovery from an injury. All families expect such events, but none is truly prepared for them. The consequence of these precipitating experiences is that the capacity of the most senior generation to exercise executive control of the family is diminished. Leadership falls by default or design to younger generations.

By the time the business family reaches the Passing the Baton stage, the complex emotional issues associated with the transfer of power and leadership from senior to junior (actually, middle) generation begin to surface in earnest. For the seniors, the signs of physical and mental decline are by now becoming increasingly inescapable. According to Erik Erikson, the distinguished psychoanalyst and theorist on human development, this era confronts seniors with an inner struggle between a sense of integrity and a sense of despair.[43] Despair can stem from deeply felt disappointment over the shortcomings and failures in their lives. The same ambitious dreams that led these individuals to begin their entrepreneurial careers decades ago can make them particularly vulnerable to measuring their accomplishments against unfulfillable goals and unreachable successes. Indeed, as Sonnenfeld points out, the relentless pursuit of an heroic entrepreneurial mission is often at the root of business owners' (particularly founders') inability to effectively plan succession in their companies.

Conversely, the Eriksonian sense of integrity emerges from a deeply rooted appreciation of the unique life course that the aging leader has followed and of his or her place in the timeless generational link between those who have come before and those who will follow. Senior leaders in business families who can realize their own particular contributions as generational stewards of the family enterprise are more able to muster the courage necessary to constructively participate in the transition to a new generation of leadership. Their ability to appreciate their own accomplishments frees them to encourage and celebrate the movement of their heirs to positions of authority in the business and prominence in the family. The possibilities for collaboration are enhanced, and the seniors can serve as mentors for several generations simultaneously.

The consequences for Passing the Baton families in which the senior generation turns toward despair instead of integrity can be significant. The seniors may keep a lock on strategic power in the business, pursuing an elusive final, grand accomplishment, which they feel will allow them to withdraw in triumph. They may justify this holding on by continually denigrating the skills or readiness of the next generation. This can not only be demoralizing to their own successors, but also undermine the confidence and commitment of nonfamily managers, customers, suppliers, and financial supporters, thereby threatening the entire system. Equally damaging, they may actually retire but continue in subtle ways to sabotage the efforts of successors. Such behavior is fueled by a need to prove to themselves and the world that they were more valuable, and more irreplaceable, than anyone imagined. These motivations may be completely unconscious, but that does not make them any less destructive.

It is in the family that the best opportunity resides to help members of the senior generation confront the conflict between integrity and despair and resolve it. The Sonnenfeld concepts of heroic mission and heroic stature are very applicable to the family's task at this stage. In many families, the best predictor of the level of ease and pleasure that is experienced in the Passing the Baton stage is the extent to which the family has found ways to protect the heroic stature of the senior generation even after family management functions have been passed to the offspring. This requires that the family find ways to help seniors relinquish the power to control events in the business and the family, while reinforcing their authority as valued elders in each system. This can happen in important symbolic events, such as the family's willingness to have celebrations and holidays on the parents' territory, even if they no longer do the organizing work.

There are, of course, senior-generation individuals and couples who are delighted to pass on the mantle of family leadership. They look forward with enthusiasm to freedom from expectations and responsibilities. Their departure from the firm is closely followed by a new, independent lifestyle of travel, investments, hobbies, a network of senior friends, and visits with family. We have encountered some families like this in the Passing the Baton stage, but not too many. The mildly enmeshed family style that served so well in earlier stages does not readily dissolve when the senior generation passes sixty. One consequence of the three interlocking subsystems—family, business, and ownership—is that roles in one area tend to be replicated in the others. Therefore, because the senior generation typically retains the chair role or an active leadership position on the board of directors, and may often maintain a link to the firm as an adviser or contact to critical customers, it is hard to let go of the leadership function in the family circle. Ironically, passing the baton in the family circle may be harder in business families than in families in general. It requires the compassionate collaboration of both generations.

Renewing the Cycle

As the senior generation moves through the Working Together and Passing the Baton stages, members of the junior generation begin their own cycles as Young and Entering the Business Families. As a result, after the first generation most family business systems have subgroups at more than one point on this axis. Many different issues, from several stages in the extended family, may be salient at the same time. That is part of the richness of what Brown-Herz calls "the family tapestry."[44] There is no way to reduce the complexity of these multiple-family enterprises without sacrificing their authenticity. Families are continuous; the stages of any model are arbitrary.[45] Nevertheless, our developmental model can be used to focus on one family structure at a time, and to determine where on the axis that part of the family belongs. When this depiction is combined with the ownership and business axes, the entire system can be brought into focus, and the lessons we have learned from families at similar positions can be applied.

NOTES

1. Levinson 1978, 1996.

2. In the early 1930s, an interest in longitudinal perspectives and the family's "developmental tasks" over time emerged (Havighurst 1966). Sorokin presented one of the earliest family stage models in 1931 (Sorokin, Zimmerman, and Galpin 1931). Duvall and her colleagues, particularly Reuben Hill, developed an eight-stage model in the 1940s and 1950s, which has been widely influential on family psychologists and sociologists ever since (Duval and Hill 1948; Duvall 1957, 1977). In more recent years, the models have become increasingly complex, taking into account ethnic and historical factors (Elder 1987; Carter and McGoldrick 1988). Mattessich and Hill have summarized over a dozen models that have emerged in the first half-century of work in this area (Mattessich and Hill 1987).

3. Aldous 1990.

4. The excellent work of demographers and sociologists like Paul Glick have demonstrated the remarkable consistency of age patterns for key family experiences, even internationally (Glick 1947, 1977). In addition, more recent work has greatly refined the analysis of demographic data (Spanier and Glick 1980).

5. Furstenberg 1979; Combrinck-Graham 1985; and Kaye 1985. Aldous has also written eloquently about the functional consequences of the inherently developmental nature of families:

> The nuclear family is perhaps more subject to organizational instability than other organizations because of its rapidly changing age composition and frequently changing plurality patterns. Its leaders are two relatively inexperienced amateurs in the roles of spouse and parent. They must work with a succession of followers having few skills and lacking judgment under conditions that appear never to remain stable enough, long enough, to allow for organization. The family has hardly established one set of relations based on mutual, normative expectations and agreements when some child begins demanding a reinterpretation of the rights and duties built into his roles. Yet, despite these disruptive factors, which are part of its standard operating procedures, the family somehow, in a majority of cases, manages to maintain the structured interaction patterns that enable it to continue as an entity. (1978, 36)

6. Families who own businesses have a special need for a shared sense of who is in the family because of the significant assets in common. Clarity about the family's boundary is helpful in deciding who has responsibilities to the business and who deserves to benefit from it. Are sisters and brothers entitled to employment? first cousins? in-laws? nephews, nieces, and more distant relatives? A sense of the family's boundary is helpful for small issues, such as special prices or services available to family members, and for big issues, such as who can own shares of company stock and how high an individual can be expected to rise in company management.

7. In the United States today, 64 percent of the adult population lives with a spouse, and another 20 percent lives in some other kind of familial household. Although the percentage of nonfamily households has doubled in the past thirty years,

still only about 18 percent of American adults live separate from any blood or marriage relative (Saluter 1994).

8. Hofferth 1985.

9. Walsh 1994, 176.

10. Aldous 1978; Matthews, Delaney, and Adamek 1989; Connidis and Campbell 1995.

11. Spanier and Glick 1980. Among younger cohorts the marriage rate has been declining recently, as more couples choose to live together without getting married (Saluter 1994). Of course, among those who do try marriage, many of them do not care much for the experience. In 1870 the American divorce rate was about 3 percent; it is somewhere between 35 and 50 percent today, although most of those whose first marriage fails will try again at least once.

12. Levinson 1978, 1996.

13. Minuchin et al. 1967; Minuchin 1974.

14. The most influential contemporary work on this topic is Blood and Wolfe (1960), which has been refined and expanded by Heer (1963); Centers, Raven and Rodrigues (1971); Nock (1988); and others.

15. The more equivalent the dyad's dominance structure, the more flexible their transactional patternings, the more frequently discussions about who is to do what when take place, the greater the conflict potential of dyadic conversations, but the more understanding is experienced in marital negotiations. In contrast, the more one spouse is clearly more dominant than the other, the more rigid their transactional structurings, the less frequent discussions about who is to do what when, the more apparent "harmony" in their conversations, but the greater the "rebellion" potential of marital negotiations and the less understanding is experienced by the partners. In addition, the increasing prevalence of second marriages may be encouraging more egalitarian patterns, especially among older adults. Second marriages in general demonstrate more balanced authority, with less rigid sex-role differentiation, than first marriages. (Millar and Rogers 1988, 93–94)

16. Centers, Raven, and Rodrigues 1971; Furstenberg and Spanier 1984.

17. Nelton 1986; Barnett and Barnett 1988; Marshack 1993.

18. Ponthieu and Caudill 1993.

19. Kadis and McClendon 1991.

20. Wicker and Burley 1991.

21. LeMasters, in his often-quoted classic study, found that 83 percent of couples reported an extensive or severe crisis around the birth of their first child (1957).

22. Gillis-Donovan and Moynihan-Bradt 1990.

23. Levinson 1978; Gersick 1991.

24. Despite its frightening reputation, the mid-life transition for most individuals is a time of heightened sensitivity and perhaps anxiety, but not really a crisis. Most people, with some bumps and ambivalence, manage to cope with these intense demands, make some level of change, and move ahead into the calmer waters of the late forties and fifties. In fact, it is a unique opportunity to make the midcourse corrections that can dramatically enrich adult life in the years that follow. For others, however, the life structure that was in place in the thirties proves seriously inadequate for the future, and more revolutionary changes are attempted. The marriage may be

reevaluated, sometimes painfully. Business decisions may become more impulsive and less carefully planned, in an effort to reinforce an image of youthful adventurousness. Parents experiencing a difficult midlife transition may resist the entry of the younger generation, refusing to acknowledge their readiness and insisting that they are too young or immature for serious responsibility.

25. Osherson (1980) explores an adult development perspective on this dilemma.

26. Thornton, Orbuch, and Axinn 1995.

27. Thornton, Young-De Marco, and Goldscheider 1993; Mitchell 1994.

28. Adams 1968; Rosenberg and Anspach 1973.

29. Hines et al. 1992.

30. The literature on adult sibling relationships, after many decades of slow growth, has many new and exciting contemporary streams (Bank and Kahn 1982; Cicirelli 1985; Bedford 1989). Also, there are many classic contributions in Lamb and Sutton-Smith (1982). Carroll (1988) and Friedman (1991) offer excellent explorations of sibling relationships in business families.

31. Primogeniture has been less formalized in the United States than in European and some Asian cultures. More flexible social classes, abundant land, relatively early recognition of property rights for women, and an open commercial economy have provided ample opportunity for later-born sons in America since colonial days (see Auwers 1978), and for daughters in this century.

32. Bossard and Boll (1960) present an excellent discussion of sibling role differentiation. Schachter and his colleagues (1982) developed the concept further, into sibling "deidentification." See also Bowen 1972; Kepner 1983; Dunn and Plomin 1990; and Hetherington, Reiss, and Plomin 1994.

33. Lansberg, forthcoming.

34. Duvall 1957, 420. Family development in these later stages has been profoundly affected by demographic changes over the past century. Until the late 1800s, the prospect of family life after the departure of all children was not a common concern. A century ago, most women who survived the birth of all their children were widowed before the youngest reached adulthood. Today, both members of the average couple survive more than fifteen years beyond the departure of the youngest from the parental home.

35. Harvey and Evans 1994.

36. Jaffe 1990; Kaye 1991.

37. In fact, some intriguing research by Simonton (1983) on hereditary monarchs suggests that leadership is modeled more strongly from the grandfather than from the father.

38. Lansberg 1988. See also Handler and Kram 1988.

39. Sonnenfeld 1988; Sonnenfeld and Spence 1989.

40. Lansberg 1988.

41. Kasl 1980; Beehr 1986.

42. Levinson in Lansberg 1991, 60.

43. Erikson 1963.

44. Brown 1991.

45. Hareven 1978.

3

The Business Developmental Dimension

ALL FAMILY COMPANIES may have much in common, but it is also clear that the corner store and the multinational corporation are different in important ways. Alongside the ownership and family developmental dimensions, it is necessary to take into account the size, age, structure, and financial performance of the business itself in order to understand how the system is currently working and how it needs to develop further. Young, small, simple firms make certain kinds of demands on the family and ownership groups. They are preoccupied with survival; most often they see the family primarily as a source of cheap, dedicated labor and badly needed cash. Mature, large, complex companies face a very different set of challenges, such as business unit coordination and strategic planning. The family still plays a critical role in ownership, and often in management, but the presence of nonfamily professionals is likely to be much larger, and the interrelationships of the three circles are much different. The third dimension of our model describes these different stages of business development.

Thinking Developmentally about Business

Business development in family companies is a special case of the general topic of organizational change, about which there is a rich literature of theory and research. Our model takes into account both of the primary perspectives on why and how organizations change over time. The first perspective focuses on the effect of external economic and social forces on organizations. These models, including institutional theories, resource dependency, and ecology, suggest that we look to the world in which the business is trying to survive—the markets, supplier costs, customer tastes, business cycles, industry characteristics—to see where pressures to change are coming from.[1] Some of these models suggest that organizations are relatively limited in their ability to change. A process of natural selection takes over, so that the overall field of organizations changes because individual businesses will either thrive or die as a result of environmental factors. Other models propose that organizations can adapt to the environment if they pay attention well enough and early enough, and if they have exceptional leadership. With this focus on external forces, it is possible to describe the process through which an organization responds and adjusts to its environment, but it is very hard to predict what changes will occur or when. The role of leadership is mostly reactive. Each business's internal developmental path appears idiosyncratic, without a generalizable sequence or time interval, or common events and tasks along the way.

The second perspective, on the other hand, sees organizations as changing in a predictable sequence of stages, driven in part by conditions in the external environment but primarily by complex maturational factors inside the organization. Such models focus on organizational life cycles. They talk about organizations as if they were biological organisms: they are born, they grow and change, and eventually they must deal effectively with maturity or they will decline and disappear.[2] Like all organisms, companies in this view go through a relatively predictable series of stages over the course of their lives, each stage carrying with it a predictable set of challenges.

Most models of internally driven development agree that there are characteristic strategic, structural, and managerial issues with every phase. However, there is no consensus among scholars as to how many phases there are or what they should be called; different research efforts have proposed anywhere from three to ten distinct developmental stages. Some focus on a series of functional problems that the organization faces: for example, adequate capitalization, functional diversification, new product development, or marketing.[3] Other researchers have created frameworks based on organizational size and complexity, on management structure, or even on member psychology.[4] There are many other qualifications and details of specific models: the process of moving from one stage to another, the universality of stages across many types of organizations, and whether a particular organization can move up or down or skip stages.[5]

In creating the business developmental axis for this model, we concentrated on the common elements from research and theory that are most relevant for family business. Of all the potential indicators of organizational development, two emerge as the most comprehensive and the most applicable to family firms. The first is *growth*. Growth is relatively easily quantified and intuitively appealing. There are many ways to measure growth—sales volume, number of employees, asset value, market share, product lines. Taken together, they form a core indicator of the firm's stage of development. Growth is the measure by which owner-managers assess the progress of the company in the past and plan for its short- and long-term future. Although there is great variability in growth patterns and timing, the importance of level of growth to the nature of the business— and in particular to the relationships among the company, the family, and the ownership group—is clear.

The other measure of business development, *complexity*, may be highly correlated with growth, but it captures a different aspect of change. Complexity is a particularly useful measure of business development in a stage theory, because the distinctions between one organizational structure and another are easily apparent. Businesses in the early stages most often adopt simple structures, with unitary control and communication systems, and close individual management by the leader. Nearly all sole proprietorship family businesses—restaurants, retail stores, single service agencies—have this kind of structure, at least when they begin. If the company survives these early years, it usually begins to differentiate its structure with distinct functional units or product lines, a growing layer of middle management, more formal control and human resource systems, and more decentralized, although still tightly coordinated, organizational processes. Family businesses in manufacturing or services, especially with multiple sites, well-dispersed customers, and more than 100 employees, are more likely to have moved toward this form. Companies that continue to grow and diversify develop even more complex structures, with more independent divisions or operating companies, multiple cost and profit centers, a separation of strategic and operational leadership functions, and elaborate policies for human resource management, marketing and sales, research and development, and so forth. These are the most complex family businesses.

The Business Developmental Stages

Each of these measures of development—growth and complexity—contributes to an understanding of change in family firms. Therefore the three developmental stages for this dimension—Start-Up, Expansion/Formalization, and Maturity (figure 3-1)—use criteria from both indicators. Each stage has characteristics of both size and structure.

The first stage, Start-Up, covers the early life of a company and includes two steps: formation and survival.[6] This includes the period in which the business is just an idea, attempting to be realized, as well as the period in which the entrepreneur and (often) family members are living the start-up business around the clock. The second stage, Expansion/Formalization, may be a brief, explosive period, as the company rides a hot idea or product like a rocket, or a very long phase of gradual evolution. Again, although other, more detailed models often subdivide this stage into early and later periods, for our three-dimensional model it is sufficient to focus on the general characteristics of family businesses that are growing and developing more complex structures.[7] The final stage, Maturity, is reached when the organizational structure and the key products have gradually slowed their evolution. It is in the Maturity stage that businesses face an inevitable dilemma: renewal or dissolution. In keeping with a true life cycle perspective, our model assumes that organizations will die if they attempt to continue indefinitely in the Maturity stage without a major renewal effort.

Change from stage to stage can be gradual or dramatic. Our observation of family companies is that change often occurs suddenly, and often in response to trigger events. A wide variety of events in the business arena—the sudden opening up of a new market, for example, or the acquisition of an important new customer—can launch a company down the developmental path. In addition, changes in ownership and family relationships can also trigger (or delay) organizational growth. Examples include a sudden influx, or a negotiated or unplanned withdrawal, of

Figure 3-1 ■ *The Business Developmental Dimension*

significant family investment capital. More gradually, the succession process—sometimes, just explicit talk about succession—may trigger the business to move to the next stage. The actual passing of ownership and management control to younger generation family members can propel a company quickly into a growth phase.

The business developmental dimension, like the other two, needs to be applied appropriately to family firms. Although distinct phases of business development can be identified, most real-world companies are more complicated than the models we use to describe them. The word *development* may imply that there is an inevitable direction and destination for a start-up company. In our experience, there is nothing inevitable about the life course of a business. Companies can leap across stages, move backwards, stall in one place, or be in several stages at the same time. In fact, as companies move through later generations and Sibling Partnership and Cousin Consortium ownership stages, it is almost inevitable that they will be in more than one (and often all three) business developmental stages at the same time. Some parts of the business will be expanding or mature, while new ventures re-create start-up dynamics in other parts. Determining one stage for the company as a whole is not the point. Instead, this dimension is most helpful as a general guide to the common sequence of business developmental stages in family companies. Like the family dimension, which also describes a typical sequence of stages within what may be a complex network of developing families, the stages in business development have two primary uses. First, the model can be applied to an identified subunit of the family enterprise, which will be at a particular developmental stage. Separating the business into its component parts and looking at the different stages that each part is currently experiencing can help sort out the conflicting perspectives of the family members identified with each part—for example, a nephew who is responsible for a new overseas office (Start-Up) versus a daughter who is rising in the ranks of the home office of a mature parent company. In addition, the company as a whole may be *primarily* in one of the three stages, dominated by the issues characteristic of that stage. Thus a large, complex Cousin Consortium company may be locked into a Start-Up or Expansion/Formalization culture, for example, even if there are many parts of the company that should be attending to other developmental issues.

It has been our experience that the most successful family business owners and managers use concepts of business development as they adapt their behavior to the current stage of their company. They are aware of the typical issues associated with each phase of growth; they understand how business development interacts with family and ownership development; and they periodically analyze their own company's development in order to determine what they must do differently to meet the particular challenges accompanying each phase. Ironically, this means that, to best meet the needs of their companies, managers need to be prepared to change structures, policies, and practices that have worked well in the past and may still be adequate in the present. If organizations change along broadly predictable developmental progressions as they age, then management can anticipate and be prepared for these changes.

The Start-Up Business

Characteristics

Companies begin as ideas. In its earliest stage, a business is rarely much more than a dream or a project that its creator is testing, to see if it can come to life. The variation in the details of these individual enterprises is almost unlimited. Nevertheless, whatever the industry, location, or market, start-up companies generally share two characteristics. First, their owner-managers are at the center of everything, investing a great deal of time, energy, and, often, most of their resources. Organizational structures are minimal and informal; procedures are usually worked out as they are needed, and often modified. Most communication runs to or through the owner. Second, in most cases the company is focused on one product or

The Start-Up Stage of Business Development

Characteristics
- Informal organizational structure, with owner-manager at center
- One product

Key Challenges
- Survival (market entry, business planning, financing)
- Rational analysis versus the dream

service. It is hoping to find a niche where it can hang on long enough to get established for the long run.

West Indies Shrimp Company (WISCO)

Owning their own business was the dream of Deke and Matilde Boncoeur even as college students in the States before they were married. A year after Matilde graduated with a business degree, they returned home with their two infant children to the West Indies. Deke, who had an undergraduate degree in marine biology, had been working on water quality with an environmental group. He wanted to come back to the island on which he had been raised. His mother was still there, running her famous island hotel. He felt the pull to be with her, and he also saw the chance of a lifetime to do what he had always wanted to do—run a shrimp farm.

Deke and Matilde found a perfect location on the island: a freshwater pond near the ocean, which allowed the right influx of salt water into the mostly freshwater shrimp ponds. With the help of local laborers, they dug the ponds and built a crude concrete hatchery/laboratory structure. During that same first nine months, they surveyed the island's restaurants and hotels, their primary potential market. Would they buy local shrimp if it was available, and how much would they pay for it? The results were overwhelming: most said they would feature shrimp in at least three menu offerings at lunch and/or dinner. With an analysis of demand and a break-even figure, Deke and Matilde had the beginnings of a business plan.

Having borrowed from family members to investigate the viability of the business, Deke and Matilde went looking for investment capital. Institutional investors were frightened by the risks associated with an aquaculture business. Eventually the Boncoeurs got a small U.S. AID Caribbean development loan. This allowed them to buy several small stocks of shrimp and to experiment with breeding conditions in the laboratory, with salinity in the ponds, and with harvesting techniques.

Almost two years after they had arrived on their home island, and a year after they had secured their loan, a hurricane blew through, breaching the dunes that separated the sea from the freshwater ponds. Most of the maturing shrimp were lost. The Boncoeurs had a choice: reconstruct and restock the ponds, or give up. They decided to persist—after all, hurricanes were not part of the business plan. However, they were stumped on how to raise the capital to rebuild. Although they had begun to successfully sell some shrimp to local vendors, their track record was far too limited for WISCO to attract funds for reconstruction. Deke and Matilde borrowed another $50,000 from their families. Deke made necessary changes in the design of the ponds, a process that delayed the restart of their production for a year. In the meantime, they discovered they could profitably import U.S. shrimp to satisfy their customers' newly created demand for fresh shrimp. However, with debt and rebuilding costs, they were still deeply in the hole and could not afford to invest much time and capital into this related business.

The final blow to the shrimp farm came with the second hurricane, almost two years after the first. This storm again flooded the shrimp ponds with salt water but also knocked down the laboratory. Unwilling to ask Deke's family for more money, Deke and Matilde searched among their aquaculture network for a buyer and sold off the equipment. Bootstrapping on credit cards, they then focused intensively on the shrimp importing business, which ultimately produced a modest profit for several years. However, the growth of that company was severely constrained by the plateaued number of hotels and restaurants in the immediate area. Following the death of Deke's mother, Matilde and Deke sold the importing business and moved with their two, now-school-age children back to the States.

Key Challenges

WISCO was a company that never quite made it past the Start-Up stage. Although the company existed on paper for about seven years, the enterprise was never much more than a dream, a project that *might* have developed into a business but never proved completely viable. Because WISCO was relatively long-lived as a start-up, the Boncoeurs' experience can provide us with important lessons on the general characteristics and challenges of this phase of the organizational life cycle.

In the Start-Up stage, the owner-manager is central—often, there *are* no other employees. Typically for start-ups, there is no organizational structure to speak of; the owner-manager may hire a supervisor, but all the other employees may work and be paid by the day. And most start-ups are one-product ventures. All of their energy and resources are focused on an attempt to sell one product at a profit. If their entry product is not profitable quickly enough, they may not be able to hang on long enough to try alternative ideas.

Survival. The central survival question is: Can the product find a successful market at a competitive cost? Deke and Matilde worked hard to establish WISCO's chances for success in several areas:

- *Market entry.* They learned that there was an eager initial market for their product and no competition.

- *Business planning.* They learned that they could, under ideal conditions, produce and price their product at levels that would allow them to make a profit. They also understood their technology: the production systems they needed to generate appropriate levels and quality of production.

- *Financing.* They were able to combine personal assets and a loan into enough start-up capital to open the doors.

Their success in developing a reasonable business plan and in gaining market entry was what sustained WISCO initially. Unfortunately, what Deke and Matilde did not factor into their analysis was risk—the riskiness of all aquaculture enterprises and this one in particular. The shrimp farm business looked good on paper, but their ability to produce a product at all was terribly dependent on conditions beyond their control. If it had not been the hurricanes, their shrimp crops could have been damaged by disease or predators. Under any scenario, their risk level was more than most start-ups could survive, whatever their financing scheme.

Success in this kind of venture is based on deep pockets (which the Boncoeurs did not have) and/or good luck (which they also, unfortunately, did not have). Many founders assume that adequate financing means having enough capital to set up a basic operation, buy materials, produce a product, and get it to market. In reality, in WISCO as in most start-up ventures, adequate capital to get the initial product to market would have required enough resources to withstand setbacks that were not specifically foreseeable. Even in the import company, financing also made the difference; they didn't have the capital to expand the business to the point at which it could have generated substantial profit.

Rational Analysis versus the Dream. Psychological issues are inextricably intertwined with the business issues, as illustrated in this example. Founders must walk a fine emotional line between staying neutral about their project and keeping their ability to analyze objectively, and feeding their passion for it. Clearly, most business ideas are not viable and would be rejected in a perfectly rational evaluation process. But some prospective business owners jump too quickly toward an idea because they feel excited, not because they have analyzed all dimensions of the business situation.

When the start-up is a family business, either a new independent venture or a spinoff, the new business ideas may have more to do with personal, family, or lifestyle dreams than with objective business projections. Deke and Matilde were clear that they wanted to operate a shrimp farm. They had talked about it for years. Perhaps the specificity of this personal vision kept them from considering other, related business ventures that might have been more successful (such as shrimp importing). At many points in this book we talk about the importance of having a dream and being aware of it. However, that is not to say that all dreams are realistic. In fact, overcommitting to a personal or family dream without thinking through the constraints of reality can easily lead to premature commitment to an untenable business idea.

Other unexamined goals can be problematic. For example, was the shrimp farm an excuse for Deke and Matilde's move back to the islands? Was it connected to the role of being an "essential supplier" to Deke's mother's business—close at hand and highly valued? If they had started with the idea of the shrimp farm and then done the analysis and risk assessment, they might have decided on a different geographic location altogether. In this case, the business came about because of a personal decision, not because analysis showed in advance that this location was optimal. Other projects are developed because a couple, for example, wants to work together, or because the owner-manager wants to change careers. All of these projects can turn into viable companies, of course. The challenge is to keep personal hopes and family agendas from clouding judgment about the viability of the business itself.

On the other end of the scale, there may be family pressures away from entrepreneurial dreams. Some owner-managers, feeling the weight of the family's financial needs, are reluctant to give up their "day" jobs in order to invest time and energy in the analysis of new business ideas. Their start-up projects, unlike WISCO, are likely to stay on the drawing board forever. There is also a classic dilemma for second-generation leaders in successfully continuing family businesses. They grew up watching the business capture the previous generation's full investment in its Start-Up stage. At least some part of their parents' heroic stature probably comes from their entrepreneurial triumph.[8] But the second generation is caught in a bind. Its history, inclination, and desire to either impress or surpass the parents pushes it to strike out with a start-up venture of its own at a time when the business needs successor-leadership.

A final aspect of the interaction between family dynamics and the Start-Up stage has to do with children. Even as preschoolers, the Boncoeurs' children were aware that their parents were busy with the business. Both their parents made time for them, but Deke's time in particular was rushed. In this family, the children were too young to be involved in the company—neither Matilde nor Deke wanted them playing around the ponds or the laboratory. Children in entrepreneurial families, even after they can understand their parents' physical absence and psychological distraction, sometimes feel deprived of attention and affection. Children of any age can conclude that the start-up business is really the most-loved child. Jealousy of the business can persist for decades and can cause difficulty in the succession process. Deke and Matilde often worried that their intense involvement in a start-up firm was unfair to their kids. It may well be that the fact that the children were reaching school age was as influential as the capital constraints in Deke and Matilde's decision to give up WISCO and return to the States.

The Start-Up stage is a gamble; you have to "know when to hold 'em and know when to fold 'em." Of course, some people don't care about winning as much as about making the effort to realize a dream. On this level, Deke and Matilde may consider WISCO to have been a great success.

The Expansion/Formalization Business

Characteristics

After weathering the uncertain years of the start-up period, a company may progress into a second stage, characterized by expansion in a number of arenas (such as sales, products, and number of employees) and by more formalized organizational structures and processes (adding human resource policies, differentiating marketing and sales, on-site production controls).[9] At this stage, the Start-Up issues may not be completely resolved; the owner-manager may still be trying to raise enough capital to keep the business running at a sustainable level and to get the company's name out to prospective customers. The transition from Start-Up to

---

The Expansion/Formalization Stage of Business Development

Characteristics

- Increasingly functional structure
- Multiple products or business lines

Key Challenges

- Evolving the owner-manager role and professionalizing the business
- Strategic planning
- Organizational systems and policies
- Cash management

Expansion/Formalization may not even be noticeable, or it may be abruptly marked by the opening of a new facility, hiring professional management, or introducing a new product. Usually, it is only when owner-managers recognize that they have created a viable company and are now facing *new* challenges that they believe the Start-Up stage is behind them.

In the Expansion/Formalization stage, the importance of both growth and complexity as measures of development becomes clear. Some companies may grow significantly and change their structures very little, whereas others may actually stay the same size or grow slowly, but go through significant restructuring for the long haul. The first type continually seeks expanding markets; the second type tries to consolidate its niche in the market and routinize its ways of operating. The ProMusic case is a company of the latter type.

ProMusic, Inc.

Sarah Greenberg had been passionate about music her whole life. It was a strange choice for the daughter of an accountant and a tone-deaf real estate broker, but her focus had been unwavering—through childhood piano lessons, an undergraduate degree at Oberlin, several jobs at record stores, her own radio show, a stint as music reviewer for a city newspaper, and, later in life, a master's degree in music theory and composition at Columbia. Stimulated in her master's program by more academic perspectives, Sarah decided to combine her interest in music with her long-term entrepreneurial inclination to start a business. Her firm, ProMusic, would be a resource for composers, teachers, and performers, with several lines of business: providing rare recordings by direct mail, offering online research on composers and compositions, creating and distributing software to allow composers to score and orchestrate their compositions via computer, and (her real dream) operating a small recording studio.

Sarah researched the opportunity and found no competitors in her niche except for music stores and libraries, which were unresponsive to customers' needs for speed and specialized expertise. She put together a business plan and talked to family and friends, raising some initial capital to create the first business line: a direct mail catalogue for rare recordings. Sarah, her husband, Aaron, and a graphic artist worked for several months to design a vehicle to let their target market know about ProMusic services (which did not yet exist) and order specialized recordings, each of which was reviewed briefly in the catalogue by a specialist. At this point, they also had no inventory. Sarah's plan was to fill orders through a special rush arrangement with distributors she had located, who were willing to provide this service at a discount price to ProMusic in exchange for what they saw as free marketing and potential higher sales volume for their merchandise.

Sarah spent most of her $50,000 start-up money on the catalogue, then crossed her fingers and waited. The orders rolled in, and over the next two years, the company made a small profit on sales of about $250,000. They opened an office, developed an information system, and began to stock inventory. During this Start-Up stage, Sarah felt busy all the time with the company. Aaron picked up the slack with their two young sons, and Sarah waited for things to calm down. She had no idea that the stress would get worse, not better, as the company grew.

When it was clear that ProMusic was a going concern, Sarah moved quickly to grow the business. The family moved back to the New Jersey suburb where Sarah had grown up. She opened a retail record store, created a consulting and information service via online links to publishers and distributors for specialized services, and bought a small recording studio. Each of these new divisions had its own general manager, but none of them made important decisions without checking with Sarah first. Sarah intended to have weekly meetings of her executive team, but travel and work demands made that very difficult. She hired office, research, retail, software development, and studio production staff. They were growing; however, costs were also growing, and because they still weren't making much money, the company's balance sheet performance was declining. Every two years, Sarah would put together yet another business plan that laid out the need for several million dollars' worth of capital investment. Each time she would make a connection with a publisher or venture capitalist with deep pockets, and each time she would come away from the deal with $200,000 or $300,000 instead of the several million she needed.

What Sarah found was that the potential investors wanted control, which she was not yet willing to give up. She also found that the projects that *she* liked—the retail store and the recording studio—were not projects that thrilled potential investors, because of their low margins. So she kept turning to her and Aaron's family for short-term operating loans, and the business bumped along without sufficient capital.

Ten years after the company's founding, Sarah was becoming discouraged and worn out. She closed the consulting business, which had never found its market and only broke even in its best years. The record store was about to be the next closure, until the manager convinced Sarah to move to a smaller location with a much more specialized jazz inventory, and focus on supporting the mail order catalogue. Then ProMusic had a sudden and unexpected breakthrough. Her software designers developed a product which was a major improvement on the programs currently in use. Before she had to worry about production, she received an offer from a major company to buy out that division at a very generous price. Sarah took the proceeds from that sale and purchased three recording studios in the metropolitan New York area. In the course of six months, ProMusic's cash flow doubled, Sarah could retire most of her debt to nonfamily members, and the prospects for the future looked much improved. Sarah immediately began considering new ventures, like producing CDs of local talent at the studios or sponsoring major musical events.

ProMusic is still in business, but in a form significantly different from that of its Start-Up years. Sarah has turned most aspects of the company over to professional managers. The retail store and mail order service have been combined into a separate subsidiary company with its own president. Sarah is chair of the board and continues to run the original recording studio. This decision reflected a fundamental change in her approach to the business. Initially, she made the decision to do what *she* wanted, rather than to please investors, and was happy to work hard for relatively low returns. She did not start the business to get rich, after all, and they were living a comfortable lifestyle in a place they loved. After several years, though, she had become burned out. Each of the five product lines of the business required huge amounts of time and effort to develop. Sarah needed time to see her family and to have a life of her own. With the buyout of the software division, she was tempted to try again to run things herself, in all three directions at once. But with Aaron's help, she recognized instead that neither the company nor she could survive if she did not formalize the structure, hire senior managers, and begin to act more like the owner of a complex enterprise and less like a hands-on entrepreneur. She is now more realistic about her own role and more optimistic about the prospects for the business. ProMusic has found a surprisingly solid niche in its current businesses, and has the opportunity to leverage modest continued growth in the coming years.

Especially in its early years, ProMusic did not sound like the typical example of the Expansion/Formalization stage. What about all those high-tech companies that double sales each year? Some companies *do* grow that fast, but most family companies do not. The difference lies in financing and ownership. Start-ups headed for the fast track often go public to raise capital; after the IPO, the founders may retain a significant ownership interest, but the company is publicly traded. As we discussed in chapter 1, all family businesses must either rely on family investment or gain access to outside sources of capital. This puts many family companies in the position of ProMusic—ready to grow but constrained by the absence of investors who are willing to take a minority position. Thus growth proceeds much more slowly and is driven as much by reinvestment of the cash that the business generates as by significant outside capital.

ProMusic leapt quickly through the Start-Up stage, and then remained in the Expansion/Formalization stage for almost ten years. And ProMusic raises the interesting question that many owner-managers have to answer: What constitutes success? Is it sufficient that the business just supports the family? Is it sufficient that it satisfy the owners' professional self-image? Or is it necessary that the business bring significant positive change to the economic status of the family? Sarah was certainly hoping for the latter when they started but, with experience, she is happy to have the first and second criteria met.

Key Challenges

Evolving the Owner-Manager Role and Professionalizing the Business. In the Expansion/Formalization stage, businesses typically evolve from a founder-centered structure to a more formal hierarchy with differentiated functions. At some point in this phase, the pressure builds to hire professionals to fill key managerial and specialist roles, and for the owner-manager to start delegating significant authority to nonfamily members.[10] This is often not easy for the owner-manager, especially in the founder generation. At ProMusic, Sarah hired professionals in each business line—direct marketing (a graphic designer), consulting, retailing, and software development. The realities of diversification gave her little choice, even though she was uneasy with the way that decentralization diminished her direct control. Her challenge was to gain a strategic advantage in the specialty music services business—to establish a strong foothold in that market—by virtue of providing many products and services at once.

The Expansion/Formalization stage puts the owner-manager in a difficult squeeze. She or he may hire professionals to staff the business but usually stays directly involved with day-to-day operations. Ambivalence about delegating authority often leads to some confusion or conflict, so that the professionalizing process happens in a "start-stop" pattern: hiring new managers, reassuming control, delegating again, and so forth, until the owner-manager gets used to the new role. In addition, the company must develop sufficient product quality and availability to meet customer needs and satisfy the growing customer base. Relationships with suppliers and customers are under stress, as cash needs have multiplied and products or services cannot always be delivered when promised. Accounting, information, and communication systems may not be sophisticated or fast enough to keep up with the company's increasing complexity. In this case, ProMusic had all the costs and operational needs of a retail enterprise, a software R&D firm, a production studio, and a direct marketing business.

Often, as was the case here, all this development must be done with insufficient funds. The owner-manager, who is watching the funds drain out of the account every month, is also spending a great deal of time and energy revising the business plan, locating potential investors, and trying to secure the funding that will allow more unencumbered growth. The time and attention of the owner-manager, therefore, is one of the key bottlenecks of the Expansion/Formalization stage.

Strategic Planning. ProMusic exists because the Greenbergs' first line of business, the catalogue, was a moderate success for the first seven years. This means that Sarah successfully identified a market and a service that the market would buy. She also had good ideas about other, complementary lines of business; however, her strategy consisted mainly of developing a presence in *all* the areas where products and services for music makers intersected. She did not consider the competitive advantages of ProMusic in the strategic environment of each business line separately, nor the benefits of a staged entry plan, nor the impact on the company of trying to develop all those business lines at the same time. Two of the five lines proved unsustainable in the long term, but for very different reasons: the retail store, because the margins were too thin, and the consulting business, because they could not develop a cost-effective marketing plan to target a specific customer base. Arguably, either of these businesses *might* have succeeded had Sarah been able to focus her management time and capital exclusively on them.

There are many opportunities for strategy formation in the Expansion/Formalization stage. Since the 1960s, a major theme in management science has been exploring the complex relationship between strategy and structure as companies grow and age.[11] The key issue here is not which strategy is chosen (high volume, specialty market, cost or quality focus) or what type of expansion predominates (functional, multidivisional, decentralized), but rather that these are challenges that must be addressed much more fully than in the Start-Up stage. Owner-managers who restrict information gathering and analysis, and who resist critical reflection on the personal vision that sustained them in the earlier stage, will be working with a truncated range of options. This may well lead to a mismatch of resource investment with strategic opportunity or, even more likely, to a failure to see the new opportunities that are available in the Expansion/Formalization stage.

Organizational Systems and Policies. True to form, Sarah did everything herself in the early days. However, she moved very quickly to hire outside expertise for the specialized, value-adding touches that made the catalogue work—the graphic design, the short album reviews in the catalogue text, and the consultants for specific problems. The Greenbergs also built a computerized accounting and inventory system early in ProMusic's life. Thus Sarah began to move away from the hands-on management mode earlier than most founders do. However, it took her almost a decade to move fully into a functional organizational structure and to set up integrative systems and policies. Sarah's centrality in operations remained, despite the fact that she hired other professionals, because the diverse business units remained in business-building mode for so long. As the key resource allocator among the five enterprises, Sarah could not move out of the center until there were enough resources to permit full delegation. Unfortunately, neither internal nor external sources of revenue were sufficient to grow all the businesses comfortably, until the software company was sold off. The resulting cash supported a major jump in business system development, as the organization finally caught up with the needs of its diverse operations.

Cash Management. ProMusic clearly acquired funds sufficient to make the business go in the Start-Up phase. Sarah invested her original stake wisely, and the first business provided enough cash to move the company into expansion in just a few years. However, Sarah still had to spend months of her time in the first ten years trying to "sell" the company to outside investors. Had she been willing to make the company more commercially attractive by traditional business standards, Sarah might well have been successful earlier and at a grander scale than has been the case so far. However, she felt strongly about keeping control and was committed to a diversification growth strategy. As a result, ProMusic had to weather continuous cash flow crises. She could never invest in people or systems fully enough and always had to fend off her family's needs for cash because of the constant need for reinvestment in the company. In the end, Sarah may conclude that it was her faith in the range of services that led to the software success and the dramatic improvement in her company's cash position. But Sarah is also a seasoned enough businesswoman to realize that this is no ultimate resolution. She has only moved up the line of business development, and ProMusic still faces critical choices on strategy and cash management at this point in the Expansion/Formalization stage.

Business development in Expansion/Formalization affects the family in a variety of ways. During the early part of this stage, Sarah continued to live the life of the entrepreneur, even though she didn't quite accept this identity and had a significantly expanded cadre of managers. She worked long hours, traveled away from her family, worried about the business all the time, went through periods when she did not sleep well, and, most painfully for her, did not have time to do other things she loves—rafting trips, camping, and extended periods in the wilderness. ProMusic took a heavy toll on her.

The demands of the company have also consumed Aaron. He is an active participant in the company—hardly a silent partner, as he sits on the board—but he works only part time. And he works, one feels, as much to stay connected to Sarah and her passion as to satisfy his own needs and interests. Early on, of course, he was working for free; now he is paid. An observer would speculate that the business has intruded into their marriage; they are connected now through the business, especially as the children grow close to college age. Members of Aaron's family of origin are still key investors, so his own and his sons' financial security is inextricably caught up in the company. It is tempting to wonder what kind of business Aaron would choose to run, if the pair had followed his dream instead of Sarah's. The challenge for this couple, then, is how to maintain the marriage enterprise that they have chosen in the face of the entrepreneur's urgent passion for the business and the business's overwhelming need for cash and attention.

Sarah and Aaron are about to confront another family issue that sometimes appears when a company is growing—the potential entry of the children into the business. So far, neither of their sons has expressed an interest in joining Sarah, and she has not given much thought to the idea of passing the business along. After all, it is *her* dream, and one that she has not yet fully realized. Still, the boys will be in college within two years, and she knows that they will all need to sit down and talk about whether there is room for either of them in the business. And the vision of her sons in college has also provoked a new round of anxiety about tuition. Although the boys will probably go to state schools, Sarah recognizes that her family is also facing significant financial needs, at the same time that the business has reaccelerated its growth and requires a cash infusion. She knows that she and Aaron must make major estate planning decisions, which she has avoided until now, in order to be sure that their family will be secure financially if she should die prematurely. Sarah is more pragmatic than she was ten years ago, and she has broadened the range of scenarios she is considering: continued rapid expansion, settling down into a more restricted niche and moving the company to maturity, or even, for the first time, putting the company up for sale.

The Mature Business

Suddenly or gradually, a business eventually enters yet another, sometimes final, stage. Maturity in relation to the market becomes apparent when healthy margins start to thin, when competitors multiply, when the flagship product is no longer distinguishable from others on the market, or when sales plateau or drop. Even a company with a successful product or service gradually finds its success harder and harder to repeat. This may happen

The Maturity Stage of Business Development

Characteristics

- Organizational structure supporting stability
- Stable (or declining) customer base, with modest growth
- Divisional structure run by senior management team
- Well-established organizational routines

Key Challenges

- Strategic refocus
- Management and ownership commitment
- Reinvestment

after ten or fifteen years, or after fifty. Successful companies will recognize that the period of Expansion/Formalization is coming to a close. Some companies are able to protect a sufficiently adequate market share to remain in the Maturity stage for a very long time. In most cases, however, the organization must adjust and renew itself, or face decline.

Characteristics

There are mature companies that have held to very limited product lines. They still command a position in their market that allows them to perpetuate many of the same ways of doing business they have always employed. Most firms, however, have gone through a sequence of increasing organizational complexity. Some companies will experience a traditional functional differentiation, with departments such as sales, marketing, finance and accounting, human resources, and manufacturing. Others will treat each plant, product line, or brand name as a business unit, with or without functional subunits inside it. Still others will experiment with other models, such as flat organizations, inverted triangles, clusters, and so forth. Regardless of the particular form, the hallmarks of the Maturity stage are that the purpose of the organizational form is stability; expectations for growth are modest; and, specifically in family businesses, a group of managers have authority and responsibility for many executive functions without the direct input of owners.

The mature family business offers many unparalleled rewards to its owner-manager family. It has survived, grown, and found a place for itself in its industry and in its community. If the company deals directly with the public, particularly if the company bears the family name, the family may be widely recognized as successful and influential. Many families adopt a highly visible role in the community, sponsoring activities with a joint purpose of civic philanthropy and good public relations. Family managers have probably attended dozens of conferences and industry or trade association meetings, assuming a leadership or mentoring role in relation to younger owners of Start-Up firms. Senior family members may sit on boards of other companies, as well as public and cultural organizations. These are the rewards of maturity that were only a vague image to owner-managers in the Start-Up stage: stability, recognition, and an identity with its own unique history and traditions.

But Maturity is also a stage, not a final destination. In theory, a purely mature firm is a dinosaur waiting for extinction. Most organizational experts argue that new ventures and spinoffs, anticipating new directions in the market, are essential to fend off obsolescence and decline in mature companies. We have found this to be true in many cases, but not in all. Some family firms hold remarkably tightly to their organizational traditions. They may modernize, but they do not seek new opportunities. Still, it is relatively rare for a family firm to be completely in the mature stage for an extended time. Some portion of the company will typically begin a recycle by spinning off a new start-up venture, acquiring a subsidiary in an earlier stage, or establishing remote or foreign branches that exhibit some of the Start-Up or Expansion/Formalization characteristics.

FP Construction Company

Frank Pineo and George Tecce are looking forward to their retirement. The brothers-in-law have run the family's construction-related companies together for thirty years. Francesco Pineo, Frank's father, arrived in New

York in the early 1900s and worked with relatives in the construction industry as a laborer. Soon he was foreman and, over time, he accumulated enough money to take on some of his own work. He leased the equipment he needed from his cousins until he could afford his own fleet. FP Construction Company (FPC), a general construction firm, was born in 1928 in southern Connecticut.

Having weathered the depression, Francesco decided to focus on a new specialty—highway construction. By opportunistically entering every new market, Francesco built FPC into a diversified construction company capable of everything from complex bridge jobs to simple parking lot paving. He also acquired property of all descriptions: vacant land, strip malls, urban office buildings. Frank and George, who is married to Frank's older sister, followed in Francesco's tradition: they have taken the construction company to $100 million by running a trimmed-down, honest business. Their philosophy is that they will never underbid a job—they would rather lose the business than lose their margin. The company now owns a sizable fleet of specialized heavy equipment and a large repair facility, run by Frank's son as a separate business. The real estate is also held in two different corporations, and the brothers own a majority interest in a real estate management business as well.

FPC did very well during the highway boom of the sixties and early seventies. However, the company struggled during the recessions of the eighties and nineties. Federal cutbacks of highway funds posed major obstacles to the construction business, and the plunge in the real estate markets jeopardized some of their larger properties. In the mid-1980s, they hired a specialist to bid their jobs, in part to prepare for the time when George, the master bidder, would retire. Their choice was Bill O'Day, a diligent and intuitive bidder himself, who was also good at supervising jobs. Impressed with Bill's ability to find the jobs that were scarcer every month and to bring jobs in on cost, the brothers-in-law soon promoted him to president. Frank stepped into the chair role, and George became CEO.

Frank and George also encouraged their own sons to join the business; two of Frank's children tried, but only Frank Jr. stayed on. George's son James was a "natural," having worked in the company since he was a teenager. Both young men had proved themselves in laborer and supervisor jobs when Bill O'Day came on. And, to everyone's surprise, Bill took an interest in the development of the younger Tecces and Pineos, considering their training part of his job description. Frank Jr., who shared his father's love of hands-on work, became head of the garage; James, a capable estimator and foreman, moved into the office. His job was to unravel the administrative systems that their longtime CFO Bernie had left behind after a heart attack had forced his sudden early retirement.

Frank and George, after attending a seminar on continuity, brought in a family business consultant to evaluate their progress toward succession. Reassured that they were on the right track, they also took the consultant's advice and established a board of advisers that included outsiders to the company. In its first year, the board looked carefully at the real estate companies and strongly advised Frank and George to hire a real estate specialist to clean up the problems. Within two years, the properties in crisis were either turned around or sold; however, the portfolio was not generating much cash. This was a concern, because Frank and George intended to leave the real estate companies to their five other children (on the assumption that Frank Jr. and James would have the construction businesses). Their concern was compounded when the real estate manager left suddenly, apparently miffed that Frank and George wanted to hire George's daughter, Linda, a property manager who had returned from graduate school with her MBA. On the board's advice, they gave the senior job to Linda, who immediately drew up a strategy for the portfolio and formed a working advisory group of siblings and cousins for the real estate.

Meanwhile, Bill O'Day continues to worry that they can no longer hold to the Pineo philosophy of never underbidding a job. The industry has changed, and huge firms with lower overhead costs are taking a good share of their business. The fewer jobs they bid, the more their equipment fleet sits unused. Frank Jr. wants to launch an expanded marketing effort for their equipment repair operation and to jump into the equipment leasing business. And James is encouraging him to form some kind of joint venture arrangement with a firm in New England, which might allow them to bid work in a larger geographic area. Bill has to choose between the perspective of the second generation, which ran the company in the founder's tradition, and that of the third, which has new directions in mind.

Key Challenges

The decisions that Frank and George face with FPC are typical of those facing the owners of a mature company. Margins have thinned, competition is fiercer, and old formulas for success have become threats to innovation. The problem facing the younger generation of family and nonfamily managers is how to maintain tradition while moving beyond it. In part, they must honor tradition because they must satisfy the older-generation owners; however, they must also understand analytically what the company's competitive strengths have been, in order to build a solid base on which to move forward.

In the Maturity stage, a business has grown into a complex enterprise. Even in the relatively small FPC structure, there are different companies and differentiated estimating, administrative, and construction functions. The company depends on nonfamily professionals (Bernie, Bill) as much as on key family members, and operating strategy is forged by a senior management team. Although Frank and George are indisputably "more senior" than the others, they are also happy to have their professional managers make the decisions within their areas. If they have substantial disagreement with Bernie or Bill, Frank and George typically take the issue to the board.

At this stage of life, even smaller companies frequently have multicompany structures like FPC's. One of the two real estate companies is owned by Frank and George and the other, by all their children except Frank Jr. and James. In this case, the board was instrumental in getting Frank and George to treat their real estate like a real business; nevertheless, they have significant assets invested in that company, and their real estate problems are jeopardizing the construction business. Like other companies in this stage, FPC needs to look for new lines of business and new ways to generate margin in their current operations. Their success depends on three key variables.

Strategic Refocus. Creating a board of advisers was the first of several steps Frank and George took that *could* lead to a strategic refocus for the company. Planning for the turnover of the company to their sons is also an important step. However, there are still at least two steps to go for FPC. First, the senior management team and the board have not done any systematic analysis to generate options for new business. Frank Jr. believes that the garage can become a revenue-producing division and wants to experiment with leasing underutilized equipment. However, the group has not discussed this proposal seriously nor considered investing company resources in this new project. Second, Frank and George have not blessed the effort to find new lines of business. Although they are open to new ideas, they continue to focus their own energies on improving operations in the construction business. They need to send the signal to their sons and to nonfamily managers that searching for new sources of revenue is an important priority and that they welcome this refocus as part of the succession process.

Family firms are sometimes slow to acknowledge the complexity of the strategy process when they reach the Maturity stage. Ward has found that both strategy and organizational structure in family firms are influenced by a wide mix of forces.[12] Some of these forces are the same as those experienced by all firms (such as organizational mission, industry and company analysis). In addition, family businesses need to factor in the influence of the founders' legacy, family values and goals, and history of the firm. Even the most enlightened family leadership needs help from a strong board to manage this complicated strategy process in mature companies.[13]

Strategic refocus also operates on a different timetable than it did a generation ago. In the middle part of this century, the life expectancy of a major innovation or technology was about twenty-five years—nearly identical to the typical span of control of one generation in a family business.[14] New ideas and systems entered with the new leaders. Now the typical product life cycle has shrunk to four or five years (and, in some industries, to a matter of months). No generational leadership can coast on its entry improvements for very long. Most leaders will have to guide the company through the business cycle, from Start-Up through Expansion/Formalization to Maturity, several times during their tenure. This uncoupling of the cycle of family succession from the business's development is an example of why it is so important to consider developmental stages separately for each of the three axes.

Management and Ownership Commitment.   Because Frank's and George's own personal assets are invested in FPC, they are making a strong statement of trust in turning the business over to their sons, who will eventually own the company fifty-fifty. Likewise, Frank Jr. and James are sending the signal, by their decision to accept the FPC mantle, that their generation is committed to keeping the business in the family. However, this family has not sat down and openly recommitted itself to the company.

For Frank and George, this may seem unnecessary; they never considered any alternative for themselves except running Franco's business. However, for their children, it may be an important conversation. In particular, nonemployed children need to understand and accept the continued dedication of significant family assets to the company.

One advantage of the Mature firm is that it offers a variety of different career advancement opportunities for both family and nonfamily managers. Nonfamily managers become increasingly important to all family businesses as they move through the business development stages. Nonfamily leaders are sometimes a forgotten issue in the analysis of family firms. Beginning in the Expansion/Formalization stage, few families can staff all management positions themselves. Nonfamily managers provide essential resources, especially for expertise and experience that is not included in the family. They can be a buffer against inappropriate family influence in management. They can be an encouragement to lower-level nonfamily managers and staff because they symbolize the opportunity available to successful employees. Finally, they can play an essential role in the supervision and mentoring of the next generation of family managers.

The contribution of nonfamily managers cannot be taken for granted, however. A comprehensive career development strategy for the company's leadership should include incentive and recruitment tactics that will locate and retain the best available nonfamily management. Many family owners worry, especially in the early stages of the family business's development, that it will be difficult to attract and keep ambitious nonfamily managers because of the family control. As a result, they avoid clarifying career opportunities and restrictions for young nonfamily managers. Dealing successfully with this issue requires the owner-managers to first make some important decisions: Are there positions that are reserved for family members? Why? Are there policy issues and information that are to be decided by family members only? Why? Will nonfamily members be moved out of positions to provide opportunities for developing family managers to get essential experience? Is the family ownership prepared to offer competitive compensation to nonfamily managers, even if family members are willing to work for below-scale salaries? Once the leadership is comfortable with its policies on these issues, it is almost always a better strategy to discuss them openly with key nonfamily managers. Their fears may be worse than the reality of their opportunities. In any case, understanding what the rules are and what to expect from each other is better than surprises.

Reinvestment. FPC is facing a critical juncture in the succession process, and part of the transition's success will depend on how the leadership (senior and junior) balances the financial needs of the family with the business's needs for reinvestment. Strategic refocus typically requires investment—in new products, in new people, and in new equipment. However, when a company is mature, there is often a temptation among the owners to treat the company as a static and automatic source of income. Continuous capital reinvestment does not carry the same excitement or feeling of creativity as investment in new ventures. Some businesses whose products are potentially viable far into the future make the mistake of continually deferring needed upgrading. This can push equipment, marketing strategies, facilities, and product lines beyond their optimal life. Then, if everything falls apart at once, massive reinvestment is needed on a crisis basis, and by then it is often no longer feasible to rebuild. If a company hopes to maintain all or part of its operations in the Maturity stage for some time, it needs to accept a psychological commitment to feed the cow as well as milk it.

The challenge of reinvestment can become complicated if the Maturity stage in the business dimension coincides with the Passing the Baton in the family dimension. Psychologically, it may be more difficult for a senior generation to embrace a strong reinvestment policy, especially if it means significantly increasing debt, during their last few years of active involvement in management. They may have spent years improving debt-to-equity ratios and working off long-term obligations. Starting over is a hard choice to make.

There may also be cash considerations during this time. One of the financial challenges of the Passing the Baton stage is financing the retirement of senior family members. There is sometimes simply not enough surplus cash or retained earnings to buy out the interests of the retiring generation and to pay for major rebuilding at the same time.[15] The problem is compounded if there is also pressure to cash out nonemployed siblings or cousins in the younger generation. The result of these forces is that many companies are left in the Maturity stage a little longer than is financially prudent by senior owner-managers who convince themselves that major change is the prerogative (and therefore the responsibility) of the next generation. Sometimes the new leaders have the skill, judgment, authority, and cash to begin strategic reinvestment as soon as they assume leadership. Sometimes they do not.

Moving through the Stages of the Business Dimension

In addition to the characteristics of the stages, it is also important to consider the factors that speed up or slow down the business life cycle, or push a company to jump forward or backward. Although each company has its own pace, there are general factors that will influence any business's developmental timetable. First, external factors such as industry conditions and the general economic cycle can have a determining impact on business development. Industries vary widely on product life cycles, dependence on new technologies, and the nature of the competitive environment. For example, in environments in which new product life cycles are short, companies often cannot afford to enter the Maturity phase; if they do not have new products constantly under development, they will be left behind. In industries in which new technologies are critical, the demands for continuous investment in new product development or new generations of equipment may actually constrain growth by swallowing all excess capital. Finally, government policy or general recession may raise the cost of capital or force long delays in expansion plans. Spurts in general economic growth can carry companies faster along the growth path; stalls in recessionary times can retard business development. The life cycle of a family business often is determined by the luck of the timing of the general business cycle.

Second, the interaction with the developmental stages in the family and ownership dimensions can control business development. In the WISCO and ProMusic cases, the ownership structure (Controlling Owners) limited access to capital. The Boncoeurs could not find sufficient outside investors who wanted to own even a minority share of the company, and they tapped out their own and their families' resources. Sarah Greenberg found outside investors willing to take a majority interest, but she was not willing to change the ownership structure of the company she had built. In a different dimension, we have discussed that Working Together families sometimes accelerate the structural formalization and differentiation in their companies in order to give rising family managers separate organizational units or functions to run. On the other hand, a Passing the Baton family with a previously expanding business may become tentative about new ventures and slide into Maturity if the senior generation is reluctant to start something it will not be able to finish or to tie its successors' hands with debt.

The business developmental dimension completes the three-dimensional model. Each of the dimensions has a slightly different quality; the pace and pattern of development over time is different for shareholders, families, and businesses. But knowing the current stage of each contributes to understanding the unique character of the family business. In the next part of the book, we combine stages across all three dimensions to generate portraits of the most common types of family businesses—in effect, putting the model to work.

NOTES

1. DiMaggio and Powell (1983) and Scott (1992) argue that organizations change as a result of their membership in an industry or other large group of organizational actors (called a "field") that move in the same economic arena. As economic, market, and regulatory forces act on that industry or group, organizations change to remain competitive, but also to be able to do business easily with each other. For example, if a powerful institution like a government regulatory agency requires an organization to report a new kind of information, then all the organizations affected will adjust their information and management systems, usually in similar ways, to provide the data required, in the format requested. Another school, called "population ecology," uses the biological model of natural selection to argue that individual organizations cannot change fast enough, but that the environment will choose which businesses survive (Hannan and Freeman 1977). Those that best fit their environmental niche will survive, and others will fail. From this perspective, external forces (markets, suppliers, costs, customer tastes, and the like) again are the primary shapers of the mix of successful firms. Thus the combination of organizations in an arena at any point in time is the product of quasi-biological forces weeding out the weaker players. One outgrowth of the pure ecology models are the resource dependency theories, which acknowledge a greater ability of management to read the environment and adapt to it (Pffeffer and Salancik 1978; Van de Ven and Walker 1984; Sharfman, Gray, and Yan 1991). Of course, not all proactive adjustments to the marketplace make the difference between company life and death. For example, companies that predicted consumers' positive response to environmentally sensitive packaging (refillable detergent bottles, for example) gained an edge; however, they have not by any means put their competition out of business.

2. Organizational development, from this perspective, is a process parallel to individual development (Piaget 1963; Levinson 1978; Erikson 1980) and group development (Bennis and Shepard 1956; Gersick 1988; McCollom 1995). One of the most interesting conceptual conundrums is the issue of the end point of an organizational life cycle. The concept of lifespan without end is in some ways an oxymoron. Therefore, the immortal and regenerative capacities of organizations illuminate the limits of the application of the biological metaphor to organizational life cycles.

3. Greiner 1972; Flamholtz 1986; Dodge and Robbins 1992.

4. Christensen and Scott 1964; Steinmetz 1969; Torbert 1974; Katz and Kahn 1978.

5. There is also variation in the envisioned "shape" of the organizational life

course. Some of the models conceptualize development as essentially continuous growth; the graph depicting the company's path through time looks like an ascendant straight line (Greiner 1972; Barnes and Hershon 1976; Churchill and Lewis 1983). Others picture the life cycle as a rising and falling curve, tapering to eventual decline at the end of the organization's life (Adizes 1979; Miller and Friesen 1984; Poza 1989). Some of the researchers also conclude that organizations must address and resolve the issues of each stage before they can successfully move to the next (Lippitt and Schmidt 1967; Greiner 1972). Others portray more skipping around. This is a strength of Churchill and Lewis's work (1983), which provides a realistic picture of the possibility of plateauing, backtracking, or failure at every stage. Finally, much of the research on organizational growth and change treats all types of organizations, including governmental agencies. In choosing our stages, we have paid most attention to the writers who have focused specifically on closely held companies (for example, Churchill and Lewis 1983; Flamholtz 1986; Olson 1987; Scott and Bruce 1987). Unfortunately, the researchers who have written specifically about family businesses are few in number (Barnes and Hershon 1976; McGivern 1989; Poza 1989). We have drawn most heavily on the work of these latter thinkers.

6. Some models have separate stages for "early" and "later" start-up. Churchill and Lewis (1983) make this distinction (their phases are existence, survival, success, take-off, and resource maturity), as do Scott and Bruce (1987), whose model includes inception, survival, growth, expansion, and maturity.

7. Barnes and Hershon (1976) and Poza (1989) have particularly good models that subdivide this stage into sequential parts.

8. Sonnenfeld 1988.

9. Berenbeim 1984.

10. Dyer 1989.

11. Chandler 1962; Bolman and Deal 1984.

12. Ward 1987; Harris, Martinez, and Ward 1994.

13. Ward 1991.

14. Barnes and Hershon 1976; Ward 1987.

15. Cohn 1990.

PART II

Four Classic Family Business Types

THIS SECTION looks at family businesses in four of the most typical, and most interesting, combinations of ownership, family, and business developmental stages: the first-generation, founder-run business owned and managed by an individual entrepreneur; the established business owned by a Sibling Partnership and experiencing rapid growth and change; the complex, mature Cousin Consortium; and the business at the brink of transition, controlled by a Passing the Baton family. Each of the following four chapters is designed to show how the dimensions interact in shaping the character of actual family businesses. The chapters also present, in turn, four of the most important themes of family business: entrepreneurship, organizational change, networks, and succession.

4

Founders and the Entrepreneurial Experience

THE FIRST-GENERATION Controlling Owner company is one of the most exciting types of family businesses. New ventures not only are critical to capitalist economies, but they also have an important symbolic identity as the society's stairway of opportunity for individuals and families. The entrepreneur is a complex figure in our cultural mythology: part adventurer and part misfit, part benefactor and part exploiter, part genius and part fool.

Founders of family companies can have a profound influence on the organizational cultures of their creations as well. The founder's beliefs, business acumen, decision-making rules of thumb, and values are part of the basic structure of the enterprise, and they are perpetuated through the developmental cycles of all three dimensions. In that way founders can remain a presence for generations beyond their own lifetime.

This chapter reviews the issues faced by a typical, newly founded family business: a Controlling Owner, Start-Up business, with a founder in the Young Business Family stage. A family company can return to the Controlling Owner stage of ownership and the Young Business Family stage many times in its long history, and there will be issues in common in all of these periods. But the founder (first-generation) experience is unique, and all of the subsequent stages are affected by what happens during these first few years of the business's life.

It is reasonable to ask whether Start-Up ventures are really family businesses at all. In the initial stages, most Controlling Owner founders do not significantly involve their families in employment or ownership (companies that begin as Sibling Partnerships or Cousin Consortiums are, of course, different). Some new businesses remain the individual domain of one founder, never employing or sharing ownership with relatives, and are sold or liquidated without a thought of continuity in the family. However, the fact that many Start-Ups do not become family businesses does not diminish the critical importance of this stage in those that do.

Factors Leading to the Founding of a Business

There is a rich literature about the motivations and personality styles associated with starting a business.[1] A long list of variables have been investigated in conjunction with entrepreneurial activity: internal locus of control, inability to adapt to system roles, early family experiences, lack of traditional economic opportunity, and many others. These factors are often grouped into "push" forces (psychological dispositions and life events that drive the entrepreneur into a need for or a readiness for starting a business) and "pull" forces (economic and environmental conditions that make new ventures attractive).[2] There is also increased interest in entrepreneurial networks and support systems, as opposed to the traditional focus on independent entrepreneurs, which has particular importance for the founding of a family business.[3]

There are two general motivations of founders that have a particularly lasting impact on the businesses they begin. First is the desire, however measured, to be an owner-manager instead of an employee. The motivation for personal independence, to be one's own boss, and to have control over one's life has been widely connected with the desire to start a business. Most founders of companies leave other jobs to start their own businesses, sometimes moving from one unsuccessful job to another before deciding to create their own company. Frustration with bosses, lack of career progress, and a desire for more decision-making power have all been noted as encouraging entrepreneurial careers.[4] This characteristic of founders can become institutionalized into those aspects of the organization's culture that are tolerant of individualists, resistant to rigid authority hierarchies, and reluctant to formalize organizational structure. That may be why family businesses tend to have less rigidly defined job descriptions and more powerful informal hierarchies than nonfamily firms.

The second key motivation is the desire to seize opportunity and to exploit it. As much as founders are driven away from their old jobs by frustration, they are equally attracted to the challenge and excitement of their new venture. Entrepreneurs are often inspired by the achievements of other company founders.[5] A high percentage of the stories we have heard over the years about how a company has started begin with, "Somebody gave me a chance to . . . , and I couldn't pass it up." It is the entrepreneur's version of the adage, "If life gives you lemons, make lemonade"—in this case, "If you get an opportunity to buy lemons cheap, *sell* lemonade." This characteristic of founders becomes reflected in the opportunism of their companies. They often grow by taking advantage of a series of "good deals," whether or not the opportunities are guided by an overarching strategic plan.

These two founder characteristics require a catalyst to result in the start of a business: the timely availability of financial resources. In chapter 1 we discussed the problems of inadequate start-up capital and overly optimistic market assessments and cash flow forecasts. The entrepreneur's personal resources are usually the main funding source, and funds from lending institutions provide additional capital.[6] A survey by Coopers & Lybrand in 1994 reveals that by far the largest sources of start-up capital were personal savings and other family members (73 percent) augmented by other investors and bank loans (27 percent).[7] The availability of family capital (including free or cheap labor) and the family's willingness to sacrifice financially while the company is being established are two of the most important financial resources available to most founders.

The New Venture's Transformation into a Family Company

Whatever the entrepreneur's motivation for starting the venture, the odds are against success. In the United States, 40 percent of businesses fail in the first year, 60 percent fail within two years, and 90 percent fail by the end of the tenth year.[8] The competencies of the founder in several critical areas—especially leadership, managerial, marketing, financial, and technical skills—will influence whether the enterprise will be successful or not.

In some ways, the role of entrepreneur seems incompatible with the role of family business leader. The classic view of entrepreneurs emphasizes their individualism, self-determination, comfort with rapid change, and obsessive immersion in the enterprise. The head of a family business, in contrast, is supposed to be group focused, collaborative, committed to long-term continuity, and equally immersed in firm and family. It is true that some successful founders are ill equipped to manage their businesses after the Start-Up stage. In other cases, however, what appears as a contradiction is instead an aspect of the stage of the system's development. The founder may begin as an entrepreneur, displaying all of the first set of qualities. At some point, a transition in his or her values, visions, identity, and behavior occurs, and the family business is born.

The transition from a Controlling Owner new venture to a family business requires both concrete actions and a psychological step. The concrete actions include one or more of the following: hiring family members, preparing them for management positions, distributing ownership to family heirs, and, typically, anticipating a transition of management control within the family. The psychological step is in the controlling owner's perception of the company, changing from seeing the business as a personal activity to seeing it as a family asset that has an existence and a life expectancy separate from the founder's individual life course. The psychological redefinition can come first, and the concrete actions follow. In other cases, oddly enough, the founder takes the concrete actions long before thinking of the company as a family business. He or she may not consciously recognize that the company is becoming a family business and may deny it if asked.

On the other hand, sometimes the vision of family involvement and continuity is part of the founder's dream from the beginning—or even before the company is founded. This seems to be especially prevalent when there is a family business tradition in one's family, community, or society that encourages a founder to think of the business as a family company.[9] In these cases, the choice of the right entrepreneurial opportunity may depend more on its long-term viability or its fit with family resources rather than on the founder's individual preference. Founders who dream of dynasties from the beginning are likely to be very inclusive of participation from many family members, which can increase the broad family's identification with the firm. However, unless the founder's offspring are already adults and have joined very explicitly in the formation of the dream, these founders may also be setting themselves up for disappointment if other family members do not share the same enthusiasm for the company or the idea of a family business.

The desire to have one's company be a family business may also grow as the family grows up. When the children are young, founders may have no interest in bringing them into the business or passing ownership to them; but when they and their children get older, several dynamics may increase the founder's interest in making the company a family business. The company may grow beyond the founder's expectations. The founder may recognize a surprisingly good fit between the company's needs and the interests and abilities of the children. As founders mature, they may develop a desire to have a legacy that will outlive them. Finally, family members themselves may exert pressure for the opportunity to have careers in the company. Suddenly, or gradually, the Start-Up firm becomes a family business.

Controlling Owner–Young Business Family–Start-Up Business

Characteristics

Although it is simplest to conceive of a new business venture as emerging from scratch out of the ideas and energy of a single entrepreneur, that is not the typical story. Most businesses are started as part of a process that includes many smaller efforts, some successes and some failures, from which the founder learns what he or she needs to know. Other people contribute ideas, capital, or encouragement. The story of George Pilgrim and Agricultural Publishers, Inc., captures this "accumulated learning" idea of the founding of a family business.

Agricultural Publishers, Inc.

George Pilgrim was born in 1917 and raised along with his younger sister in towns in Indiana and Illinois. His father was a successful industrial designer and mechanical engineer (as well as a political cartoonist for the local paper), whose inventions included, among other things, putting light-bulbs inside refrigerators. George found in his father a model of independence, successful entrepreneurship, and close involvement with family. He admired his father a great deal, and they achieved a kind of colleagueship, which was very important to George's success at several key points in his career.

As a child, George developed an interest in poultry agriculture. His father was ready to acknowledge that George had not inherited his mechanical aptitude or interests, but no one could understand the fascination with farming. George raised pigeons, the closest thing he could find to chickens in a city. "I called it the Healthy Pigeon farm, and every pigeon

was named for a famous cartoon character. Obviously, I wasn't too sophisticated about life in those days because Moon Mullins and Dick Tracy
were some of my best egg layers." George was a reasonably good student
and an excellent athlete—also strongly encouraged by his athlete father.
He was competitive and "didn't see any reason to come in second" once
he started something. He had a good sense of humor and was known for
his practical jokes, which usually stopped short of getting him in trouble.

George attended the University of Wisconsin. He began as a major in
poultry husbandry, then shifted to agronomy. Hybrid corn was just beginning to make its mark, and George saw that bigger opportunities lay in
improved strains and new seeds, not poultry. He gradually modified his
boyhood vision of creating a large-scale egg operation into a more general
interest in farming. George's father, anxious to move his design studio out
of the city and interested in supporting George's enthusiasm for farming
as a commercial enterprise, bought a farm in northern Illinois and hired a
manager to operate it. When he began to confess that he did not see the
attractions of farming over mechanical engineering ("This whole operation
would make a lot more sense if you could do it indoors," he told George),
his son decided he should leave college after his junior year to assume
management of the farm.

The farm was diversified, giving George experience with poultry, grain
and feed crops, dairy cows, and even sheep. George wanted to make the
farm a financial success as soon as possible so that he could marry his
college sweetheart, Dorothy. "She was a city girl, so whenever I called back
to her at school and described the farm, I emphasized the long afternoons
riding our horses. I didn't talk as much about the dairy cows." Dorothy
and George were married in June 1940. From the beginning, they were "a
farm couple." There was only one hired hand. Dorothy kept all the books,
drove the trucks, and did whatever else was needed. George had the 200
sheep sheared and the wool sent to Ohio to be made into virgin wool
blankets; Dorothy sold the blankets at country fairs and craft shows.

George's and Dorothy's talents and the welcoming economy at the start
of World War II led to steady growth. Primary annual financing came from
the Production Credit Association, an agricultural financing agency with
a nationwide network of county-based offices. At first George could not
sell much seed for cash, so he bartered it for other grains and feeds,
machine parts, and agricultural supplies—which conserved his own cash.
Gradually, as a cash market developed for various seed varieties, George

began to contract with other farmers for their acreage to produce seed, which he sold in a continually increasing geographic market. At its peak, George's farm of 450 acres was augmented with contracts for over 10,000 acres, and he was selling seed all over the United States, primarily in the East. They also operated a grain elevator, for which Dorothy did the accounting until their sons, David and Jon, were born in 1942 and 1944.

The next entrepreneurial leap was a contract to grow certified seed from the foundation seed of a new barley being developed at the University of Illinois College of Agriculture. This seed was rationed according to the number of acres of certified seed that farmers had produced in the prior two years. George was able to get enough foundation seed to plant about 40 acres—at that time the largest share in the country, but only marginally profitable. Instead of waiting for spring to plant his allocation, George leased land in California's Imperial Valley and took a chance by planting in October, hoping to have a much-expanded crop of seed to plant the following spring in the Midwest. Everything went wrong. The irrigation water had wild oats in it, which had to be removed by hand after they sprouted. In the much longer winter growing period before the seeds matured, the barley grew seven feet high instead of four; the combines were not equipped to harvest such excessive straw. Once the seeds were harvested, there was no time for a conventional winter dormancy period. George had to rely on the commercially untested theory that the trip back to the Midwest in a refrigerated truck would suffice. Each problem was solved in time. The original thirty-six-bushel allocation was multiplied to enough seed for 4,000 acres of spring planting. His confidence had been so high that he had not only precontracted for the 4,000 midwestern acres before planting the California experiment, he had even presold the following year's crop from all 4,000 acres to Cargill. After a second year of similar success with a new variety of oats, the other certified seed growers cried "foul" and pressured the University of Illinois to withdraw their permission for George to use their foundation seed that way for another season. George looked for another opportunity.

He used the seed profits to buy a grain processing plant in Racine, Wisconsin, and began to manufacture and market oatmeal at retail as Pilgrim Oats. This effort was as much a disaster as the seed business had been a success. George realized he had been incredibly naive to attempt to compete with a giant like Quaker, which controlled shelf space in the retail markets. He had counted on export sales but found the international regulations, duties, and currency exchange eating up all his profits. His only redeeming experience from the oatmeal business was Dorothy's idea about what to do with a train car full of unused, brightly painted metal oatmeal containers that were intended for export use. They invented a game, which they called Holi Boli, using ten of the cylinders held together in a triangular box, and a shipment of red and white Ping-Pong balls that George had bought from another failed entrepreneur. George took his sample product to the home office of a department store chain in Racine and convinced the managers to buy all of them—several thousand games. "That helped get us out of the hole and salvage something," George says. "But I'm sure it was a little confusing when, somewhere in the Midwest, the day after Christmas that year, some kid accidently broke open the triangular box and found himself surrounded by metal cans with a Pilgrim hat painted on them and directions for making oatmeal in eight languages."

David and Jon, now in junior high school, had their first real jobs in the family business at this stage. They were responsible for putting the cans into the Holi Boli boxes. They also had to open thousands of unsold, prepackaged cardboard containers of oatmeal and put the contents back into 100-pound bags for resale overseas. "They were on their own paths. Their jobs were to take school seriously, do sports, find out what they wanted to do. I remember David leaning over to Jon after a day of emptying those oatmeal cartons and saying in a well-reasoned voice, 'Something must have gone really wrong here.' I remember thinking he had a pretty good business head on his shoulders."

"It's hard to think of any way to put a good spin on the oatmeal experience," George remembers. He converted the now-inoperative facility into a commercial grain elevator, which Dorothy managed until George hired a general manager who eventually purchased the facility. Meanwhile, George pursued his new idea. His experience with the Production Credit Association (which accounted for over 30 percent of all short- and intermediate-term credit to agriculture) convinced him that there was a need, and a market, for a good-quality magazine covering the business concerns of farmers. "Farming was becoming capital intensive. Farmers needed to know more about pushing a pencil than about operating a tractor. As it was, the only publications were very general. A melon farmer in South Carolina could read about sheep ranching in Wyoming, but hardly anything about the financial side of running his business." George went on the road to recruit individual offices of the PCA to subscribe to a new magazine that he intended to publish. At that time he met two experienced publishers who were ready to leave the companies they worked for, which put out established magazines on country life, and to join in a new venture. George put in what he had salvaged from the oatmeal business, and they formed a three-way partnership. The two partners concentrated on sponsored farm publications for corporate clients such as Ford Motor Company and Massey-Ferguson. George traveled to individual PCAs trying to sell the magazine concept.

"I made my first sales call on a PCA office in April 1957. We put out our first issue that fall, with twenty-three offices signed on and a circulation of 35,000." George's new idea was to have a shell of national business news, with a core of local news and advertisements generated by that particular association (typically serving five counties). George actually traveled to every individual PCA in the United States. Even though the idea caught on immediately and new association offices were signing on every day, George's two partners thought it was too complicated to continue. Printers were not friendly to so many different versions of the same magazine; the concept of regional editions, let alone local versions, was not yet accepted. They worked out an amicable separation, with George intending to develop the local news and advertising as a newsletter service, and the partners keeping the general magazine part.

Within three months, the newsletter had grown to the phenomenal size of 300,000 circulation. When the former partners approached George about buying the original farm magazine back from them, George knew he should make the deal to keep them from evolving into competitors, even though the asking price was exorbitant. To raise the capital, George made a deal with an Iowa agricultural company to set up a new company, Farm Credit Services, Inc., half owned by them and half by George. George would have complete control; Farm Credit would in effect be silent financial partners. Once he had the magazine back, its growth exploded. Within a year, annual sales had reached $3 million. In only a few years, he built circulation to 600,000, representing 94 percent of all the Farm Credit Associations nationwide. Through the various buyouts and restructurings that have occurred since them, the agricultural publishing business has been the heart of George's work for almost forty years.

Ownership Issues

The ownership of a first-generation Controlling Owner business is in the hands of the founder (sometimes shared with a spouse or a minority partner). The founder's ownership control allows control over strategic and operational decisions and often gives control over family decisions as well. George Pilgrim had experience with a number of ownership combinations. At first he developed a farm that was actually owned by his father. This is especially common on family farms, where ownership characteristically does not change hands until the death of the senior generation, but operational control may be passed down to the next generation much earlier. In the grain and oatmeal businesses, George was the controlling owner. His experience with nonfamily owner partners in Agricultural Publishers lasted only five years. Although in the end he had built a business that required more capital than he could generate himself, he was able to structure a deal with a new nonfamily financial partner that gave him the capital he needed while leaving him with complete operational control.

As discussed in chapter 2's introduction of the "marriage enterprise" concept, the role of the spouse in the Start-Up stage may be that of a silent and supportive partner, or of a copreneur. Working in the business together does not necessarily make the business copreneurial. Only if both spouses have significant management authority and feel empowered to make decisions is the business truly copreneurial. These equal partnerships are becoming more common in family businesses, but they are still the exception. More commonly, the spouse is an owner in name only, especially if some of the start-up capital came from the spouse's personal funds or extended family. In those cases, it is very important for there to be an explicit agreement on the spouse's appropriate role. A spouse will occasionally serve as an adviser to the founder and even comment on operational issues, but the couple's division of responsibilities makes it clear that the business is in the founder's domain. The Pilgrims had that kind of arrangement. Dorothy was as influential in the family as was her husband and was also an important business adviser to George, in addition to being a key manager at times, but he was the business leader. Their marriage enterprise involved them both in the business and the family, and they made a good team.

In other cases, the understanding may not be as clear. Some spouses can confuse their shareholding with management authority in the business and may attempt to make decisions or direct employees. This confusion of management and ownership responsibility or authority can lead to friction within the marriage and the company.

At the Young Business Family stage, the children are typically too young to be involved in ownership in any significant way. The only reasons for the controlling owner to put shares in the name of children would be for symbolic or tax purposes. Minority shares held by the founder's children are not likely to have much effect until late in the Young Business Family stage. But at that point, the passing of even token ownership to the children can signify a coming of age for the younger generation and their parents' conferring of trust. Then, if young adolescent children are made aware of their ownership, it may increase their interest in the company and engender a greater sense of responsibility.

Finally, the impact of nonfamily shareholders in these founder-centered companies varies greatly. In this variation on the classic Controlling Owner stage, there is always the potential for conflict if owners with small or token shareholdings try to exercise too much (in some cases, any) influence on the early development of the company. There are entrepreneurs with a collaborative style, who welcome input and gladly share control, but they are in the minority. Most founders want to see minority shareholders as loyal—and silent—investors. These feel gratitude for the financial support and for the confidence and optimism that it represents, but they expect the investors to step back and let the founder create an enterprise that will benefit them all. When the investors can no longer go along with the founder's clear vision, as in Agricultural Publishers, then it is time to dissolve the arrangement.

Family Issues

Many of the family issues that are most important in Start-Up, Controlling Owner businesses were discussed in chapter 2. The nature of the marriage enterprise, the disengaged or enmeshed style of the family, the distribution of authority between the spouses, and the relationships with the extended families are all variables that shape this type of family business. The place of work in the lives of founders is particularly important. Within the founder's family in general, the owner-manager is very often at this stage an absentee parent. This absentee role can cause the children to feel resentment toward the business, as if it were a powerful sibling competitor. These feelings of rivalry can, in fact, discourage children from having anything to do with the company in the future.

In addition, the tensions of the Start-Up stage can easily affect moods and anxiety level of the parents in the business. If it is the founder's style to bring home the frustrations and problems of the firm, then the children's early impressions of the family business may be negative. If the founder decides not to share anything about work with the family, the children and spouse can feel excluded from the most compelling part of that parent's life. Although this was a very busy and stressful time in George Pilgrim's career, his sons remember their father as upbeat and confident. George and Dorothy were open with their sons about the problems the business was having, but also confident that the problems would be overcome.

On the other hand, some founders experience such a high degree of satisfaction and accomplishment from the role of controlling owner that it invigorates their role in the family. In these cases, the family can be invited in as participants in the drama of the Start-Up business. The pioneering or adventurous aspects of the founder role can lead young children to create a mythical image of the parent that is part cowboy, part pirate, and part king or queen. If children are allowed to come to the workplace and become familiar with it, they sometimes see it as a natural extension of the home. This may lead to a much greater chance that the younger generation will seriously consider careers in the company when the family matures into the next stage, Entering the Business.

George Pilgrim was unusual in his skill at balancing the intense demands of his various entrepreneurial ventures with a high-involvement definition of parenting. During the farm and seed days, he had the benefit of working and living in the same place. Farming is one of the few family enterprises that carries some of the lifestyle of preindustrial families, where the children are observers of all aspects of the parents' work. When George began the publishing business, all that changed abruptly. He was on the road, eventually coast to coast, selling his new product. He states that however much he traveled, he always insisted on being home by Friday night and would not leave again until Monday. David and Jon also remember their father driving all night to make it home for a Little League game or a special event. Even so, the business's demand put some strain on the family system; they were used to having him around all the time.

Business Issues

At this early stage in the business, the owner-manager must work to establish with customers that the company has something valuable to sell. Sometimes this is relatively easy, but rarely do we see a "better mousetrap" phenomenon, where the product is so clearly desirable that the customers beat a path to the start-up's door. As the owner-manager builds capacity to produce or provide service, with little secure revenues, the management of cash flow is critical. As in the WISCO case (chapter 1), even if there is enough investment capital to begin to produce and market the product, business survival is very much in doubt until there is a stable revenue stream that more than covers operating costs. The energy required to pull off this early business development effort is generally astounding. For several years, most of the owner-manager's waking hours are spent managing the business to the point where there is a reliable cash surplus at the end of each pay period.

In the Start-Up stage, the controlling owner as a business leader must work very hard to establish loyalty among customers, employees, and other key stakeholders, such as the family, the bank, and suppliers. A loyal following is typically patched together first by spinning a compelling vision that allows these critical constituencies—especially employees—to believe that the company has a chance to survive and prosper, and therefore that it is worth their efforts. The founder may have to cut special deals with key players in order to secure their commitment. Financial institutions may need extraordinary loan guarantees. Nonfamily candidates for key managerial positions may negotiate special benefits or incentives to leave secure jobs and take a chance with the new venture. Potential major customers may demand price considerations; unethical purchasing agents may ask for kickbacks. Family members and others may be offered influence in return for investment. These deals are most often secret and nonuniform. Although expedient in the short run, they also become part of the founder's legacy that may complicate the introduction of management systems into the business as it progresses to the next stages in business and ownership.

Founder controlling owners in our experience often do not choose an organizational structure that encourages teamwork among the key players in the company, often preferring to foster close relationships with the top managers individually. They feel most comfortable with the business in a hub and spokes organizational structure, in which the owner-manager, at the center of the wheel, is necessary for all key decisions and is an intermediary in all communication. This hub-and-spokes design—with information flowing in and decisions flowing out—can generate a highly innovative, customer-responsive culture. It can be successful as long as the organization does not get too large and the owner-manager remains physically and mentally vital, in touch with the market, and fully competent in the company's technology. If these conditions are not met, the hub-and-spokes design can inhibit company growth and profitability. Because of the fluid and centralized nature of this organization design, all eyes tend to look to the owner-manager for direction. His or her vision drives priorities and activities, and his or her behavior drives company decisions and values.[10]

None of George Pilgrim's businesses except the magazine got very large or had many full-time staff. Still, George definitely involved himself with every aspect of each business, down to the smallest detail. He was the primary salesman, product designer, production manager, marketing expert, and financier. Dorothy handled accounting whenever possible. He always felt that he knew what would work, even if it was a tough sell to others. When printers fought with his idea to put different advertising sections in each of four county editions for each of the 400 credit association districts, George kept shopping until he found shops that would just do what he wanted. "I didn't understand the technology of printing, and I didn't care. I knew what the market needed, and I was right."

In the Controlling Owner–Start-Up business, the two most important requirements for the business's survival are that it flexibly responds to customer needs and remains very cost-efficient. The owner-manager must select adequately skilled employees who can take direction, find financing for investment and operating capital, carefully manage cash flow, and budget for various company projects. In this early period of business life, the business must be able to adjust quickly to growth opportunities and cutbacks. Upturns and downturns can be dramatic and unpredictable for these smaller companies, and they must learn how to meet expanding or declining orders for what they sell.

The personally involved style of most founders can work well in creating an initial customer base. George Pilgrim wanted to know every branch manager in the Production Credit Association, and he worked hard at creating a personal relationship with each of them. He was on the road selling the idea so that he could talk to the association directors face to face. In the car after each meeting, he made notes for a card file, so that when he came back through the same territory six months later, he could ask the right questions and renew the conversation. He knew that his main selling advantage was himself—an experienced, knowledgeable farmer, not an advertising or publishing man from the city. The personal loyalties of customers are often what primes the initial cash pump of the new venture. It is also true that these individual connections to the founder have to be modifiable, and eventually transferable to the company itself, if the business is to make the transition into the next stage of Expansion/Formalization.

Policies and procedures within the Start-Up–Controlling Owner organization are typically not formalized. This lack of routine and controls can work in support of flexibility if employees are of good quality and empowered to act independently within the limitations of overall company goals and values, and if communication is good enough for the company to learn quickly and continually adjust. However, more often the vagueness of authority, policies, and even direction of the company can implicitly make employees even more reliant on the owner-manager, keeping him or her in the center of the company. Lack of operating systems can also indicate weak management skills of this individual. These companies demonstrate limited delegation to others, a poorly skilled group of other managers, and authoritarian decision making by owner-managers.

In summary, the Start-Up stage is a time when the foundation is laid for three core aspects of the family business: company culture, strategy, and asset management values. A company's *culture* (like the culture of any social group) is its strongly held values and assumptions about correct behavior in a number of areas: proper decision-making authority (hierarchical, collateral, or individual), the role of management, ideal leadership style (autocratic, consultative, participatory), norms of openness versus secrecy, people versus task orientation, loyalty to the leader versus loyalty to the organization, respect for management hierarchy and structure, the role of the family in the business, and the time orientation of the company (focused more on the past, the present, or the future). These values and assumptions are identified through visible cultural "artifacts," including myths and stories about the founder, dress codes and physical features of the company, the written philosophy of the organization, and traditions in the company and the family. The founder also symbolizes or directly articulates, through words and behavior, these underlying values and basic beliefs. They become ingrained in the company, because it is part of the founder mythology that the early success of the organization depended on them.[11] Company cultures can endure for a long time without major changes when there are reliable methods for faithfully transmitting their essence. That is certainly the case in family firms; the family is perhaps the most reliable of all social structures for transmitting cultural values and practices across generations.

Dyer observed four kinds of cultures in family companies. The most common form, *paternalistic,* is characterized by hierarchical relationships and centralized authority. The leaders, usually family members, make all significant decisions and closely supervise employees. The second pattern, *laissez-faire,* is similar to the paternalistic culture, but employees are instead seen as trustworthy and are allowed to make some decisions. The family still determines what needs to be done, and the employees decide how to accomplish it. The *participative* culture, a rare form in family companies, is radically different. It is group oriented, structured to involve others, downplays the power of the family, and encourages the growth and development of employees. Dyer labels the final cultural pattern *professional,* a form usually found in firms being run by outside professional managers. It is characterized by individualism, competition, and impersonal employee relations.[12]

The founder also has a strong influence on the enduring *strategy* of the company.[13] There is often in family business a strong and sometimes irrational loyalty to the original business or businesses started by the founder. The founder may convince his family and managers that success depends on being in a certain line of business or running that business in a certain way. When, in later generations, the value of the original business is questioned or there is a drive to sell or diminish the business, some family members may see this as an affront to the original founder and may fight to maintain these original operations. Beliefs about growth, diversification, debt, ownership control, competitive positioning (in terms of quality, price, service, and so on) can all be heavily influenced by the founders' original tenets about smart business practices. The founder may also have strong loyalties to the community in which the business originated and to the original customers or markets served by the company. Finally, the founder generally has a philosophy about the extent to which the company is to serve the needs of the family. All of these original philosophies can have important influences on the current strategy of a family company. These philosophies can be functional or dysfunctional in the current business environment.

Third, founders can affect for generations a family's shareholder *asset management values* and related practices. A family's orientation toward preservation versus consumption of business capital and family wealth is generally initiated by the founder in the first generation of the business. Shareholder loyalty to established businesses, interest in entrepreneurship and new ventures, the commitment of ownership to family and nonfamily management, the separation of shareholder and management roles, the responsibility of the business to shareholder needs, and the management of information to and involvement of shareholders are all initiated by the actions and attitudes of the founder. All of these practices in turn greatly influence how shareholders are treated, how they treat the business and its capital, and the ultimate harmony of the family in the company.

NOTES

1. Some of the best recent work in the extensive literature on entrepreneurship include Brockhaus and Horwitz (1986), Bird (1989), Timmons (1989, 1994) and Birley and MacMillan (1995). Our family business and developmental approaches to entrepreneurship are particularly influenced by Dyer (1992), Kets de Vries (1985), and Stevenson (Stevenson and Sahlman 1987; Stevenson, Roberts, and Grousbeck 1994). In addition, the special issues of women and ethnic minority entrepreneurs are reflected in a growing literature (see Shapero and Sokol 1982; Bowen and Hisrich 1986; L. Stevenson 1986; Aldrich and Waldinger 1990; Brodsky 1993; Loscocco and Leicht 1993).

2. Many environmental factors have also been identified as influencing and encouraging the founding of a company. Macroeconomic factors, such as levels of consumer spending and disposable income, and rates of inflation and unemployment, can create either opportunities or limitations for the founding of a business. Broad availability of employment in established companies and industries depresses entrepreneurial activity. Certain industries present better opportunities for small companies, often in niches that are relatively protected from the larger players (Covin and Slevin 1990). The economic infrastructure of a country also influences the ease with which new companies can be created and function. The availability of venture capital, a technically skilled labor force, accessibility of suppliers and customers, favorable government policies, availability of land or facilities, access to transportation, and availability of support services all encourage the founding of companies (Bruno and Tyebjee 1982). These factors apply equally to all types of businesses, family or not.

3. Reich 1987; Cramton 1993; Copland 1995.

4. The life and career stages of individuals also influence the founding of a business. Many founders do not create companies until they are in their mid- to late thirties, when they have established a sense of their interests, style, and competence. Not coincidentally, this is also the time of life when individuals become less comfortable taking direction from others and are highly motivated to "become their own man (or woman)" (Levinson 1978; 1996).

5. Dyer's work suggests five factors motivating an entrepreneurial career: early childhood experiences, need for control, frustration with traditional careers, desire for challenge and excitement, and role models. According to Dyer, entrepreneurial behavior can be recognized very early in a person's life. In his research, many entrepreneurs reported creating business ventures when they were young. Perhaps successful experi-

ences at a young age encourage more substantial entrepreneurial ventures in adult life (1992).

6. Dyer 1992.

7. Mangelsdorf 1994. See also Harvey and Evans 1995.

8. Timmons 1994.

9. The culture may include a norm of family mistrust of outsiders, which influences the founder to prefer dealing with relatives in commercial matters. Sometimes the family or society confers upon the founder special social status for owning and managing an enterprise. The culture can also include norms about ownership rights in families who pool their resources and hold assets in common, including family companies. The typical progression in the United States is for individuals to start owner-managed businesses that are later owned more broadly by the founder's family. In other parts of the world, such as Asia, there is a greater tendency to involve siblings at the start of one's business and to share ownership and control with them. This leads to more Start-Up Sibling Partnerships and even some Start-Up Cousin Consortium companies. Some excellent recent explorations of Asian family companies include Panglaykim and Palmer 1970; Wong 1985; Cushman 1986, 1991; and Chau 1991.

10. Zaleznik and Kets de Vries (1975) have explored motives for the creation of a business from a psychoanalytic perspective. They conclude that entrepreneurs have a desire to re-create a father or nurturing image, and to reconnect with a more idealized version of their family of origin. In this reconstructed family, founders can be in the center of the social system and receive the nurturance and adoration they strongly desire. By encouraging others to depend on and be loyal to them, they achieve substantial control over their most cherished social structures. Obviously, if this unconscious wish to be both nurturant and controlling is too strong, the development of the business will be constrained.

11. Schein 1983.

12. Dyer 1986.

13. Ward and Aronoff 1994.

5

The Growing and Evolving
Family Business

I N T H I S C H A P T E R , we take a closer look at the challenges and opportunities facing family-owned companies that have moved beyond the entrepreneurial enterprise profiled in chapter 4. In other words, the business has moved from Start-Up into the Expansion/Formalization stage, ownership has passed from a Controlling Owner to a Sibling Partnership form, and the family is at the Entering the Business stage, where the children are roughly fifteen to twenty-five years old and the parents are at or just past midlife. The businesses and families that have reached this stage, different as they may be, share a number of common challenges: finishing the consolidation of ownership control in the sibling generation, developing an entry process for the next generation, and restructuring the business and its systems to initiate and sustain growth.

The largest number of closely held companies in the United States are of the type described in chapter 4: first-generation owner-managers running small, sometimes struggling business ventures. As we have learned, many of these companies never make the transition to the second generation for many reasons. Some were never intended by their founders to be passed on as family businesses. Even when the owners would like the firm to continue, most Start-Up companies fail for business reasons long before succession becomes an issue. Some others cannot find a way to complete the ownership transition within the family and sell the company instead.

Therefore, the type of family business profiled in this chapter—a second- or later-generation Sibling Partnership in the Expansion/Formalization stage, with the third generation ready for Entering the Business—is not statistically the "typical" family business. However, this *is* a critical stage among those family companies that survive and thrive. Within the family, the increase in scale of the business probably means that more family members are connected to the company, either as shareholders or employees. The business is becoming a central component of the family identity.

These companies face important organizational, strategic, and psychological challenges. It may be that these are the most vulnerable family firms, as they try to make the difficult transition from a company controlled by one person to a more complicated organization managed by many. The theme for this stage of business development is collaboration. A company that could be a one-person show at an earlier and less complex stage, now *must* be a partnership, in the psychological as well as the literal sense. Sibling owner-managers must find ways to run the business together and to develop constructive working relationships with their young adult children. Family members of both generations must form cooperative and trusting relationships with key nonfamily employees. Now, more than in earlier stages, the family business is a team effort. Solo performers may succeed in the short run, but they will usually hit difficulties as the next generation begins to enter the business.

This psychological transition—from the individualistic quest of the sole owner to the team effort of the sibling partnership—is a theme that echoes through all three dimensions of the family business. Coordination, communication, and planning are crucial skills for managers and family members at this stage. The increased complexity of the company sometimes requires the formalization of many guidelines and policies that could remain informal before; the same kind of changes may be useful in the family, to achieve the experience of fair treatment for all, to manage inevitable conflicts, and to clarify expectations about third-generation involvement in the company.

Novelty Imports illustrates well the challenges and dynamics of this stage. It is a company run by a Sibling Partnership but depended on by three generations. It is a particularly good illustration of how dynamics from all three dimensions—ownership, family, and business—interact to create challenges.

Novelty Imports, Inc.

Novelty Imports, Inc., is run by Bernie and Mitch Kopek, who have recently been given fifty-fifty ownership of the company by their mother, Miriam. At age seventy-five and widowed, Miriam is still active in the business and has no plans to retire. Bernie (age fifty) and Mitch (age forty-seven) have had a contentious work relationship for twenty-five years. Bernie handles the finances and office administration; Mitch handles operations, buying, and sales, traveling more each year as his mother decreases her own buying and account management activities. Bernie is divorced and lives alone. He has one son, Benjy (age seventeen), a high school student whom Bernie sees on weekends. The oldest of the third generation is Mitch's son, Mark, who is twenty-five. He studied business as an undergraduate and has just finished law school. He has a younger sister, Abby (age twenty), who is in college. Mitch's wife, Betty, works as an operator supervisor for the local telephone company.

Novelty has done well over its forty-year lifespan. Miriam started the company out of her home when her husband was incapacitated with a chronic illness. In the beginning she sold holiday ornaments that her cousin found in Poland. After her husband died, she traveled to eastern Europe to find more suppliers of a broader range of products, which she successfully sold to several large department store accounts in the United States. By the late 1960s, when Mitch and then Bernie joined the business, Novelty had plateaued at a comfortable $15 million in sales. During the 1980s, however, largely due to Mitch's aggressive sales efforts and his mother's extensive contacts in the retail industry, the company landed two major department store accounts. Sales doubled in two years, causing the three principals to scramble to find suppliers. In the late 1980s, the eastern European supplier market opened up, and once again sales jumped. In 1994 sales reached $45 million, and the company employed sixty people, fifteen in the controller's and administrative offices under Bernie and forty-five in the sales, distribution, and buying functions under Mitch and his mother.

Ownership Issues

Ownership structures at this stage of family and business development may be simple or extremely complex. In chapter 1, we identified the defining characteristic of the Sibling Partnership stage: two or more primary owners from the same generation of the family. The issues facing a particular family business at this stage will be influenced by which specific variety of Sibling Partnership has emerged. How many people hold ownership rights? What is the mix of voting and nonvoting shares? What is the norm concerning dividend distributions? How much autonomy does each sibling have to make decisions about how to handle his or her ownership share?

The ownership issues most common in this plane fall loosely under two themes. The first comes from the interaction of the business development stage—Expansion/Formalization—with the ownership stage—Sibling Partnership. It has to do with how well ownership interests and company needs are being integrated to make growth possible and to encourage professionalization of the management system. The second theme comes from the interaction of the Sibling Partnership with the family development stage: Entering the Business. This theme is related to planning for ownership distribution among the younger generation, who are now making career decisions. How are the current and future needs of the family weighed against the needs of the company? What ownership structure do the principals want to see, and how will they accomplish this objective?

Sibling Partnership Issues in the Expansion/Formalization Business

It is easy to see that a growing company needs cash. Reinvestment of profits seems like an automatic decision from the business perspective. However, as we have mentioned earlier, families at this stage face an extremely difficult squeeze, as the family also has pressing current and future needs for capital. Consider the various legitimate competing demands for cash that these families face in the short term:

1. Reinvestment in the company.

2. Launching the children (education, help buying a home).

3. Other lifestyle expenses (mortgages, health needs, travel).

In addition, there is the issue of asset diversification. Families at this stage must consider the wisdom of having all their assets tied up in one investment, the business.

The financial requirements of the Expansion/Formalization stage will almost certainly require a combination of reinvestment and new sources of capital. One advantage of the Sibling Partnership stage is that, if the company has managed its transition from the Controlling Owner stage well, there should be solid professional relationships with lending institutions that can be used to generate appropriate debt. With the institutional lenders looking over the family's shoulders, the pressure is increased in the Expansion/Formalization stage to put profits back into the company, for the expansion of capacity, acquisitions, new product lines, or marketing. Owners in management often find themselves trying to "sell" conservative dividend policies and reinvestment within the ownership group.

Two of the primary competing uses for earnings in the Entering the Business stage are the expenses that the parental generation incur helping their children get established and supporting an increasingly luxurious lifestyle. If the business is successful, there is the natural inclination for its owners to want to experience some of the benefits of that success. That often emerges as a desire to give the younger generation a boost. The family dynamics may work in favor of cash as a reward to those offspring who decide to enter the business, in the form of educational support, help with a home, underwriting of recreation and travel, and many others. On the other hand, the parents may feel inclined to compensate those offspring who choose not to work in the firm (or, even more so, those who are not invited to join). This may take the form of other kinds of educational support, the bankrolling of some other business or professional venture, or a lump-sum compensatory gift.

At the same time, the parental generation may feel that it is foolish to wait any longer to upgrade their own lifestyle in keeping with their seniority in the business. This may be the time they want to move to a more luxurious home or an upscale neighborhood, travel, or take a more visible philanthropic role in the community. Now that the children are gone, a spouse not in the business may want to invest in education or a new entrepreneurial venture of her or his own. All of these investments and expenditures require cash. Each owner will be in a different situation depending on the spouse's desires, the number and ages of children both inside and outside the business, and his or her values about lifestyle. The debates in the ownership group about dividend policy and public image may become very heated at this stage, even if there has been consensus and harmony in the past.

In many firms, one of the consequences of the transition into the Expansion/Formalization stage of business development is that unspecified "partnerships" are replaced by more formal hierarchies or divisions. This often means that the distribution of power, authority, and autonomy in the management structure is different from the distribution of ownership shares in the Sibling Partnership. This can be a major source of strain and a real test of the family firm's ability to assess the needs of each of the three dimensions separately. In sibling groups with equal divisions of shares, for example, it is obviously in the company's best interests to assign management roles according to ability, instead of mirroring the ownership distribution by maintaining equity in management seniority and the size of the division managed by each sibling partner. In those Sibling Partnerships where one or two siblings hold larger blocks of shares, it is also in the company's interests for minority sibling managers to be allowed to grow and rise in the hierarchy according to their performance, not their shareholdings. Unfortunately, many Sibling Partnerships at the Expansion/Formalization stage cannot manage this tension, and some siblings feel undervalued and overrestricted. If enough of them feel unfairly treated, they may seek to leave the company or redeem their shares, sometimes forcing a sale. If the business survives the loss of capital, it may revert to the Controlling Owner stage of ownership development.

Finally, an additional stress on capital reserves may come from the retirement needs of the generation that preceded the Sibling Partnership. In the Kopek family, Bernie and Mitch are aware that the company will pay generously to support Miriam for as long as she lives. This is money that will not be available for reinvestment in the company to support growth. Asset diversification may not seem like a real option to the founding generation, but it is a clear option for sibling partners. Careful planning is needed to minimize the impact on operations when cash is diverted to fund current and anticipated retirements.

The needs of nonemployed children must also be considered in investment and estate planning. Parents have several options: to split the ownership of their share between their children or to accumulate other assets, which would go to the noninvolved child. In the Kopeks' case, to split Mitch's stock between Mark and Abby would leave Mark without voting control and could disadvantage Mitch's branch (assuming that Benjy got all of Bernie's 50 percent). In addition, Mark would have to deal with an uninvolved family member as a significant coowner.

In a second option, Mark would get the company and Abby would get perhaps a small share of the company but also something else. The "something else" is elusive, however. Mitch and Betty both have small IRA accounts, and they own a heavily mortgaged house in need of repairs. All of their discretionary income has gone to pay college bills. In addition, they are in their late forties, and there is not much time left to build a nest egg for Abby, while they are funding their own retirement.

Sibling Partnership Issues in the Entering the Business Family

The second ownership challenge that arises at this stage is planning for the future ownership structure in light of the younger generation's transition into adulthood. Will ownership become more or less concentrated? How and when will stock be transferred to the new owners? Generally, despite the warnings of some family business consultants, stock ownership tends to become more dispersed at each generational transfer. This happens partly because families often translate treating children "fairly" into treating children "identically." This is obviously how Miriam viewed the situation. Miriam could have acknowledged Mitch's greater leadership responsibility and commitment to the business, but her parental value of not differentiating between her sons held her back. As a result, she left neither of her feuding sons in control. Now the second-generation sibling partners must make their own decisions regarding ownership, and the decision is complicated. Coordination between sibling partners is usually challenged by a number of new factors when the family moves into the Entering the Business stage.

First, most sibling partners are eager to see their branch retain at least as much control of the company in the future as it had in their sibling generation. They are unlikely to disadvantage their own children, even if all partners agree that consolidation of the stock would be desirable. For example, even if Mitch had the capital to buy Bernie out (he does not), he knows that Bernie will never sell. Despite his own unhappiness, Bernie wants his son to have every possible advantage in the business. Without explicit rules about entry and career criteria—and even when those rules exist, without confidence that they will be fairly enforced—hanging onto all your shares is the best protection of your offspring's interests.

Second, sibling partners often have different financial planning needs, which affect how they want to treat their ownership interests. In this case, Mitch must think about Betty's and Abby's future needs; the stock has to be considered as an asset for their future support. Bernie, however, with fewer family obligations, is not thinking about his stock in the same way.

Third, siblings frequently approach estate planning differently. They may have different values, for example, which could influence their views about gifting their stock versus having the next generation buy them out. Also, as in the Kopeks' case, the financial status of each sibling may be quite different and thus require different estate planning strategies.

Finally, many sibling partners, even those who get along better than Mitch and Bernie, do not think to discuss their estate plans with their siblings. Their stock, after all, is theirs. It takes a broad perspective on ownership and a cooperative relationship between siblings to develop a shared vision about future company ownership structures.

Family Issues

The family developmental challenges in the Entering the Business stage spring from the varying degrees of emotional, financial, and professional interdependence among all three generations. The challenges facing the individuals in the entering (younger), midlife (middle), and retirement (older) generations influence how they respond individually and collectively to decisions about how the younger generation will join the company. The needs of the three generations can be at odds, and family relationships can suffer under the strain.

Individual Life Cycle Transitions

The Entering the Business stage catches all three generations of family members at major transition points. Mitch, Betty, and Bernie have recently been through midlife—the years between thirty-eight and forty-five. As discussed in chapter 2, the individual development task at this age is a reevaluation of life arrangements and structures, to prepare for the journey into middle age and beyond. The strain on the family business system can be significant, as leaders of the business whose children are considering joining the company question their most fundamental life structures. Some divorce, splitting the family unit in which their children have grown up. Some leave jobs; others go to work for the first time. They sense that time is limited to accomplish their dreams, and they feel a sense of urgency.

Mitch's marriage survived the midlife transition, but Bernie's did not. His wife left him in a contentious divorce after he began an affair with a younger neighbor. Bernie is still recovering from the divorce and the loss of his son. Thus he has a strong interest in cultivating Benjy's interest in the company. Bernie is clear about his agenda: to get his son back, through the business. Mitch understands this, having watched the turmoil around him.

Betty has also been through some changes. After the initial shock of seeing her daughter, Abby, go off to college, she was surprised at how happy she felt with her newfound independence. She knows that Mitch is counting on Mark's return after law school, so she feels uncomfortable telling Mitch that she really does not want Mark living in their house.

Mark, his sister, and their cousin are just passing out of the adolescent stage and into early adulthood. The task in the early twenties is separating from the parents' family and establishing an individual identity in both personal and professional arenas. To test this emerging sense of individuality, young adults typically make temporary commitments in their twenties. They sometimes try different jobs or move to new geographic locations. They fall in love and try a serious romantic relationship. Young adults also articulate a preliminary vision for their lives in the future, which encompasses work and family dimensions. This dream (using Levinson's term) becomes the benchmark for their later assessment (and reassessment) of their own success and the impetus for growth and change.[1]

Mark's own feelings of ambivalence are almost overwhelming. His father, while sounding a constant theme of how overworked he is and how much help he needs, complains endlessly about his older brother, Bernie. Mitch frequently tells Mark, "You'd be crazy to come into this company," but Mark knows that he doesn't mean it. Nevertheless, on some days, Mark feels that he *would* be crazy to do so. The practice of law would give him the secure income and professional identity that he wants. On other days, Mark has ideas that he knows would improve the company. He feels that it would be shortsighted to walk away from the opportunities the business offers him.

Adolescence was a rebellious time for him. He fought with his father all the time. This makes him wonder whether they really could work together. Their relationship seemed to improve dramatically during the year he took off from college to work in Canada. As close as Mark is to his family, he also feels that his college and graduate school offered interesting new perspectives on who he is and what he might do in his life. He feels a strong need to shape his own sense of himself. Could he do that if he came home to the business? Is his current relationship with his father and the other family members the way it would be forever?

Davis's pioneering work in this area is the best possible example of the application of adult development concepts to work relationships in the family business. He has used Levinson's life stages to predict periods in the lives of fathers and sons when they are likely to develop good collaborative work relationships, and periods when their relationships are likely to be full of conflict and incompatible agendas. His predictions based on adult development stages are highly correlated with individuals' self-reports of smooth and rocky periods.[2] Family members in the Entering the Business and Working Together stages are often relieved to learn that research suggests some of the conflict they are experiencing is neither chronic nor due to irreconcilable personality differences, but rather is due to the stage of development through which one or both of them are passing—and as a result, it may ameliorate with time.[3]

Miriam, the sole living member of the founding generation, faces her own issues of retirement: a decline in health and vitality, an uncertain future, the need to find some activity that can capture her imagination and commitment as the business did, and the challenge of potentially facing financial and emotional dependence on children and grandchildren. She knew that her sons were too old for her to hold onto the ownership indefinitely, so she made arrangements for her financial welfare and passed the shares on to them. Now she is struggling with forming a new role. She fears that, like King Lear, without the power of control she will have no influence at all or, worse, become invisible. Like others of her age, she has the challenge of finding both purpose and stature in the family circle, without the foundation of authority in the business and ownership circles that used to be the core of her identity.

As individuals, then, the Kopeks are experiencing a complex array of emotional pushes and pulls. The business can become the means of moving family members to the next developmental stage, when parents support their children in establishing their independence and competence through their work in the company. However, the business can also be the way a family gets stuck, as Mitch and Bernie might characterize their own experience. They never left home, remaining under their mother's strong control for most of their adult years. Although they developed clearly differentiated areas of responsibility, they are still locked in an undifferentiated fifty-fifty ownership arrangement that neither of them wants. Neither would say that Novelty Imports represents their dream.

This family is close and comes from an eastern European tradition of family cohesiveness that leans toward enmeshment. Other families from different cultural backgrounds would make different decisions on how to handle the complex forces of this stage. Some parents actually drive their children away, out of fear of too much involvement. Another factor complicating the situation is generational differences in values. Family norms, strong as they may be, can change when children are exposed to a variety of social classes and ethnicities, at college, work, or other social settings.

Occupational Choice in the Family Business

How does the typical family business heir make the decision to enter the family business? The contemporary view of careers portrays occupational choice as a search for the best fit between an individual's personality and the job.[4] Some believe that certain personality types are most happy in particular occupations (artistic types in advertising, for example, or enterprising types in business). This explanation assumes, however, that young adults from business families have an accurate understanding of who they are and what they want. One of the challenges of the Entering the Business stage, for parents and for children, is to clarify whether the business is really what the younger generation wants.

Gender, social class, and family background exert a strong influence on people's beliefs about who they are and therefore who they can become. Mark, for example, may set off down the path of enterprise because he has learned to see himself as a part of the business, not because it fits his realistic and analytic personality. Unfortunately, many young adults do not truly choose the business; instead, they feel as if they have no choice but to join. The absence of choice at the Entering the Business stage is what can cause disappointment and a sense of resignation, rather than fulfillment, later in life.

Mark's situation illustrates well the forces that threaten to rob young adults in a family business of their choice. First, family roles and expectations are a crucial influence on a young adult's self-concept. Mark is the oldest of his generation and thus is perceived as the leader of that group. Second, Mark is male. Even though Mark's grandmother started the business and is still active in management, their family assumes that only males will be interested in business. Thus Mark's younger sister, Abby, has experienced no pressure to join the company; in fact, she feels left out because no one seems to care whether she works for the company or not. Third, Mark's branch of the family, through his father, is perceived as the "competent" branch. Mitch was the workhorse of the company and his mother's right-hand man. Thus Mark is automatically assumed to be more capable than his cousin. Finally, as the firstborn grandchild, Mark is Miriam's favorite. Since he was a child, she has been enthusiastic for Mark to come into the company. These characteristics of the family structure (birth order) and dynamics (affiliations and roles) create powerful forces that pull Mark almost unthinkingly into the business. None of these forces has to do with a fit between the skills required to run the business and Mark's personality and talents.

Business families in the Entering the Business stage also carry strong assumptions about the relationship between the business and the family—assumptions that sometimes propel young adults to join, despite the absence of a real fit between the individual and the situation. One assumption is that to be a *real* family member, one must also be a member of the business. There is a concern that those who stay outside the firm will get less attention, status, and family identity than those who are employed. A second assumption is that joining the family company is an obligation. Many young adults feel an unspoken message that they "owe" their parents. It feels disloyal to walk away from this family responsibility.

In some cases, there is also a third assumption: if the younger generation does not enter, the business will fail. This guilt-inducing assumption is based, paradoxically, on the family's perception, sometimes unrealistically fantasized, of a child's competence. Especially in enmeshed families, where the boundary between family members and all others is very sharply drawn, there can be the principle that "no one else can possibly do it as well." Therefore an offspring's decision to do something else is seen as a decision to let the business die. This pressure is intensified by the company's needs in the growth phase, as the sibling partners may turn to their own, unprepared children as an alternative to hiring outside professionals.

Sibling Relationships

At the Entering the Business stage, the sibling partners need a relationship that can withstand stress, which usually means a relationship in which the partners can communicate openly, resolve conflicts, and support each other's decisions. For example, sibling partners in this stage almost always have to deal in a new way with fairness. When a controlling owner and his or her spouse strive to create fair conditions for all of their children, they presumably have control over their assets and can make decisions that take the interests of the whole nuclear family into account. When the business is a sibling partnership, achieving fairness is more complicated.

Inevitable competition arises between siblings regarding the opportunities available for their own children. Perceived differences in lifestyle among the nuclear families fuels concern that one's own branch of the founding family will suffer. This concern, if well managed, can motivate families to create explicit policies and guidelines for the conditions under which the third generation will join the business. If unmanaged, it can lead to endless comparisons and bickering.

Bernie and Mitch are a long way from being able to manage their own conflict and create policies to assure fair treatment. The structure and dynamics of their own nuclear family have predetermined, to a large extent, their inability to create a constructive working relationship. For one thing, their hierarchical relationship is complex. Bernie, as the oldest, was close to his father Jacob and assumed the responsibilities of the firstborn. Mitch, Miriam's favorite, was always dynamic and outgoing. As their father's illness became apparent and Miriam took charge of the family, Mitch became the unspoken leader of the two brothers. After Jacob's death, Miriam was stuck: she could not unseat Bernie, her husband's choice, but she could not forsake Mitch either. Thus the brothers inherited a conflictual relationship.

The other key sibling relationship in families at this stage is between siblings involved in the business and those who are not involved. In the Kopek family, given that Bernie and Mitch have no other siblings, this dilemma has become located in the third generation, between Mark and Abby. Parents whose children are at the Entering the Business stage need to attend to how siblings who are not interested in the business, or who have not been invited to join, may feel about their siblings' involvement. These feelings can have major impacts on the family business for years into the future. If Abby feels she has been treated unfairly, for example—if she is not encouraged by her father and uncle to join the business—will she express this resentment toward Mark? If she inherits stock, will she support Mark's decisions? Will she pressure him to pay higher dividends? And, later, will she want her children to have the opportunity to join the business? Even if Abby stays out of the business, her relationship with Mark will have an impact on the company.

Other Family Relationships

All of the extended family relationships we discussed in chapter 2 are in evidence in the Kopek case. First, grandparent-grandchild relations can shape the family's expectations about which members of the third generation should join the company. Miriam had always assumed that Mark would want to run her company. His fear of disappointing her contributed significantly to his ambivalence. Second, the next-generation cousins, who grew up at a greater psychological distance from each other than Mitch and Bernie did, are already having an impact on their parents. How well do Mark and Benjy know each other? Could they trust and respect each other if they were partners someday? Sometimes these relationships are easier than sibling relationships, because they are less intense. However, Mark and Benjy have listened all their lives to their fathers' complaining about their uncles; they might carry this conflict into their own relationship. This is especially likely to happen if Mitch and Bernie "appoint" them to fill their roles, rather than if both partners welcome and support both cousins.

The relations between in-laws and family members also present challenges for families at this stage. As we discussed in chapter 2, spouses of sibling partners often become the loudest voice of the conflict between the siblings. Also, they may resent each other because of fears that their children may be disadvantaged professionally or financially in comparison to their cousins, as the next generation enters. In-laws may also carry conflict between the sibling partners and their retired parents over financial and other matters.

Because of the emotional complexity of family relationships at this stage of family development, and because of the critical nature of the decisions that must be made, Entering the Business families sometimes seek help. Consultants often recommend the creation of a family council, a representative group of family members who meet regularly to discuss concerns created by the family's involvement in the business and to develop guidelines for family decision making. This structure (which is discussed in more detail in chapter 8) helps keep family conflict from spilling over into the business by providing a forum for family members to express their views and work out policies that they consider fair.

The Kopeks probably could not start a family council without the assistance of a facilitator, who would identify key areas of conflict in the family and set the ground rules for how this conflict could be addressed. This family's entrenched dynamic of avoidance between Bernie and Mitch and the polarization of the family branches would make such an effort difficult. However, their collective unhappiness with the current situation, their sense of urgency about growth, and their desire for the children's fair treatment might motivate them to make a family council work.

Business Issues

The timing of the transition from the Start-Up to the Expansion/Formalization stage on the business development dimension varies. Some companies achieve the second stage within several years of their start-up. This requires the owner-manager to move quickly to resolve the organizational and strategic challenges presented by growth and complexity. Other companies, like Novelty, hit a growing streak later in life, when a combination of internal and external conditions alters their market, their product, or their costs. In those cases, expansion and restructuring may coincide with the entry of the second generation.

Whenever the company hits its growth phase, family owner-managers will face the same general challenges. On the organizational side, professionalization is the watchword. Managers usually need professional knowledge and skills; organizational structures and processes must align more closely with industry norms; and systems, particularly information systems, become important to improve coordination. Strategically, growing companies can face difficult long- and short-term problems: capitalization, cash management, new product development, competition, and diversification. As we saw in chapter 3, this may be the first time in their life cycle that they have had to attend seriously to strategic planning.

Formalization in the Sibling Partnership business typically means that management must undergo significant change. Owner-managers were accustomed to a hands-on style of management in the Start-Up stage; now they feel more pressure to delegate. They simply cannot manage all the pieces of the organization themselves any longer. Organizational structures evolve as well, creating more formal hierarchical and functional differentiation. Finally, the organization discovers the need for new formal systems of all types, particularly to manage information and human resources, and to allow managers to analyze business performance and coordinate work in different functions.

Management Changes in the Sibling Partnership
Expansion/Formalization Business

Novelty is only beginning the shift to professional management that is required for companies to grow successfully. Bernie and Mitch are not delegators; they prefer to manage every detail of the business themselves. Bernie, whose work style is more relaxed than Mitch's, has begun to rely on his two key subordinates, the company controller and the office manager. Mitch, the more intense of the two, is overworked. He has complied with his mother's belief that a family member must do the buying but, as their suppliers and product lines have grown, Mitch's travel schedule has become impossible. He was hoping that Mark, his son, would join the business and relieve some of his burden. Mark, who is not ready to make a commitment to the business, believes they should hire a professional buyer for the transition period during which he would need to learn the buying trade. However, his father and uncle are skeptical about turning such a crucial function over to an outsider.

Observers would say that the Kopeks need to go quickly down the professionalization path on which they have haltingly embarked. The demands of the Expansion/Formalization stage are putting pressure on the traditions of their Sibling Partnership. The brothers do not have the resources to run the business by themselves; they need a team. However, like many other Sibling Partnerships, there is some ambiguity about how much true interdependence and collaboration is involved in this operationalization of the word *partnership*. Essentially, they have divided between them the tasks that their mother used to do. As the company has grown, Mitch's half has grown faster than Bernie's. Thus Mitch has become the leader of the company, but neither Miriam nor the brothers themselves can acknowledge this reality, nor its far-reaching consequences for the nature of the partnership.

One obstacle to creating a management team, then, is that families may be reluctant to allow the entry of nonfamily professionals, sometimes to avoid having their contentious family relationships or their management skills scrutinized by an outsider. The strongest support for bringing in outside professionals may come from the entering generation. They may have learned the value of professionalization in college or business school; they are less defensive about family dynamics because they see the problems as existing largely in the senior generation; and the buffer of nonfamily managers would give them some protection from the expectations of the senior generation, as well as needed time to learn the company.

The key problem facing management, then, is building the mix of skills needed for leadership continuity. In some Sibling Partnerships, either sibling could run the company alone if the other were incapacitated. In the Kopeks' case, neither has voting control. And, although Mitch could run the company, Bernie could not and Mark is too young. Thus, without outside professionals in key roles, the business is vulnerable.

Structural and System Changes

Novelty's structure badly needs an overhaul as well. Along with professional management comes differentiated roles, and the company's formal structure should reinforce those roles. Before the growth spurt of the late 1980s, Mitch's and Bernie's areas of responsibility were better balanced. However, with the opening of a small European office and warehouse operation and the increase in U.S.-based account representatives, the operations staff has increased significantly. Miriam's decreased involvement has also left Mitch with more to cover. Whereas Miriam used to watch all the account reps and buying staff closely, Mitch doesn't even know the names of all the warehouse workers.

Companies at this stage often begin the formalization process by adding to middle management; for example, a head of distribution and a supervisor of the account reps. At some point, the old organization chart absorbs as much growth and as many new positions as it can. This can trigger a more comprehensive reorganization, by business unit, product type, or geography, for example. This is one point in the development of the business when an outside consultant can be very effective, helping define formal job descriptions, firm up an organization chart (or, in some cases, create one for the first time), and add formal cross-functional lines of communication and accountability.

Like other companies at this stage, Novelty also needs a variety of new management systems: a larger and faster information system with the ability to track products more accurately; a more sophisticated cost accounting system (to assess the profitability of each product); and, most important, the capability of connecting its financial system to its operations system. Mark argued these changes, but his father and uncle did not see the benefits of such a "fancy" system and responded that it would be much too expensive. Mark feels they do not take his education seriously and is frustrated that they don't understand how much a good information system would improve customer satisfaction. He suspects that, although money and skepticism were part of the story, they actually opposed the system because they *didn't want* to coordinate their two areas too closely.

Aside from information systems, companies at this stage also need professional human resource policies. Like many other entrepreneurs, Miriam had been reluctant to pay the salaries that well-qualified workers expected. At Novelty, as in other companies moving out of the Start-Up phase, employee salaries were determined as much by history and carelessness as by merit. Another important task of the Expansion/Formalization stage for companies of Novelty's size is the creation of formal compensation, promotion, and hiring policies, as well as a formal evaluation process. These policies are crucial to recruiting and retaining talented outside managers. Besides their actual human resource value, they signal a commitment on the family's part to run the business professionally and to create fair career opportunities for nonfamily talent.

Mitch and Bernie are also facing the crucial human resource issue of whether and how their own children will join the family company. Most families begin to discuss options on a case-by-case basis as their children reach college age. However, what is needed is agreement on a range of questions, including qualifications, compensation, evaluation, and training. For example, will children have to demonstrate that they are qualified in order to join? What does "qualified" mean? How much school and how much work experience are required? Should they work outside the company before returning to the company? Most observers agree that outside experience benefits the business and also gives the younger generation a sense that they have options outside the family company. Will all children have an equal opportunity to run the company?

Once the younger generation does join, how will they find a role in the company that meets their skills? How will their performance be evaluated? Companies like Novelty often declare that they support open and fair treatment for all members of the next generation, but family politics may undermine the creation of the necessary formal human resource procedures. The younger generation will watch carefully to see if the power relationships in the senior generation will determine opportunity, or if children from all sibling branches are given equal opportunity to prove themselves. In the Kopeks' case, the fact that Mark is Mitch's son and the oldest cousin might effectively close the door for Abby and Benjy if policies are not in place to allow all the cousins a chance to show their talents and interests in the business. In chapter 8, we present some of the techniques family businesses can use to oversee the career development of both younger-generation family members and nonfamily managers.

Strategic Challenges

Most business owners look forward to the time when their company's growth takes off, seeing it as a time when doing business itself will no longer be a problem. However, ironically, business conditions can be extremely tough for the Sibling Partnership in this phase. These Expansion/Formalization companies face serious new challenges because their success and growth have put them up against different, usually stronger, competitors. The best-established of these competitors will have been riding the growth curve for some time already. They usually have cash to reinvest, have secured market share, have developed a strategic focus, and if they are well managed, are actively involved in developing new products to balance their mature ones. Companies like Novelty must learn to play with the "big kids" fast, and they must have a clear understanding of how they can compete against this new and stronger opposition.

The strategic challenges of family businesses in this situation can be broken into three main areas: capital/financing choices; market and product issues; and planning, particularly strategic planning. In Sibling Partnerships at this stage, decision making is a critical capacity. Effective sibling teams usually follow one of three models. The siblings may make all major business decisions jointly; they may divide the company into clearly demarcated areas of responsibility and each cover his or her own area; or they may set up a top management group to decide with them on major issues. Whatever process is followed, coordination is crucial.

Coordination with younger-generation members who are thinking of entering the business is also important. Sibling partners who function well together, especially in the second or third style described above, often discuss with their children major strategic decisions that will shape the future of the company. This gesture indicates an understanding that the business will be, in the future, a collaborative effort and that the older generation respects the younger's opinions. However, parents at this stage can also make the mistake of pressuring their children into joining the business immediately, because they are anxious about the strategic decisions that they face.

One issue where business development and ownership development interact at this stage concerns financing. Like many entrepreneurs, Miriam hated debt. However, most Sibling Partnerships in the growth stage badly need capital to finance growth. When Miriam ran Novelty, she refused to deal with banks. Bernie had to twist her arm to set up a line of credit during their first growth spurt in the 1980s. At several points during that time, when they ran short of cash, she stretched payments to suppliers and postponed paying family salaries to meet payroll. Bernie gradually stabilized the cash flow, but their seasonal business pushed his talents. Faced with more growth, he worries that they will lose control again.

In addition, Mitch has been pushing Bernie on the need to expand their European operation. He wants to buy a warehouse and a small fleet of trucks, to protect them against the vagaries of the eastern European delivery companies they have been using. Bernie argues that the idea would cost millions, which they don't have, and require them to go to the bank for a *real* loan. Bernie knows that the company could afford the extra debt load, but he worries about the impact of their cash flow instability on their credit.

The Kopeks face the challenge of matching the selected strategy to the family's ability to generate capital, either by minimizing withdrawal of retained earnings or by accepting an increased level of debt. Unless the business has a dominant position in a very well protected niche, the Expansion/Formalization stage and the demands of competition almost always require a more aggressive approach to investment. However, this is a time when cash needs in the family are high: children are in college, and retired parents like Miriam may still receive dividends plus a generous salary from the company. The constraints on options may also depend on the norms that the founder established. Miriam was always clear that, after the business's basic needs are met, all the extra cash should go to the family. Since the company has always operated that way, it will take a good collaborative process for Mitch and Bernie to evaluate whether or not those norms still serve the best interests of the family business at this stage.

Often the growth stage is sparked by a company's entry into a new market or the launch of a new product. Entering a new market places strains on operations and cash flow. For example, Novelty has made a practice of buying from craftspeople in small towns, mainly in Poland, but also recently in the Czech Republic and Slovakia. Given the recent surge of interest in eastern Europe by U.S. consumers, their large department store accounts have been ordering more and with greater frequency. However, Mitch and his mother are aware that they might soon become victims of their own success. Larger, diversified importing companies have already approached some of their suppliers. While working to keep their suppliers' loyalty, Mitch and Miriam also considered broadening their reach to some formerly communist countries, particularly Bulgaria and Romania.

In some ways, all of these operational and investment decisions stem from a central strategic choice that the family must make: to reinvest in an effort to sustain the Expansion/Formalization process into the future, or to pull back, letting the company move into the Maturity stage and redeploying family capital and the talents of the younger generation into other ventures. Family owners like Mitch and Bernie Kopek may suddenly recognize the need for strategic planning at this stage of development in the family and the business. Whereas company operations may have appeared relatively straightforward in the past, the changes we have described here can make essentially the same operation astonishingly more complex. Suddenly, an imprudent decision can have catastrophic consequences. The strategic process requires developing a variety of future scenarios for the company and analyzing the potential risks and rewards of several paths to growth.

In Novelty's case, the company is being increasingly squeezed between folk art importers and diversified novelties suppliers. To compete successfully against larger players, they need to clarify the focus of their business, analyze their strengths and weaknesses in comparison to their competitors', and then decide how they are going to compete. Perhaps the single most important change they are considering is creating a board of directors to help them through a stepped-up strategic planning process. That could add significantly to their chances of successfully negotiating the Expansion/Formalization stage and emerging at a new level of operations.

NOTES

1. Levinson 1978.
2. Davis and Tagiuri 1989.
3. See also Levi, Stierlin, and Savard 1972; Dumas 1989.
4. Holland 1973; Kotter, Faux, and McArthur 1978; Greenhaus 1987.

6

The Complex Family Enterprise

THE TYPE OF COMPLEX family enterprise described in this chapter—a multigenerational, cousin-owned company that has reached a mature stage of business development—is a rarity among family companies. Probably no more than 5 percent of all family businesses in the United States reach this stage of development. Companies of this stature, however, have a unique importance in our model. The very fact that they have reached this stage means that they have successfully responded to challenges that scuttle other family companies. They contribute mightily to the GNP, employment, exports, and innovation in all market economies. The fact that they are more common in the older economies of Europe and parts of Asia suggests that they may be the future of some of the best of the post–World War II American firms, which are now making the transition from Controlling Owner to Sibling Partnership. They also represent many founders' ultimate dream (or fantasy), which shapes the family policies of many businesses at earlier developmental stages.

These companies are among the icons of American commerce. Cargill, Inc., the largest privately owned company in the United States, is an example of a fourth-generation Cousin Consortium family business. Cargill's product line, accounting for $47 billion in revenues, consists of commodities trading and transport, food processing and production, and agricultural products. The company has 63,000 employees working in forty-seven business units in fifty-four countries. Incredibly, 87 percent of the ownership, and complete voting control, still lies in the hands of three family branches, led by four cousins descended from the company founder, W. W. Cargill. The current CEO, Whitney MacMillan; his brother, Cargill MacMillan, Jr.; and two cousins, James R. Cargill and W. Duncan MacMillan, have run the business for the last twenty years.

Campbell Soup Company, another Cousin Consortium, is a $6 billion business that employs 47,000 people. Although its well-known soups control 75 percent of the domestic market, its other popular products include Swanson frozen foods, V8 vegetable juice, Prego spaghetti sauce, Vlasic pickles, and Pepperidge Farms baked goods. Four branches of the Dorrance family, including nine cousins and their children, control the company through their 51 percent ownership stake. The well-publicized dissension within the Dorrance family, in which one branch tried to force the sale of the company, illustrates one of the key challenges of managing these complex family enterprises.

Family businesses that have reached this stage must contend with considerable complexity in all three dimensions. The Cousin Consortium stage of ownership development not only suggests a larger number of individual family owners, but often includes trusts, holding companies, employee stock ownership plans, and even, in some cases, publicly traded shares. Although some of the business units have reached the Maturity stage of business development, other product lines, divisions, or subsidiaries are likely to be at other points. Finally, in the family dimension, the range of ages in each generation typically means that there will be different nuclear families within the clan in each of the family development stages, from Young Business Family to Passing the Baton.

This increased complexity can be difficult to manage, but it also generates opportunity for family members and owners, which energizes the relationships among members of all three circles. As illustrated in figure 6-1, the relationship between family and business complexity creates for family members an environment of financial and career opportunity. In family business systems in which business complexity exceeds family complexity, sufficient "opportunities per family member" will be greater within the family business. These opportunities can be in terms of jobs, dividends, executive or board positions, compensation, and management development roles. More opportunities per family member helps to keep the peace within the family and keeps family members interested in and loyal to the business. Loyalty in turn helps the business to keep growing. On the other hand, when family complexity exceeds business complexity, opportunity

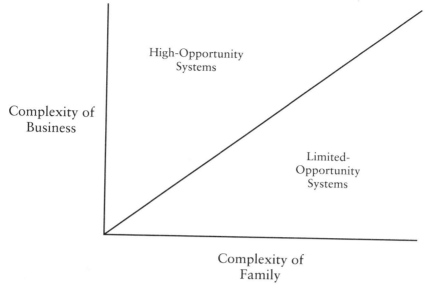

Complexity of
Business

High-Opportunity
Systems

Limited-
Opportunity
Systems

Complexity of
Family

Figure 6-1 ■ *Level of Individual Opportunity in the Complex Family Enterprise*

per family member will be lower. There is greater competition within the family over scarce opportunities and less incentive for the entire family to be loyal to the business. Family companies need to learn how to accurately assess the degree of opportunity provided to family members in these complex Cousin Consortium systems, and how to manage the consequences. If the ratio suggests severely restricted opportunities, then either the business can be reviewed for its growth and renewal potential or consideration can be given to reducing the complexity of family ownership by pruning the shareholder tree.

This chapter explores the typical issues faced by large, complex, dynastic family enterprises, focusing on the family business at the Cousin Consortium stage of ownership, with the core business at the Maturity stage and the dominant families in the Working Together stage of family development.

Hartwall Group Ltd.

Hartwall Group Ltd., a $400 million fifth-generation brewer and bottler located in Helsinki, Finland, is an encouraging example of a professionally run, complex family company. The company was founded in 1836 by Victor Hartwall, the great-great-grandfather of Erik Hartwall, the current managing director. Hartwall Group is structured as a holding company, totally owned by thirty-six Hartwall family members. The group in turn owns bottlers and brewers in Finland and Latvia, as well as a brewery machinery holding company in Holland. The principle products of the operating subsidiaries are several brands of beer for domestic and export sale, Coca-Cola and Schweppes products, and a variety of soft drinks and bottled waters. Since 1989 they have held a steady 67 percent of the Finnish beverage market, and they currently employ about 2,500 people.

The Hartwall family shareholder group has grown from one shareholder in the first and second generations, to three in the third, four in the fourth, nine in the fifth, and twenty-four in the sixth. There are three classes of stock: one nonvoting class, and both "strong" (twenty votes per share) and "regular" (one vote per share) voting classes. Some 10 percent of the company is publicly owned, nonvoting stock, which has provided the company with important capital for growth, but has not diluted family control of the enterprise. There are buy-sell agreements among the family shareholders, which control the distribution of the strong voting shares. Relatives are free to sell the regular shares. In the past, some shareholders were bought out to check the expansion of the ownership group, but there are no immediate plans to further "prune the tree."

Through the first three generations, the company was controlled only by family members. Erik's father, the fourth-generation leader, expanded the board to include nonfamily directors. Today the chair of the board of the holding company is a nonfamily member, as was once required by Finnish law and is now perpetuated by choice. Erik feels that differentiating the roles of chair and CEO has strengthened the leadership group, and he is eager to acknowledge the mentoring he has received from the nonfamily chair. The board is very active, meeting six to eight times a year. The board is credited with not only steering a sensible course for the company, but also allowing the nonemployed shareholders to feel that company actions are rationally arrived at and not just the desires of the management team.

Overall, shareholding has evolved so that no one branch has ownership control of the business. Three generations of shareholders are alive and very much interested in the company. In a culture that places a high premium on respect for seniority in the family group, this multigenerational work group has been able to interact in a cooperative, problem-solving manner; there is little visible competition within this closely knit group. Through several generations the family has followed the norm that reinvestment is a higher priority than dividends. Years ago, they established a formal limit on the amount of dividends as a percentage of earnings. Because the younger generation learns early that the company is not expected to be the sole financial support of the family, they pursue their own careers, in or out of the company.

Erik Hartwall leads the principal operating company as CEO. Erik's family branch has been in management control of the company for three generations, but all four of the family branches are represented in the management of the company. Three fifth-generation cousins occupy key management roles, and an equal number of sixth-generation members have entered the company and are working their way up the ranks. At the initiative of the two generations active in management, the family recently began to respond to the challenges of the Working Together stage by clarifying employment expectations. To qualify for employment in the company, family members must complete their university degree, demonstrate that they have skills and interests that will contribute to the company's performance, and express a long-term commitment to the company. An independent career psychologist counsels all sixth-generation members on their careers and deliberates with Erik and the board chairman about the suitability of potential family employees. Professional management standards are adhered to rigorously regarding all family managers.

In the last five years, as international competition has increased in Nordic countries as well as all of Europe, Hartwall has dramatically stepped up its already-respectable investment program. Following acquisitions of breweries in Latvia to increase its capacity, Hartwall completely reengineered its distribution system, including building a state-of-the-art warehouse at company headquarters. This new warehouse processes several times the volume of beer, mineral water, and Coca-Cola as the traditional warehousing system, lowering unit costs and providing faster information on sales. This innovation was complemented by a new management information system. Hartwall has not lost sight of what it is good at or how to make money. It has combined its tradition of strong customer relationships and market responsiveness with an increasingly analytical approach to decision making. In this way, the company has managed to fight off rigidity and bureaucracy and to maintain an entrepreneurial, professional spirit.

With all branches of the family represented in management, family members feel reasonably well informed about company performance and activities. But as the family grew, Erik understood that more formal mechanisms would be necessary to keep the family united behind the company. In 1991 he organized a family meeting to introduce family members to the academic topic of family business (they were well acquainted with the reality). At this two-day gathering, they instituted a representative family council. The council meets quarterly to plan for family meetings, develop family policies regarding the business, and discuss current issues facing the family and the company. The progressive approach has paid off. The younger generation in particular has appreciated being included in discussions about the business and having written policies about employment, promotion, and venture capital opportunities.

The long history of the Hartwall family has provided opportunity for each generation to learn from the mistakes and successes of its predecessors. Particularly in the last two generations, the family has been able to maintain an atmosphere of mutual support and respect, and has articulated family values that stress industriousness and modesty. The distribution of employment opportunities and ownership power reinforce a healthy balance among the family branches. Because there is little feeling of unjust treatment in the past and little sensitivity about being diminished in status now, family members express open support for one another and do not appear overly competitive. At the same time, they do not hide disagreements over policies or plans. In-laws have not had a fragmenting effect on the Hartwalls, in part because they have been brought into family discussions and are treated as first-class citizens in this system. The family works hard to stay aware of its internal politics and to maintain its family identity and support structure. This has been aided by the fact that the family is largely Helsinki based, and relatives see one another frequently in a variety of business and social settings. The family also no doubt benefits from the presence of leaders in the fourth generation who, now in their nineties, still appear at family gatherings to inspire even the youngest of the clan.

Ownership Issues

By the third or later generations, a business family can have grown quite large. Fifteen to twenty-five grandchildren in the third generation is not unusual; we have worked with several families with more than fifty members of the third generation, including grandchildren and their spouses.

Later generations in dynastic business families may easily exceed one hundred relatives and in-laws. All of these relatives could be shareholders.

With most shareholders at this stage not employed in the business, nonemployed owners now have less direct information about company matters. Fewer family members now have a parent, sibling, spouse, or child to keep them informed and to guard their branch's interests. To keep shareholders informed requires thoughtful information management—a requirement that, oddly enough, catches most family companies completely off guard. Getting enough of the right kind of information communicated to one's family shareholders in a timely manner is no easy task. The task is made more difficult by three factors: geographic dispersion of the family (sometimes over continents); wide differences among family members in terms of skills, interests, income, and other factors; and the attitudes of different branches of the family toward the ruling coalition in the company.

As families grow and age, they become more diverse. Family members and branches differ in their incomes and income needs, wealth, social standing, political philosophies and affiliations, educational levels, careers, physical and mental health, and a variety of other factors. Most important, the branches of a family vary in their connection to and feelings about the business. By the third generation, one branch of the family generally has assumed management control of the business. The other branches will be more or less allied with this ruling branch. Often, another branch assumes the role of chief critic of the ruling branch. Typically, this critic's role comes about because of feelings of being mistreated in the past; one generation's sibling conflict can become a deep-seated antagonism between branches and cousins who may never have met. The "critical" branch is typically only marginally involved in the management of the company, if at all. It challenges the policies of the ruling branch and tries to get the support of other branches. This politicization of the ownership group is almost inevitable in Cousin Consortiums.

With or without a critical branch to galvanize opposition, family business leaders need to recognize that nonemployed shareholders have an important ownership and emotional stake in the business. They need to be informed of key events and have a legitimate right to a voice in the direction and policies of the company. The resolution of natural and created differences between the employed and nonemployed shareholders, between the ruling and critical branches, involves first recognizing the legitimacy of differing points of view. This is a difficult realization, especially if the family has operated under the belief that only those active in the business need to know about the sensitive issues in the company. In particular, if the family is organized in the Sibling Partnership stage into a quasi-parental system (as described in chapter 1), the transition to a Cousin Consortium may be especially difficult.

The key to effective management of shareholder issues is to develop a system of involvement and governance that informs and educates family members (shareholders and nonshareholders) and gives the family a real role and voice in the company, while shielding the business from the excesses of family politics and maintaining the business's integrity. This lofty goal is, in fact, realizable through the efforts of a well-designed family council and board of directors. Boards at this stage generally include outsiders but still can be dominated by family members. This can work fine, or it can hobble the board if the family members act primarily to protect their branch's interests rather than to look out for the general long-term interests of the business. Board structures that choose members only as representatives of family subgroups and without regard to their potential contribution to the real work that the board must accomplish generally work against both the business's integrity and, ironically, family harmony.

Beyond the issues of family favoritism and inclusion, which are often present in these mature shareholder groups, both employed and nonemployed owners also tend to wrestle with the balancing act between dividend payouts to the family versus reinvestment needs of the business. As a family grows to this point, the number of family shareholders seeking dividend income will usually grow as well. The axiom we ask families to remember is "Families grow faster than businesses," which is generally true. The family's expectations about lifestyle have probably also grown, nurtured with each passing generation. The result can be a shareholder group that thinks first and foremost of its own personal financial needs and little of the financial needs of the business. It has taken the Hartwalls generations to come to grips with this dynamic and to find a way to manage it, but it still takes continuous reinforcement and reeducation of the younger generations about the limits on the company's ability to support the family financially.

Balancing the financial needs of the business and family at this stage requires planning, a concern for both entities, a view that the business's needs must come first, and a healthy dialogue between family and business members. Dividend policies must be established that allow healthy business reinvestment and give family members a predictable dividend income stream. Dividends may be traditionally high in some fortunate companies and may have high periods in many companies, but generally businesses cannot afford to sustain high dividends with a very large shareholder group. One role of leadership is to keep an expanding family's dividend expectations realistic. Families must educate their members that the business will probably not be able to support them in the lifestyle they have seen in their parents' smaller generation. As in Hartwall, family members must be encouraged to earn their own living and rely on dividend income only as a boost to their earned income.

If information to shareholders is not managed well or if shareholders feel their financial needs are not being fairly considered, the desire to sell out usually grows. Even when adequate and timely information and reasonable dividends are given to shareholders, some shareholders may not want to or be financially able to keep all of their shares. When this occurs, the ownership group must be prepared to buy out those who want to cash out all or part of their shares. A company may not be able to meet all shareholder demands for buyouts in a timely way. Long-term buyout agreements may need to be arranged to allow family shareholders to sell shares at a fair price and to help the company finance this activity. This, of course, necessitates the creation of a fair internal market (as discussed in chapter 3), where share price is agreed upon on a regular basis, typically annually.

To develop policies that protect the interests of the business, guard it from the excesses of family politicking, and treat the family fairly, nothing is more beneficial than a professional board of directors. Such a board should have ample nonfamily, nonexecutive "outsider" representation; we prefer to see a majority of outsiders on such a board. Family representatives on the board should be limited to the chair or CEO, the designated successor or successor candidates, and family council representatives. These structures and the relationships between them will be discussed in chapter 8.

Family Issues

Like any good Shakespearean play, the family drama at this stage of development has to do with its internal struggles over recognition, power, and money. By definition, families at the Cousin Consortium stage have at least two definable family branches and by the third generation can be very large. The largest fifth-generation family we work with, for example, has over 200 members. Families have a history, an accumulation of experiences, each of which is interpreted in a variety of ways within the family. The interaction of the family history with its current situation creates the context of family life.

Cousin Consortium families, really more clans than families, are political structures.[1] Each branch and each family member has its own agenda. These agendas sometimes overlap and complement each other, and sometimes conflict. With each generation, a wave of in-laws joins the family, adding strengths and weaknesses to the skill base, sometimes helping to solidify the identity of the clan, sometimes diluting its identity, and certainly adding to the number of agendas the family will attempt to satisfy. To the extent that the multitude of agendas can be recognized and satisfied, the family can be satisfied and at peace. To the extent that the family company is seen as facilitating the satisfaction of family needs, the family can feel loyal to and proud of the business.

As noted earlier, by this stage one branch of the family has typically assumed dominance in management and may even include all the family members still employed in the company. In many cases the family is reassured that one branch is in firm control and that the performance of the company is not undermined by conflict fostered by uncertainty. This dominance structure can be welcomed by relatives who are glad that some family members are keeping the wealth and the commercial name of the family intact. But the way the dominant branch uses its authority will determine the reaction of the rest of the family. If relatives believe that the choice of successors, managers, and employees, and the resulting distribution of income, have unfairly favored the dominant branch to the detriment of another branch, resentment is likely to result. This is the situation that can lead to the emergence of the critical branch discussed above—nonemployed owners who try to reduce the power of, or unseat, the dominant branch. Similarly, the branch of the family most identified with senior management can feel misjudged by other branches and resent the lack of appreciation it feels it has received. When this occurs, family tensions can be magnified and carried on for years.

The general emotional fabric of Cousin Consortium families varies widely. Sometimes family members will retain a sentimental tie to the family of origin and, to some extent, have emotion-based relationships with one another, but the emotional residue from interactions in the past (as among siblings) has died down. Although still an important factor in family relationships, emotions in these families are based less on unconscious, early relationship factors and more on the satisfaction of current personal and branch needs. This calmness is most often the emotional tone of Cousin Consortiums where the rules for employment, dividends, and other policies have been in place for a long time, and the business continues to do well financially.

But, in other families, there is no sign of such a cooling out in the cousin generation. Because it is almost inevitable that the cousins have less intense daily contact as a group than their sibling parents did, and therefore less opportunity to have frequent current issues to fight about, a high level of emotional conflict at this stage usually means that old wounds to a branch's pride are having a powerful impact on current relationships. Old wounds prepare a branch to see the current situation in a suspicious manner and expect to be mistreated by another branch. Individuals or branches who feel they have been unjustly diminished in the social order can feel great resentment. This resentment may be constant, or it can go underground for generations and emerge as covert or open conflict. Some senior family members go to great lengths to perpetuate old grudges through their (often-outdated) characterizations of other branches. Short-sighted members of the senior generation can, like effective whips of political parties, marshall support for their views and force their children to vote the party line. The junior generation of a business family must have great fortitude to defy the perceptions of the senior generation or to forgive past grievances and build solidarity among the family. This is why it is so important in every generation, if the family intends to keep a shared financial interest in the company after it has reached the Cousin Consortium stage, to reaffirm the identity and membership of the broad extended family outside the business, and to give younger generations a chance to gather their own data about more distant relatives.

For a family to have a sense of itself, it is necessary for it to have leadership. Such family leadership can be the same individuals as the business leaders when the family is united around the company and feels fairly treated. But it is often useful, and sometimes necessary, to encourage separate leadership of these two entities. The leadership of the family (one or more persons, none of whom must come from the senior generation) can help the family develop a mission that includes but extends beyond the business. Given the diversity of the family, it has a variety of interests outside the business that may include community, church, philanthropy, and other activities; the family may see value in acting collectively in any of these arenas. Even after several generations, the family may also share certain core values that help to define its identity; family leadership can help to articulate these and build a social structure around them. In chapter 8 we discuss the roles of the board and family council in balancing and expressing the needs of these critical stakeholders.

Business Issues

Companies that have reached the Maturity stage of business development have established their market reputations, grown beyond the cash flow crises of earlier stages to financial stability, hired professional management, and developed sophisticated management systems. Successful, mature companies are often dominant or at least very competitive in their market niches, having found ways to secure customer loyalty through cost or product advantages. This is the stage to which most family companies aspire, and for good reason. Once here, it is more possible to defend against competitive attack. A mature business generally has more leverage in dealing with suppliers, key customers, banks, and other resources. Once a business is large, it can gain the confidence of a market that can help it maintain momentum and grow even larger.

But size and maturity, like all organizational characteristics, also have potential disadvantages. Such businesses often run the risk of losing sight of two business basics they probably understood well in their earlier stages: strategic focus and market-smart innovation. Mature companies can begin to see their success as inevitable, rather than fragile, and stop listening to customers. They can close their eyes to current and potential competition and stop keeping up with technology. This turn inward generally spells trouble and sometimes is disastrous. Companies can stop innovating in ways the market appreciates and experiment with new products and services that are far from their core competencies. This loss of market focus and innovation can generally be traced to hubris on the part of leaders and to the rigidity and lack of responsiveness of a larger organization. Keeping the company responsive, innovative, and disciplined at this stage is the name of the game. Family companies are no different than other firms in this regard.

When companies reach this size they must guard against becoming rigid structures that discourage contact with the market and inhibit internal innovation. Keeping a business culture open and innovative is constantly challenging at any stage, but particularly when the company has been successful. A strong culture based on shared assumptions usually develops as a result of continued success. Organizational members are often reluctant to examine or alter these assumptions and, consequently, changes in the environment can transform these strengths into weaknesses.[2]

Leadership Resources

Because the stakes of poor decisions are substantial, mature family companies must insist on management competence throughout the organization, including the board. Competence may come from inside or outside the family, but the company has no choice but to put the best talent possible in key management positions. Family leadership of a family-owned business builds customer, employee, and shareholder loyalty *if it is competent*. Competent nonfamily leadership of a family company is preferable to incompetent family leadership, but nonfamily leaders can have difficulty keeping all of the constituencies loyal.

The family at this stage faces a critical decision: Whether to exercise its leadership and control in the future through ownership or through management, or both. If the family chooses to remain an owner-managed firm, then leadership will need to be developed in both the board of directors, representing ownership interests, and senior management. If the family chooses to withdraw from management, then board positions become the vehicle for family control, and the management task becomes recruiting and integrating excellent nonfamily managers. Family members need not occupy the positions of both CEO and chair of the board. These positions are both very important for a business at this stage and have different orientations and responsibilities. As long as a family member can fill one of these two positions, the family will probably appear to have maintained its leadership of the company.

To maintain family leadership of the enterprise requires both attracting competent family members into the business and developing them for positions of high responsibility. In the Working Together stage of Cousin Consortiums, a plurality of the individuals from both generations will typically come from the same or close branches of the family. The primary challenges at this stage are developing credibility and authority (by the junior generation), preparing the junior generation for senior management, and preparing the senior generation to let go in the future. Preparing the next generation for senior management is both more straightforward and very challenging at this stage. The professional nature of the organization usually makes it obvious that clear standards of management competence will be applied to family members as well as nonfamily managers at this stage. The stability of the mature company also helps to define career paths that can lead the successful member of the junior generation to the top levels of the company. At the same time, the level of performance that the junior generation must demonstrate is now very high. All the stakeholders—the senior generation, nonemployed family owners, and senior nonfamily managers—will be less likely at this stage to support family managers who are not the best talent the company can attract for any key position. In particular, nonfamily managers may feel more secure as the company operates ever more like a publicly owned, professionally managed firm, and may demonstrate more open competitive behavior toward rising family managers. Family successors who make it to the executive levels in this environment have truly earned their stripes.

By the time a family has reached the Cousin Consortium and Maturity stages, even if family members fill the CEO role, they are no longer supplying most of the management talent to its business and it is unlikely that many family members are even employed in the company. At some point in its history, often by the third generation, a family business leader has "cleaned house," removing family managers who contribute little and bringing in nonfamily to fill most management positions. If family norms prohibit such weeding out, then the company is almost certainly plateaued at a level of performance below its potential. Companies that reach the Maturity stage in this condition (sometimes prematurely abandoning Expansion/Formalization strategies) will gradually lose their competitive position and are candidates for eventual failure or acquisition. If they do survive to be passed on to the next generation, the chore of upgrading management will be dumped on the successors—a most difficult situation.

Capital Resources

Beyond the need for a high level of management competence, businesses at this stage require large amounts of investment capital to maintain, let alone advance, their interests. Annual investment requirements for maintaining plant and equipment are generally sizable, but can actually pale next to the investment needed for new technology, people development, and marketing programs. It is difficult to find a business dedicated to strong performance that does not have very substantial reinvestment requirements. Even service sector companies require sizable investments in training and development, management systems, and marketing programs. Few businesses today are exempt from these investment requirements. Mature businesses generally have even greater reinvestment requirements than do companies struggling to reach the mature stage.

Management's view of investment needs is generally tied to its view of the market's needs and the company's vulnerability, as well as the company's traditions regarding innovation. If management views the company as secure in its competitive position or the company does not have a strong tradition of innovation, little capital may be set aside for the future. The family's need for income can also have a powerful impact on how much is reinvested in the company.

By this stage, the business will probably have encountered the question of being able to raise enough capital for growth without losing family control of ownership. We have pointed out several times that, by the time a business is mature, its capital requirements can be huge. Debt, when available, may cover only some of a company's investment needs. The result is that many mature family companies must decide if they want to limit their growth to what they can support through internally generated funds and debt, or look outside the family for more equity capital. The two main options to raise growth capital are equity partners and a public stock offering. Each of these options will be evaluated in terms of the likelihood that they can raise the needed cash, and the consequences for family control. At this stage, family control does not necessarily mean owning a majority of the outstanding stock, or even the voting stock. These complex ownership systems may be effectively controlled *in ordinary circumstances* with a far smaller ownership share. But there is always some risk of *nonordinary circumstances,* where an effort is made to take control away from the family. Each family must assess its own comfort with various levels of risk, weighed against the capital needs of the company and the opportunity for significant increases in the total value of the shareholders' equity.

One way to maintain the family's control over the entire family enterprise while allowing outside investors into some areas of the company is to organize the family business as a holding company with subsidiary operating companies. In one design, the family members are sole owners of the holding company shares, distributed according to the family's decisions about equity and estate planning. The holding company, in turn, is the majority owner of each of the operating companies' stock. Outside investors (either a few individuals, or more through a public offering) also hold shares of the operating companies. In some cases, individual family members or branches also hold additional shares of those companies in which they have executive positions. This balance allows for spreading the returns of the whole enterprise throughout the family, but also rewarding superior performance for owner-manager family members on a company-by-company basis. Ideally, each operating company has its own active board, including individuals from the family and outsiders who are most appropriate to that particular business or industry. Some holding companies put aside a portion of earnings as a "new venture" fund. This allows for family entrepreneurs to start and grow their businesses under the umbrella of the family enterprise.

One of the main objections to a holding company is that it can encourage undisciplined diversification. The extent of diversification is an important issue that often arises at this stage. Especially if the company has been successful, there is a desire to try one's talents in new industries or geographical areas. A network of many different operating companies can provide greatly expanded opportunity for cousins to demonstrate leadership, satisfy an entrepreneurial need without leaving the family business, and have greater control over turf. It can also be a method of internationalizing a business, which can be essential for companies based in countries with limited investment capital and domestic markets.[3] However, there is a downside risk if this process is not carefully evaluated and controlled. As many studies have pointed out, broad diversification can distract a company from its successful enterprises and dilute needed investment in profitable ventures.

A related issue that often emerges at this stage involves how to treat the original business, the business that launched the company and to which most of the family is quite attached. Often, by this stage, the original business has either begun to lose profitability or is well into the red. But because the family has a sentimental attachment to this founding business, there can be great resistance to closing, selling, or even reducing the size of this business. For the sake of the entire enterprise, the poorly performing business must often be "retired," an act that sometimes involves a confrontation among family shareholders. Too often, closing or selling off the founding business is postponed to avoid family conflict, sometimes putting a drag on the entire company for years.

So that a mature business remains focused on its core competencies, the leadership of the company must form a compelling vision for the enterprise and convey that vision to a broad range of constituencies. After all, at this stage the company has many more stakeholders than just family owners and managers. There may be thousands of employees whose families are also dependent on talented leaders' making wise decisions. There are customers and suppliers who count on their relationship with the company. And there is probably an entire network of community leaders, neighbors, recipients of company gifts or contributions, and future beneficiaries who may be relatively invisible to the business's decision makers, but who would miss it badly if the company were to falter. Even if it is still completely in the family's private ownership hands, the mature Cousin Consortium business is often in many ways a public resource. Guiding it is the kind of task that takes the combined efforts of senior management, the board, and the family council.

Somewhere in the mind of many of the entrepreneurs discussed in chapter 5, just founding their Start-Up/Controlling Owner businesses, lies a dream of the companies that are described in this chapter. These complex systems can be giants, dominant in their industries and well known to the general public. Family control may be very evident in the name and leadership of the company, or hidden and only apparent upon close reading of the annual report. In some ways their complexity and typical size makes their issues unique. In other ways, however, they demonstrate many of the same family dynamics and business concerns as all of their counterparts, who are less far along the developmental dimensions. There is still the tension between family control and broad participation in management and ownership, the dilemmas of continuity and succession, and the challenges of preserving the asset base while benefiting from it. Family companies that have accomplished the double tasks of building a profitable, competitive business while maintaining a viable and compelling concept of family should be justifiably proud.

NOTES

1. Ouchi comments on family business clans in Gersick 1992.
2. Schein 1992.
3. Gallo and Sveen 1991.

7

The Diversity of Successions:
Different Dreams and Challenges

SUCCESSION IS the ultimate test of a family business. Once the business has been transformed from an individual venture into a family enterprise, its continuity becomes a unifying concern. Inevitably, individual and company life cycles must diverge. Passing the company on, profitably and in good condition, to a new generation of leaders is a goal that drives the members of all three circles. This chapter addresses a fourth classic type of family business: those in which the ownership group, the family, and the company itself are within a few years of changing leaders.

Succession is not one thing but many. It is not a single event that occurs when an old leader retires and passes the torch to a new leader, but a process that is driven by a developmental clock—beginning very early in the lives of some families and continuing through the maturation and natural aging of the generations. Succession always takes time. Even in those cases in which sudden illness or dramatic events lead to abrupt changes in individuals' titles or roles, there is a period of preparation and anticipation, the actual "handing over of the keys," and the period of adjustment and adaptation.

The process, moreover, is not always as rational and planful as described in most of the family business literature. Some family businesses work hard to be proactive about succession planning and anticipate the preparatory tasks that accompany each stage of business and family development. Other families succeed by simply muddling through by themselves, without much conscious planning until perhaps the last moment. But whether elaborately planned or responded to as needed, succession is a complex process, presenting a formidable obstacle course for members of all three circles. The owners must formulate a vision of a future governance structure and decide how to divide ownership to conform with that structure. They must develop and train potential management successors and set up a process for selecting the most qualified leaders. They must overcome any resistance to letting go that the seniors may have and help the new leadership establish its authority with various stakeholders. And, after planning, strategizing, and negotiating, they must then be prepared to deal with unexpected contingencies, which may threaten these very plans at any point in the process.

Despite the great variety of structures that are actually adopted by contemporary family businesses (collective ownership, shared management responsibilities, multifamily succession), the family business literature has tended to remain focused on a single type of generational transition, in which a father passes his business to a son. This model, rooted in the ancient tradition of primogeniture and with practical advantages of clarity and predictability, is still a common form of succession. Nevertheless, the almost-exclusive attention given to it by the classic works in the field has tended to inhibit a true understanding of the complex universe of family companies.[1]

Lansberg has identified two core concepts that expand the traditional view of the succession process.[2] The first core concept concerns the range of postsuccession options available to a business family and the fundamentally different processes involved in transitions to each of them. Some leadership transitions involve only a change in the people who are running the company, but others involve a fundamental change in the structure and culture of the company. The planning process can be likened to a journey that is shaped at every stage largely by the destination the family has in mind. In this case, the destination is the ownership and governance structure that the family envisions for the future of the company.

The second concept is that the choice of one or another structure at any given juncture is driven by a shared dream, in which the aspirations of individual family members become woven together in a collective vision of their future. Members of the senior generation have individual dreams of the company and the family after they are gone. They may see the company as a monument to their own accomplishments, with new leaders replicating their successes in a replay of the seniors' tenure. Or it could be a very different vision, correcting all the seniors' self-perceived mistakes. Each person in the junior generation will also have a vision, including a fantasy about his or her role, and the hoped-for network of relationships with all the other members of the rising generation. The ideal process of succession planning is the gradual uncovering of these individual dreams, and their integration into one goal and one course of action.

Reaching that ideal is not always easy. The individual dreams may be vastly different and even incompatible—as when the retiring leaders want to maximize continuity and the aspiring leaders are committed to dramatic change. Further, as the shared dream takes shape, it may or may not be realistic when matched with the "raw material" in the family; that is, the distribution of skills and talents in the next generation. The implementation of the dream may be hampered by the authority and influence hierarchy of the family, with the most powerful individuals favoring a solution different from the majority's. Finally, families that envision a structure different from the one to which they are accustomed often have not considered the implications of the change and the fundamental transformation of the business culture that will be required. However, all family members are driven to some degree by the shared goals of success, financial security, and fulfillment for their offspring. When these positive forces outweigh the impediments, succession planning has a fighting chance to succeed.

This chapter illustrates the process by which a shared vision of the company's future emerges and guides the transition from one generation to the next. Although succession is a process in all three circles, we have found that the transition mechanism in family business tends to begin with choices about ownership. In large public companies in which ownership is not dominated by one family or group, the stock is so fragmented that senior management has de facto control over the business's direction.[3] There, succession is about changing the CEO, not about trading stock on the exchange. But in family businesses, even if management has been passed largely to professional nonfamily executives, the family's control of ownership marks the seat of ultimate power in the system.[4] It is the often-evoked golden rule of family business: "The one who has the gold, rules." As a result, the succession process begins with decisions about the ownership form for the next generation—Controlling Owner, Sibling Partnership, or Cousin Consortium—and those decisions serve as catalysts for the other transitions in management and family leadership. For that reason, we have organized our presentation of the succession process by describing the transition toward each of the three ownership stages.

The following case is an excellent illustration of the succession process, because it describes two separate leadership transitions, one recently completed and the second already well under way. The experience of the Lombardis, a sophisticated and competitive family with a successful business, illustrates the challenges that must be dealt with as a company moves from one governance and leadership structure to another.

Lombardi Enterprises

Lombardi Enterprises began as Lombardi Foods, a small-scale produce distributor in the Sonoma Valley. Today it operates a $900 million chain of retail markets throughout the western region, specializing in gourmet items as well as the usual array of grocery products. The founder, Paul Lombardi, Sr., came to the United States from the Tuscany region of Italy and started operating a few acres as a truck farmer. He built the company and ruled it as a controlling owner for almost twenty-five years; now he is eighty-two years old and retired. For the past twenty years, the company has been run by his five children, four sons and a daughter. The oldest—Paul Jr., fifty-five—has filled the role of "first among equals" in their Sibling Partnership.

Over those twenty years, there has been a transformation in the management style and culture of Lombardi Enterprises. During Paul Sr.'s long tenure, power and authority radiated from a single source. Decision making was concentrated in the hands of one leader, who also enjoyed most of the glory for the company's successes. Under the Sibling Partnership that has emerged since his retirement, major decisions are made by consensus. Paul Jr.'s role is much more circumscribed than that of his father. Over time, he and his siblings have worked out a system in which all grant one another a certain amount of autonomy in running their divisions, and no one individual captures all the limelight. Nonfamily managers have had to adapt to a wholly new management environment, in which authority flows not just from one but from five sources and decisions at the top are often made by a group.

The first leadership transition at Lombardi Enterprises demonstrates how a near-tragic event can precipitate a fortuitous succession. While swimming at a California beach in 1977, the athletic founder was caught in an eddy, dragged down, and nearly drowned. Paul Sr., then sixty-two years old, spent almost half a year recuperating in a hospital and remained depressed for some time afterward. Meanwhile, Paul Jr. and his siblings stepped into the breach. Proving the dictum that power is seized and not given, Paul Jr. not only filled the leadership vacuum but, in a short time, was leading the company into new ventures. By the time Paul Sr. returned to the company, it was clear that members of the second generation were fully in charge and running things smoothly. The father decided it was a good time to step aside and assume an advisory role as chairman of the company.

It would be a mistake, however, to think that this first succession was entirely unplanned—or that it took place instantaneously. From the time the five Lombardi siblings were young, Paul Sr. and his wife, Anna, had envisioned that the children would one day take charge of the company and manage it as a team. In those early years, the parents tried to dampen their offspring's natural competitiveness and encourage them to cooperate and share, with the idea that teamwork would eventually be essential to their future partnership. When stock was transferred to the second generation, each sibling received an equal amount. The five now control 55 percent and will inherit the rest after their parents' deaths.

The five were well prepared for company leadership. The four sons were sent to excellent colleges and then graduated from top business and technical schools. As head of the company's markets division, Paul Jr. has demonstrated his leadership by expanding the supermarket chain from twelve California stores in 1965 to sixty-five stores throughout the West and Pacific Northwest in 1990. The only sister, Rita, is also college educated. She has traveled widely and for many years headed the company's import division. Each of the siblings had been working in the company for several years and was in charge of a division when their father's accident occurred.

It has taken years, however, for Paul Jr. to consolidate his position as leader of the sibling system. His position as first among equals was a compromise that preserved some of the appearances of his father's strong individual leadership and made the participative system more acceptable to employees and the outside world. But Paul Jr. had to gradually legitimize his leadership with his siblings, and the scope of his authority has been defined over the years by trial and error. When Paul Jr. makes a major decision without informing them first, they let him know—very point-edly—that he has exceeded his authority and that, as equal partners, they expect to be consulted. After many years of defining the boundary ad hoc on each new occasion, the partners have recently attempted to define explicitly the boundaries of the oldest brother's authority. So, for example, the partners have agreed to let the CEO make decisions on any expenditure of money below a certain amount and on ventures that do not commit the company to support for longer than two years.

The Lombardi siblings have been willing to grant certain limited pow-ers to their oldest brother because he has proven his ability to put money in their pockets. In recent years, they have recognized Paul Jr.'s need to receive more recognition for what he has achieved for the company and have been more generous with their private compliments and public credit. Nevertheless, if Paul Jr. gets too bossy or tries to act like the patriarch in any decision, they are quick to remind him of his limited powers.

Even as Lombardi Enterprises reaches closure on the first succession from Paul Sr. to the Sibling Partnership, it is moving toward a second that will be even more complex to manage. Paul Jr. has suffered a mild heart attack and, at fifty-five, is thinking of retiring soon. The sibling partners are thus at a crossroads where they must decide when the next leadership transition will occur and how the new leader or leaders will be chosen. The partners could have chosen to recycle the present structure, giving each sibling who wants it the opportunity to serve as first among equals, but they have rejected this option. Perhaps because none of the four wishes to take over the CEO's job in the shadow of the successful oldest brother, they have decided that the next change in leadership will occur when members of the third generation are prepared to take charge of Lombardi Enterprises. There is already some evidence of sibling politics. The sibling partners worry that Paul Jr. is maneuvering to position his son, Jaime, the oldest of the cousins and the one with most experience in the company, as an automatic choice for CEO.

There are twenty-five cousins in the third generation, many of whom have already expressed their commitment to the company's tradition of professionalism. They have also revealed an eagerness to take places in top management. The hard reality is that not all who want to make careers in the company and aspire to top positions can be accommodated. The seniors are thus faced with some tough decisions that the family has never had to deal with in the past. What will the requirements for entry into the company be? Because the cousins vary much more widely in age than did the siblings, how will the choice of leaders be affected by the fact that some will be old enough to take over before others? Moreover, there are more cousins in some branches of the family than in others, which raises questions about how stock should be divided. If each sibling divided his or her equal share among the offspring, some cousins will end up with many more shares than others. On the other hand, if stock is to be distributed equally to the cousins regardless of their branches, it would require a buyout process. Given that some branches would then control more stock than others, how would that affect the balance of power in the next generation?

The list of decisions that must be made is formidable. If some cousins who aspire to work in the company will not be able to get jobs, what, if anything, should the family do to support the careers of the disappointed family members? If many will be passive shareholders, what will the family managers of Lombardi Enterprises have to do to ensure their continuing support and loyalty? The growth in sheer numbers of shareholders in the third generation will also put financial pressure on the company to provide a steady flow of generous dividends to cousins not making careers in the company. Can Lombardi Enterprises enable the cousins to maintain the affluent lifestyles to which they are accustomed, without depriving management of the capital it needs to build the company?

The biggest challenge in transitions to a third generation is to set up structures to manage all of this complexity. The biggest risk is that the sibling partners will attempt to install a structure very similar to their own. In other words, they may look for a group of cousins who can work together and continue the same pattern of shared decision making that they have been able to establish. But this vision of the future probably will not fit the changed circumstances in the third generation. The kind of mutual understanding and synergistic cooperation that siblings growing up under the same roof are sometimes able to achieve is difficult to replicate in the third generation; cousins grow up in households and families that may be far apart in values and attitudes.

The seniors have other options, however. If managing complexity becomes too difficult, they might ultimately agree to return to a Controlling Owner form—under which one family would very likely have to obtain a controlling share of stock through a buyout process. This alternative would be particularly attractive if one of the cousins emerges as an outstandingly qualified leader, head and shoulders above his or her contemporaries. Or the Lombardis could conclude that, if only a few are chosen to lead, that will create bitter feelings and divide the five families. To avoid that, they might decide to go further down the road of professionalizing the business by hiring nonfamily managerial talent to take over the top executive positions. Again, these choices may not be arrived at by an entirely rational planning process. They may be the result of subtle negotiations and compromises. Whatever ownership and governance structures are chosen, however, structures such as a board of directors with qualified outsiders on it and a family council in which nonparticipating members can discuss business matters that affect them will be essential to ensuring sound, professional management and shareholder harmony.

How the Shared Dream Is Negotiated

At the heart of the notion of planning is the idea that the family can create a blueprint for the business, which will describe its future strategic direction as well as the ownership and governance structures of the organization. Long before details of the blueprint can be filled in, however, the family members need to formulate a shared dream—an energizing vision of what the company is to become that will enable the family to realize all of its individual values and aspirations.[5] This concept of the shared dream is Lansberg's adaptation of the dream concept introduced in Levinson's work on adult development. In his research in the 1970s, Levinson described the dream in the lives of his subjects as "a vision, an imagined possibility that generates excitement and vitality. . . . It may take a dramatic form as in the myth of the hero: the great artist, business tycoon, athletic or intellectual superstar performing magnificent feats and receiving special honors. It may take mundane forms that are yet inspiring and sustaining: an excellent craftsman, the husband-father of a certain kind of family, the highly respected member of one's community."[6]

Entrepreneurs and their spouses are typically driven by a powerful dream that influences the way they bring up their children, as well as the operation of the business. The shared dream usually begins to take shape when the children are young. Their parents develop a vague longing to see all they have built survive and continue after them, to provide sustenance for their families and their fundamental values. Meanwhile, their offspring are growing up in the pervasive shadow of the family company, which inevitably becomes a force in their lives, shaping their own aspirations and career choices. The juniors may decide to reject the seniors' dream and pursue their ambitions outside the family business—usually not without great psychological conflict. Or they may decide that they can realize their own ambitions and values within the family business. The process of forging a shared dream turns into a negotiation that begins in early dialogues between parents and children and continues right into the adult years, becoming more urgent and explicit as the time for a leadership change approaches.

For families that manage to forge one, the shared dream is thus a vision of the future, which all family members can enthusiastically embrace and which forms the basis of their future collaboration and provides the motivation and excitement needed to carry the family through the hard work of planning. Often it has a religious inspiration or stresses a social mission beyond profit making. However, not all families have a clear idea of what they want for the future of their families and the business. And in some families, the parents have dreams that are contradictory; for example, if one favors a system of equal owner-partners and the other wants to give ownership and control to only one child. When parents have a clear and congruent dream, it influences the way they raise their children as well as how they train the next generation to take over the leadership. When parents have contradictory dreams, however, they may avoid open discussion of their differences and send confusing signals to their offspring. Some couples discuss and reconcile their dreams as they form their marriage enterprise in the Young Business Family stage or as they revise it in later stages. Some families confront the inconsistencies in their dreams as they deal with the younger generation's initial life planning in the Entering the Business stage. Others completely avoid the process of negotiating a shared dream with the younger generation.

As the offspring grow into adults—and clarify their own dreams—the family's shared dream may have to be revised. The seniors must clarify for themselves the structure they want for the future and constantly reassess whether the talents, skills, and commitment of the juniors are strong enough to make that structure work. Likewise, the juniors' career interests evolve as they grow to maturity and experience the world and the family business. The dream of a sibling structure, owned and managed by equal partners, may have to be abandoned, for example, if only one offspring is interested in joining the business, or if only one is clearly qualified to lead it. Indeed, if none of the next-generation family members aspires to a career in the business, the owners may have to decide whether it would be feasible to hire nonfamily managers to run the company or consider selling it.

Families that aspire to a different governance structure than the one they have always known face a cognitive leap of faith. The three basic forms of governance—Controlling Owner, Sibling Partnership, and Cousin Consortium—call for very different leadership styles and structures. Business owners often cannot realize the full implications of the choice they have made, because they are unable to evaluate the evidence regarding what kind of structure is feasible for their family. That is not surprising, for the only roadmap they have is their own experience—the roadmap that has guided them to business success—and the terrain that lay behind may be quite different from what lies ahead.

Understanding the Diversity of Successions

In describing the ownership developmental dimension in chapter 1, we presented three categories of family business ownership: Controlling Owner companies, Sibling Partnerships, and Cousin Consortiums. Typically, when a company is on the brink of a leadership transition, the choice of a future governance structure involves three basic options. The first is to *recycle* the structure that has worked during the tenure of the incumbent leadership, as when a founder leaves the business to one daughter or son (Controlling Owner to Controlling Owner) or when a group of cousins passes on ownership to their children (Cousin Consortium to Cousin Consortium). The second option is to move to a *more complex* structure by dividing ownership rights and management responsibilities among a group of next-generation siblings, as was the case in the second generation at Lombardi Enterprises (Controlling Owner to Sibling Partnership), or when siblings pass on ownership to all their offspring (Sibling Partnership to Cousin Consortium). The third is to make the future ownership and governance structure *simpler,* which would be the case if, for example, the Lombardis were to return to a single owner-manager in the third generation (Sibling Partnership to Controlling Owner).

Many family business owners approaching retirement do not fully appreciate the range of choices open to them. As we discussed in chapter 1, successions in family businesses do not have to follow a progressive sequence from simpler to more complex. Many family businesses, for instance, are founded not by a single entrepreneur but by a team of siblings. In the second generation, the siblings may choose the Controlling Owner form as most feasible, with the successor and his or her family buying out the other partners' shares. A comparable change can happen in a Cousin Consortium, when cousins decide to sell their interest in the family company to a cousin in one branch, who then becomes the controlling owner. By the same token, a Controlling Owner business may skip the Sibling Partnership stage entirely and go directly to a Cousin Consortium. This rare type of succession occurs when none of a controlling owner's children is interested in or capable of leading the business, and the owner-manager thus makes plans to transfer ownership to his or her grandchildren, in the hope that they will eventually be able to take it over. (Usually in such cases, the owner-manager hires nonfamily professional "bridge managers" to run the company in the interim.)

Figure 7-1 shows a total of nine possible types of succession. Three are "recycles," involving a change in leadership while maintaining the same ownership form; three are "progressive" successions that involve a change in leadership while increasing the complexity of the ownership form; and three are "recursive" successions that involve a change in leadership while simplifying the ownership form. This typology demonstrates the true diversity and complexity of leadership transitions. When succession involves replacing the leadership without altering the basic form of the business, much of the owners' accumulated learning from the past is applicable to the future. However, when succession involves not just a changing of the guard but a restructuring of the fundamental form of the

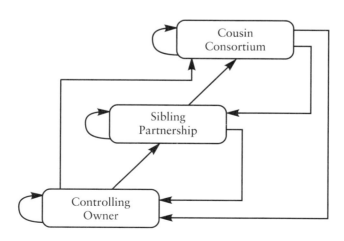

Figure 7-1 ■ *Nine Types of Succession*

business, the adaptation required of the system is of a higher order of magnitude. In this case, little of what may have worked in the past is likely to work well in the future.

All successions in family companies involve the passing of a baton from one generational leader or team of leaders to the next generational leader or team. The tasks that must be accomplished before the senior generation can depart and the junior generation can take charge, however, vary significantly, depending on where the transition starts and where it is designed to finish; that is, the governance structure employed by the seniors and the structure envisioned for the juniors.

The Transition to a Controlling Owner Business

The idea that one and only one individual should be the leader is steeped in the rich imagery of the hero in Western culture. (Given the historical biases of Western culture, the hero myth is traditionally presented as male. In the contemporary world, it obviously applies to both genders.) The king passes the crown to the crown prince. Likewise, the lord of the manor, to prevent his land from being broken up into uneconomic small holdings, turns it all over to one heir. The master's skill and craftsmanship lives on after he has gone in the apprentice to whom he has vouchsafed his sacred knowledge and secrets. It is perhaps natural for an entrepreneur, who has performed the great deed of starting a successful business and personifies this company in the community, to want to see his or her name and work carried on by a favored child who promises to become a hero in the founder's own image—to family, to employees, and in the community. There can be an intense identification between the controlling owner and the chosen son or daughter (or, in some cases, the chosen nephew, niece, or child-in-law).[7] To the extent that the senior has not achieved all of his or her own dream, he or she sees the successor as completing the holy quest. It is the ancient fantasy of immortality, to transfer one's experience and self from the aging body nearing the end of a life into a youthful and energetic figure who will continue the work.

One-person, monocratic rule also has deep roots in the hierarchical traditions of both church and state. From the management point of view, it has the advantage of being parsimonious. It permits decisive action, often critical when a company must move quickly to capture markets or beat competitors. By contrast, rule by committee is often slow and cumbersome. Controlling owners tend to believe that it is their ideas, their willingness to take risks, and their decisiveness that accounts for the company's success—and that groups are inherently incapable of those qualities. In addition, the outside world, including customers, lenders, and community organizations, is still more comfortable dealing with one individual than with a group.

Paradoxically, when the controlling owner has unshared control of both ownership and management, the very advantages of this form of governance, monolithic decision making, are also its biggest drawback. With a Sibling Partnership or Cousin Consortium, families spread the risk by placing ownership control in the hands of a group of offspring. Families that choose a Controlling Owner structure for the next generation are betting the store and the family fortune on the leadership talent, business acumen, and emotional maturity of one person—a risk that is magnified if the controlling owner is also the CEO. A poor choice can have grave consequences for the business. Moreover, the decision to have only one leader increases the risk that the choice of a son or daughter will be based on emotional favoritism rather than on demonstrated competence.

Probably the most common situation that leads to a recycling succession to a Controlling Owner form is when there is only one offspring, or at least only one who has any interest or expectation of being either a manager or an owner in the business. In the case of the single heir, there will still be the challenges that come with any intergenerational transition, but making the choice of successor is not part of the problem. By far the more complicated cases occur when there is more than one next-generation member who has an interest in the business. In those situations, when families opt to continue or return to a Controlling Owner structure, they need to devise a mechanism for concentrating the stock in the single successor's hands. For those families in which the business is the primary asset, this raises fundamental questions of fairness in distribution of the family's wealth. Parents who want to avoid showing favoritism among their offspring are strongly inclined to divide stock in the family company more or less equally among members of the next generation in a Sibling Partnership.[8] Choosing a Controlling Owner model usually means that this equal division idea has been overruled by the principle, emphasized by Danco and other advisers in the field, that the one responsible for leading the business and producing results must control the stock.[9] Otherwise, the chief executive's decisions can be constantly undermined by dissident shareholders.

Sometimes parents in a Controlling Owner generation try to hedge this issue by investing management seniority in one offspring, but dividing ownership among the sibling group, and instructing them (explicitly or, more often, with unspoken assumptions) to support the business leader "as if" he or she were a controlling owner. This is often an untenable resolution. This point was driven home by a second-generation owner-manager who had worked in his family's business for twenty years. When his parents died, they left the stock divided equally among him and his four siblings. This man complained bitterly about the injustice of the parents' decision.

> It was always understood by all that I was the one who was going to take over the family company. I loved working with my parents. I put in the time, I made the effort and achieved the respect of all employees. My parents had always led me to believe that I would control the company. However, shortly before their deaths, they felt that giving me majority control was going to be unfair to my brothers and my sister. Without telling me, they changed their will and left us all equal shares in the business. I now feel like an ox pulling the rest of the family along. The irony of it all is that they thought this would minimize the conflict among us.

It is better for members of the senior generation to be clear in their own minds about whether they want all or nearly all of the ownership shares to go to a Controlling Owner successor, where concurrence and participation of other minority shareholders (if there are any) is unnecessary, or whether they want to consider some form of Sibling Partnership, where collaboration is required. The parents' dilemma in choosing a single successor is that, while denying control of the stock to the next generation's business leader may ultimately hurt the business, concentrating the stock in the next owner-manager's hands can divide the family. Even in families that understand the distinctions between the circles, a position of authority in the business usually endows the incumbent with great power and prestige in the family as well. The elevation of one brother or sister in a group of siblings to be the controlling owner, even when other family assets more or less equalize the estate plan, can exacerbate jealousies and rivalries that go back to childhood. The controlling owner sibling's control of the business can create a de facto quasi-parental situation in the family (as discussed in chapter 1). Some older siblings already had a quasi-parental role in the early years of a family, but it normally weakens somewhat as the younger offspring mature. If given control of the business as an adult, the older sib can easily slip into a parental role again. This may be bitterly resented by the other siblings. Consider how a brother or sister will feel if, instead of going to the parent to request a loan, he or she must go to the sibling who has been named controlling owner of the business.

In certain ethnic cultures, where the rule of primogeniture persists most strongly, an oldest son is still more readily accepted as a single owner-manager than a younger son or daughter. With more daughters as well as sons desiring leadership roles in family companies today, the choice of a single successor may lead to a head-on collision between older ideas of the family "pecking order" and the new standards. Barnes, for example, has written about the problems created by what he calls "incongruent hierarchies" in modern families. If daughters and younger sons tend to rank lower than older or eldest sons in the family hierarchy, for example, but one of them becomes the CEO, "the incongruence is obvious . . . (and) can lead to family stress that becomes even more painful when older siblings are actively involved in the business."[10]

If the senior generation is firm in its commitment to a Controlling Owner succession, the system's acceptance of the decision can be greatly facilitated by educating the other family members, as well as additional stakeholders in the company and its network, of the reasons for the choice of the Controlling Owner dream, and the process by which the successor was chosen. The family leaders do not need to justify their decisions in a defensive manner; the golden rule is operative here. However, explaining the decision by explicitly describing the values and priorities that underlay it can help prevent the business ownership decision from leaving the younger generation irreconcilably divided in the family circle. For example, if a current controlling owner is able to say, "Our best prediction is that the business is headed for a very difficult period, with restructuring and downsizing likely, and I believe that it is essential for one owner to have unfettered control and responsibility for the leadership ahead," or, "I made a promise to my daughter when she started in the businesses that if she dedicated herself to preparing for the role, I would turn the company over to her in time," a dialogue can begin, which can help the family accept and prepare for the new arrangement.

The same dilemma about how severely to consolidate ownership control must be addressed in choosing whether to exclude family members from management, choose only a single family executive, or invest in a family management team with many next-generation members participating. Forming the ownership dream for second and later generations based on a Controlling Owner instead of Sibling Partnership structure usually implies a similar decision about management in the business—that is, that the family has already identified or wants to identify one executive leader for the company. In some family businesses, the choice is easy. S. C. Johnson & Son, makers of Johnson's Wax and the insecticide Raid, have had a single family member in control of ownership through four successions. Samuel C. Johnson, the fourth-generation CEO, has written, "Our firm has been fortunate in that there has been one logical successor in each generation."[11] But this is not always the case. If several more or less equally talented siblings aspire to be leaders, the choice of a Controlling Owner structure sets up a winner-take-all horse race. The more restricted the access to senior roles, and the longer the choice is put off, and the more ambiguity there is about the candidates and their relative standing, the fiercer the competition for the owner-manager position can become.

All family members know that their collective and individual futures depend on good choices. However, each generation, and to some extent different members of the generations, may have different points of view on the best process, guided to some extent by their different agendas. The senior-generation leadership is likely to want to delay the choice until one candidate emerges as clearly head and shoulders above the rest. This may require sufficient time for all of the candidates to be tested in varied positions. However, the parents of the older or leading candidates, who have a head start on experience and seniority in the company, may be more in favor of a faster timetable. In the same way, the members of the junior generation who see themselves as in the lead will emphasize early commitment and experience as critical criteria and may remind the decision makers of the disruptive effects of prolonged competition. Younger or "fringe" juniors may emphasize the value of a rational, objective process, protected from family politics and long enough to ensure that the right choice is ultimately made. Whatever process and timetable are chosen, the "tournament atmosphere" can be disruptive to ongoing business operation and put considerable pressure on the current owners.[12]

Some parents who want to put the company's future in the hands of only one leader simply put off the decision because they are unable to pick one of their offspring over the others. This is a particular problem in enmeshed families, whose members have such close and intense relationships that the parents fear that any act that can be construed as favoritism will shatter family unity. There may, in fact, be a variety of reasons why a parent is not willing to set up real tests of their offspring's capabilities. Not the least may be the founding entrepreneur's own deep-seated resistance to the succession process itself, based on fears of surrendering control of the company and facing one's own mortality. Entrepreneurs tend to be narcissistic personalities who do not find it easy to share the limelight with another, even a son or daughter. This is the theme of the classic biblical story of King Saul and his efforts to destroy David, the young warrior who enjoys such great popularity in the tribe that the king fears David may one day usurp his throne. For some of these same reasons, a founder may avoid making a choice of successor, stretching out the period of ambiguity and heating up the horse race between the candidates.

The process of transition to a Controlling Owner structure does not end with the selection of the new leader. There are several other tasks that must begin before the transition actually takes place, which continue after the new controlling owner is in place. One is to quickly put the successor into roles in the company that will showcase his or her strongest talents and provide an opportunity for quick results—ideally with good financial consequences for the company and any minority shareholders. Skepticism and resistance will begin to fade as soon as the new controlling owner can demonstrate that he or she can grow the business or produce handsome dividends in the future. There are other challenges as well. For example, the talents and performance of the single successor in a Controlling Owner to Controlling Owner transition will inevitably be compared with those of his or her predecessor. The parent must therefore pay special attention to ensuring that the successor's career development builds self-confidence and provides measurable evidence of his or her leadership ability. This is not always easy for the retiring controlling owner, caught in the "King Saul" situation discussed earlier. It takes some sensitivity to honor the senior generation's needs to have its contribution and continuing value validated, while making room for optimism that the new controlling owner will bring fresh opportunities and strengths.

The second task is the assessment of the tools, resources, and experiences that the new controlling owner will need in order to fulfill the leadership role, and providing for the development of the new leader. In a generational transition from one controlling owner to another, much of the mentoring of the successor is necessarily done by the incumbent. The process is thus intensely personal, and the quality of the relationship between parent and offspring becomes critical during the planning process. An in-depth study of successions at twenty family companies in 1988 concluded that companies in which the parent and the successor enjoyed some activity together outside the company were the most effective in carrying out the transfer of power. Whether it was tennis, or cooking, or orchard growing, the shared activity served to lessen the tensions between parent and child that inevitably arise during the planning process.[13]

The final task is the resolution of the family's financial affairs, in line with the choice to transfer ownership control of the business to one individual. For businesses moving toward a Controlling Owner structure, one of the requirements is obviously to establish, in advance, provisions—and cash—for buyouts of dissident shareholders, should a conflict arise that threatens to paralyze the business.

The Transition to a Sibling Partnership

Parents who aspire to a Sibling Partnership in the next generation usually carry the value that family solidarity is just as important as unambiguous management authority. These business owners have a strong concept of what it means to be good parents as well as successful business owners. They wish to see their children working together closely and harmoniously, a band of brothers and sisters preserving family values and carrying the enterprise to new heights. Sometimes that vision is based on optimism about expanded future opportunities for the company and the family; other times it reflects an assessment of the world as a threatening place, in which family members must "circle the wagons" and look out for one another's interests in the spirit of "one for all, all for one."

The dream of a Sibling Partnership, like the single hero model that underlies the Controlling Owner dream, has a rich cultural history, from the ancient stories of Moses and Aaron or Damon and Pythias to the French Revolution, which glorified replacing patriarchal authority with fraternal leadership based on equality.[14] The goal of interdependence requires the partners to subordinate their own ego needs and to truly appreciate and celebrate one another's triumphs. The spirit of this collaboration can be summed up: "Your win is his win; his loss, your loss."[15]

From a management point of view, multiple leadership offers opportunities for synergies from the combined talents and skills of a team, along with assurances of continuity should any one partner be disabled or die. A study of corporate CEOs by Richard Vancil shows that a number of large public companies such as General Motors now concentrate top management responsibility in an office of the chief executive, consisting of several executives.[16] In an era when corporate America has discovered the value of teamwork at every level, and in a generational cohort with so many family businesses currently passing from first- to second-generation control, Sibling Partnerships have become an increasingly attractive option.

The toughest decision for parents who envision a Sibling Partnership in the future is: Are our offspring really capable of collaborating? In the most successful cases, parents make a realistic assessment of whether their children get along well and whether the distribution of skills and talents in the group is such that they will make an effective team. The parents start early to encourage the kind of sharing and collaboration that will be necessary for a sibling system to survive when the children begin working together as adults. However, the dream of a harmonious interdependence of siblings with complementary talents has irresistible appeal for some parents, which overwhelms such a clear-eyed assessment. In these cases, parents wish so profoundly to see this vision fulfilled that they ignore evidence of deep-seated rivalries among their children. Or, as discussed in chapter 1, they may try to fabricate a Sibling Partnership precisely to compensate for the disengaged style that has evolved in the family, and which they find disappointing. The decision to create a Sibling Partnership may, indeed, be a *reactive* choice, in which parents set the offspring up as equal partners precisely in order to prevent the acrimony that is likely to erupt if any one of them is given more power than the others.

Obviously, the choice of a partnership can be destructive to the business if it locks incompatible siblings into harness together, or prevents the most capable next-generation members from assuming leadership and having a decisive voice in business operations. The Sibling Partnership is a hard system to create and to maintain in practice. These partnerships are most likely to succeed when, as in the Lombardi family, the siblings are all capable and well trained, when the talents and special skills of those who work in the business are more or less complementary, and when a career in the company is seen as an option for those whose abilities and ambitions are a good fit with company needs, whereas others can choose not to join the business without loss of status in the family. The partners not only must be willing to subordinate their egos and share the limelight, they also must be extraordinarily flexible and willing to compromise when dead-locks arise over major issues. Finally, of course, they must have a strong commitment to making a consensus-based system work.

When these requirements are satisfied, the mutual knowledge of one another's general attitudes and business philosophy, which come from years of growing up together and working within the family system, can unleash powerful synergies. Deutsch cites the example of a successful tennis doubles team: the partners are "promotively interdependent" because both play at comparable levels and yet each brings some skills—speed, a strong net game, an outstanding backhand—that raise the pair's level of performance.[17]

The early stages of the transition to a Sibling Partnership raise in a greatly intensified form the dilemma between competition and collabora-tion that was introduced in the earlier discussion of selecting a Controlling Owner successor. Some families, in an effort to strengthen bonds between the potential partners, encourage activities in which the siblings can learn together and have time to exchange ideas, such as attending an executive training seminar at a university. The members of the sibling group in the business may be assigned to special projects that test and foster their ability to work as a team; for example, the group may be asked to collectively recruit, interview, and make recommendations on candidates to serve on the board of directors. In all these activities, the juniors are assessed not only on their individual work performance but also on their ability to work within the group and contribute to building consensus.

This is in contrast to the policies in other families, which are more concerned with creating data for the differential evaluation of siblings than they are with fostering a collaborative Sibling Partnership. These families will often create competitive conditions specifically designed to see which siblings rise to the top and take control, as the parentally sanctioned quasi-parent or first among equals. Although this tournament atmosphere does sometimes help the senior generation evaluate the candidates, there are significant costs. Once the junior generation realizes that the seniors want them to compete and their futures are on the line, they are often forced to become completely self-protective in relation to their siblings. Compromise, collaboration, and sharing credit are risky, self-defeating strategies, much to the detriment of the company and the developmental progress of the successors as a group. Also, the idea that truly objective data are created in such a "dog-eat-dog" atmosphere is usually a myth. Opportunities to shine are not really equally distributed. Finally, teamwork and collaboration may be critical skills for success in the next-generation Sibling Partnership, but they are not rewarded in this environment. This may lead to the wrong sibling being identified as the first among equals or even the quasi-parent, which usually results in a breakdown of the system once the parents are no longer around to enforce it.

There are ways that Sibling Partnerships can differentiate without going too far toward destructive competition. Sibling systems consisting of equal partners who are all capable and ambitious will sometimes make concessions to the need to act decisively. This may result in one sibling's representing the business to associates, to bankers, and in the community, and another's being the voice of leadership inside the company. In a multidivisional business, each partner may be in charge of a specific division or profit center. In a functional organization, the siblings may lead separate departments. In preparing for the transition from a Controlling Owner to a Sibling Partnership system, the senior generation must find the middle ground between establishing clear boundary lines, acknowledging each sibling's autonomy in his or her own domain, and muting the competition between divisions or departments.

Even where rivalries do not exist, the siblings can become myopic in focusing on their own fiefdoms and lose sight of common objectives. Sometimes "respect for the other siblings' territory" can become exaggerated into separationist procedures that are detrimental to the company as a whole. Although a division of labor based on the individual skills and interests of the partners is desirable, the group must also stay focused on common objectives. They must coordinate their efforts on certain key functions for the whole company, such as strategy, allocation of capital, and tax planning. Some workable balance must be found between individual expression and the collective interests of the whole organization. This is especially true as the sibling partners begin to reach the Working Together stages in their individual family development, and to prepare the next generation for leadership. In one large retail company in the southern United States, run profitably by two brothers for twenty years, neither brother's children were permitted to work in the sectors of the business managed by their uncle. This was part of the policy to protect the discretion of each brother from intrusion by the other. As the brothers neared retirement, they realized too late that none of the otherwise-competent cousins was prepared to take over as general manager of the entire company.

The partners must make a pact to stick together and strongly resist any efforts by employees or outsiders to play one sibling off against another and divide the group—which frequently happens in sibling-led companies. Just as important, they must work out specific rules for resolving the arguments and breaking the impasses over major decisions that inevitably occur in any business organization. Some of the rules that we have seen attest to the flexibility and ingenuity of families in finding ways to prevent friction among people in close business relationships. One group of partners in Texas, for example, has developed a kind of lottery in which each gets a turn in having his viewpoint prevail when there is a deadlock. The brothers keep track of whose turn it is to prevail with an amulet that is worn around the neck at meetings and functions like "the Force" in *Star Wars*. Once the brother who is wearing it uses the amulet in order to have his view prevail on a major decision, he must pass it to the next brother, who also has the opportunity to use it just once. One reason this ritual seems to work is that it promotes consensus. The brother who wears the amulet wants to reserve "the Force" for a decision that he feels very strongly about, and thus is more willing to compromise with his siblings on issues of lesser importance to him. By the same token, the other brothers know that, when a conflict arises, they will lose out to the brother wearing the amulet—with whom they may vehemently disagree—unless they can reach a compromise.

We have seen in the case of the Lombardis that a partnership with a first among equals can work impressively. Although Paul Jr.'s authority sometimes appears to duplicate his father's, his siblings constantly remind him that his powers are, in fact, far more circumscribed. At the same time, the Lombardis' partnership functions effectively because each of the siblings not only acknowledges the skills and contributions of the others but also trusts the others to perform their roles and carry out their responsibilities capably. The Lombardis are highly competitive at times, but they understand that their rivalries trace back to childhood, and they are able to laugh and joke about them. Humor is one way that brothers and sisters can make a point in a nonthreatening way when a sibling's behavior provokes or offends. A sense of humor about their rivalries may be one of the clearest signs that siblings will be able to manage their tensions in a partnership. The challenge to both seniors and juniors in similar companies is to correctly assess, first, whether such a critical balance and mutual appreciation of talents exists and, second, whether each of the partners has some insights into his or her limitations. Again, this is no easy task.

The Transition to a Cousin Consortium

As companies grow in size and families proliferate in later generations, it becomes more and more difficult to preserve the family influence. The dream of a Cousin Consortium company is a vision of a network or clan of cousins with a common lineage, ancestral symbols, stories, and traditions. The dream becomes the binding force for an extended group of families—like the Rockefellers in the United States, the Rothschilds in Europe, the Mogi family of the Kikkoman Company in Japan—that traces its roots to the founders of the company and their heroic accomplishments. The different family branches and the numerous cousins may not be as intimate as their sibling parents. Only a few of them may be active participants in the business. They may live far apart and come together only for occasional clan meetings. But they provide a far-flung support kinship network whose members can call on one another for help in time of trouble and even, in some cases, for financial assistance.

Cousin Consortiums tend to be associated with families that have enjoyed considerable success in business and accumulated substantial wealth. This is largely because, below a certain threshold of resources, an enterprise cannot continue to provide livelihoods for an expanding number of family members. Interest in the legacy of the business tends to wane as most cousins must seek alternative careers and sources of income. On the other hand, if several branches of a family and numerous cousins still feel strongly about the legacy and wish to retain some connection with the company, the challenges of governing in the next generation become far more complex for those who remain involved. Some family businesses in Europe and Latin America, which have existed for three or four generations, may include as many as 200 cousins who have some equity in the company. In addition, a large number of them may hope to make careers in top management.

In chapters 1 and 6, we have discussed the many dilemmas inherent in the complexity of these Cousin Consortiums. Of the many other challenges that confront Sibling Partnerships as they anticipate a transition to a Cousin Consortium, maintaining a balance of power among the various branches is unquestionably the most critical. One significant determinant of whether such a balance of power can be achieved is the simple numeric distribution of cousins among the various branches. In most extended families, the branches have unequal numbers of offspring, and that is where trouble begins.

Often each sibling partner will divide stock equally among his or her children, because that was how the founder did it when the company moved from a Controlling Owner structure to a Sibling Partnership. Thus the family chooses a Cousin Consortium structure by default, without realizing the full implications of the choice. For example, a successful leather products company in Spain is owned equally by four brothers. Each brother plans to divide his stock equally again and establish a Cousin Consortium in the next generation. This has been one of those well-functioning egalitarian Sibling Partnerships. For thirty years the brothers have been accustomed to having an equal voice in the company's policies and decisions. In considering the ownership structure for the next generation, however, the brothers must wrestle with a different reality. The oldest brother has five children; two work in the company, and three do not. The second brother has only one son, who heads the marketing department. The third brother has four children, two working in the company and two not. And the youngest brother has five children, all of whom are still in school.

It is easy to see how these asymmetries in the next generation must be considered before beginning the transition to a Cousin Consortium. The second brother's son stands to inherit fully one-fourth of the company's stock, whereas his cousins will receive only a fraction of their father's fourth. This has naturally increased the influence of the second brother's son, who is already the odds-on favorite to be the next CEO. Fortunately, this "lead cousin" happens to be a very competent manager who has earned credibility among both family and nonfamily senior managers by quadrupling sales during his tenure as head of marketing. In addition, he has given other family members assurances that he will not abuse his advantageous ownership position. Nevertheless, his cousins privately worry that he might do so.

The fundamental dilemma in designing an ownership structure for the Cousin Consortium is whether to undertake a distribution of stock *per stirpes,* maintaining the quality of branch ownership, or to reallocate shares so that each of the cousins controls an equal amount of stock, maintaining the equality of individual ownership. This is a perfect example of how the world changes between the Sibling Partnership and Cousin Consortium stages. For the siblings, branch and individual equality were the same thing; for the cousins, unless each sibling has exactly the same number of heirs, they are mutually exclusive. Each option poses significant challenges. The resolution of this dilemma is so tricky that, more often than not, the sibling partners take the easy way out—they do not discuss it at all. As a result, everyone anticipates that a *per stirpes* distribution will take place, and the politics of the succession process occur with one eye on the new ownership power balance that will result in the cousin generation.

Although siblings are often very active in protecting the interests of their own children (as discussed in chapter 6), at the same time they usually do everything they can to avoid arguments over which of their children are most deserving and best qualified for leadership positions in the next generation. Evaluating one another's children is probably one of the most sensitive—and potentially explosive—challenges of sibling partners planning a succession. The problem is compounded when many capable cousins are competing for a few top management spots in the company and leadership positions in the ownership group, particularly on the board of directors. Sibling partners sometimes respond with structural gerrymandering that diminishes the need to make hard comparative assessments of the cousin candidates. Cousins may be dispersed to widely separated functions where they do not interact and where comparing their performance is an "apples and oranges" situation. We have described a case in which each offspring could only work in his or her father's division; in contrast, sometimes offspring are allowed to work anywhere but in their parent's domain. A growing number of families go to the extreme to avoid what they consider the inevitable destructive conflict that follows competition: they ban the cousin generation from management roles altogether. All of these solutions may satisfy some family needs, but they almost certainly interfere with the best course of management development for the cousin generation.

Furthermore, this kind of uncoordinated preparation threatens the company's ability to continue as one enterprise. Keeping the cousins apart is no way to build a foundation for a strong, collaborative Cousin Consortium. The solution is not to avoid comparisons at all costs (which responds to the siblings' discomfort more than to the cousins'), but to structure the management development process so that the best solutions for the company and the overall family can be rationally discovered. This requires the seniors to set up forums in which ownership and governance issues are confronted and procedures are worked out to appraise, select, and train successors as evenhandedly as possible. To enhance the fairness of the selection process, many family companies set up assessment committees, which include family members who are known for fairmindedness or who have no offspring involved, outside directors, and trusted senior managers (described in more detail in chapter 8). In fact, some companies, like a large Sibling Partnership in northern Mexico, turn the process over to a committee made up entirely of nonfamily board members and staffed by the senior human resource manager and the nonfamily heads of the operating divisions. In the right situation, where the nonfamily manager has considerable credibility and the family sticks by its noninterference policy, this can be a very rational and successful approach.

The options open to such committees will depend on the parameters determined by the family (ideally in a family council, as will also be discussed in chapter 8) on the desired relationship between the family and the company in the Cousin Consortium. If the family has decided that the protected role of the family members will be only in ownership (that is, through the board), then the committee may be instructed to evaluate the family management candidates in open comparison with the nonfamily talent that the business can recruit. A modified version would reserve the CEO position for a family member, but enforce no special consideration for cousins for other management positions. On the other hand, the family may want to encourage competent family participation throughout the top business management. In that case, the committee must be guided by these family goals—even if there is a cost in objectively assessing the professional abilities of the cousin participants. By custom in Japan's Kikkoman Company, for example, each of the eight branches of the owning family is allowed to designate one and only one family member in each generation to participate in the company (although a parent and one offspring, from different generations, may work in the business at the same time).

Finally, perhaps the biggest challenge for Cousin Consortiums is to keep the dream alive. With each succeeding generation, the family's influence tends to wane, and, unless the ownership tree is severely pruned, the stock will become increasingly fractionated. Cousins who want to use their wealth to pursue other careers and interests may seek to sell their shares, which makes some sort of buyout process and fund essential at this stage. Rather than too many family members knocking at the door seeking management positions, there may be too few—or none at all. The family may be held together by nothing more than their common financial interest, and if the returns on their investment are not better than what they could earn elsewhere, some stockholders may seek opportunities to sell their shares in the family company.

The gradual professionalization of management may contribute to the weakening of the family's identification with the company. The Dorrances of the Campbell Soup Company are examples of third-generation family members who have had difficulty maintaining the family legacy in the company. Although they still control a majority of Campbell's stock, they have never participated in management, and a few of the cousins have talked about selling their stock.[18] By contrast, the traditions of the Ford family remain strong at Ford Motor Company through a few heirs of the founder in every generation who have served in management and board positions.

If the family determines that it wants to keep alive the dream of the family business, then it has to recommit in each generation to put in the required effort. For many companies at the Cousin Consortium stage, this is reflected in periodic clan meetings or retreats at which the elders may tell stories that illuminate the family's values and traditions. For example, the seniors in one Canadian enterprise that has 200 cousins in the fifth generation talk at such events of the family's dogged efforts to succeed—captured in its motto, "Persistence Pays." The retreats feature ritual retelling of core myths about the family and the business: how the founders tried many beer recipes before hitting on one that became a best-seller, and how the family decided to tough out a provincewide labor crisis when other beer makers sold their plants or moved away because of the threat of violence and sabotage. These heroic stories inspire younger family members to carry on the legacy.

The company must also develop a range of opportunities for contributions by those young family members who do not want or are not offered jobs in top management. Participation on company boards of directors, family councils, boards of family foundations—all afford young people opportunities to get experience and remain connected with the family legacy even though they may not be involved in management.

The process of succession is the vehicle that moves the family along from stage to stage on the ownership and family dimensions. It is part voluntary and part irresistible; part planned and part developmental. The core perspective of our model is that succession goes far beyond unplugging the retiring leader and plugging in the new one. Succession is a transitional process along all three dimensions. It involves uncovering and examining the dreams of all the key players for the future, and forming from them a coherent dream for the family business. Then it involves understanding the requirements of whatever future is chosen and doing the necessary work to prepare the system to succeed in that future. The fascination with the succession process in family business is very understandable; it is complex and compelling. Helping it along requires an application of developmental principles of ownership, the family, and the company—a formidable challenge, but one with extraordinary rewards.

NOTES

1. Levinson 1971; Danco 1975; Barnes and Hershon 1976. Handler (1994) has prepared an excellent summary of this literature.

2. Lansberg, forthcoming.

3. The central arguments in the fascinating issue of ownership versus management power in American corporations are outlined in Berle and Means's classic book (1932) and in the counter arguments that have followed (Larner 1966; Levine 1972; Zeitlin 1975; Francis 1980).

4. Daily and Dollinger 1992.

5. Lansberg, forthcoming.

6. Levinson 1978, 91.

7. Dumas 1990.

8. Menchik 1980; Swartz 1996.

9. Danco 1975.

10. Barnes 1988, 10.

11. Johnson 1988, 10.

12. As the data gathering proceeds, in some cases the senior generation may benefit from reopening the question of whether the Controlling Owner form is really workable for the next generation. The parents may believe in one-person governance philosophically, but there may not be one sibling who demonstrates clear superiority over the others as the selection process unfolds. Estate planning advisers may make it clear that, no matter how carefully things are structured, there will be an unacceptably unequal division of assets if one heir is given controlling interest in the company. Or the sibling or cousin group may themselves convey that they would feel more comfortable in a Sibling Partnership or Cousin Consortium, perhaps with a "first among equals." Parents are well advised to stay open to modifying their dream if circumstances warrant—provided the more collaborative goal is not just wishful thinking, and the siblings have demonstrated that they can get along and work together.

13. Lansberg 1985.

14. Hunt 1992.

15. For more on this idea, see Deutsch's discussion of "promotive interdepend-ence" in the resolution of conflict (Deutsch 1977).

16. Vancil 1987.

17. Deutsch 1977, and personal communication.

18. Muson 1995.

PART III

Managing the Developing Family Business

THIS SECTION focuses on ways to guide the family business as it moves along all three developmental dimensions. Our conclusions are based on the "lessons from experience" that we gleaned from working with companies in the field, and on our own and our colleagues' research and writing about family firms. Chapter 8 summarizes the organizational structures and operational plans that we have found the most useful in companies that manage their developmental dynamics successfully. We have been as specific as possible in describing our view of "best practice" in each case, so that family business members can discuss these suggestions and experiment with them without any outside consultation, if they choose. Chapter 9, on the other hand, deals specifically with occasions when the family and the business are considering outside consultation. We have addressed the chapter both to our professional colleagues and to family business leaders who make use of their services. It presents our ideas about how to customize standard consultative practice to make collaboration between consultants and family businesses as successful as possible. It also discusses what family members should expect from a family business specialist.

8

Structures and Plans for Guiding Development

THROUGHOUT THE earlier chapters we have suggested various structures and plans, such as boards, committees, and leadership roles, that can help all three groups—ownership, family, and business—accomplish their immediate tasks and prepare for the future. In this chapter we summarize those suggestions according to the developmental stage of the business.

Each of the three subsystems of the family business can benefit from a coordinating structure, which helps it accomplish its developmental tasks. There are also plans that can guide the work on those tasks. The plans usually are the responsibility of individuals in the "overlap" sectors of the model, who are in two or three of the subsystems at the same time. The easiest way to get an overview of all possible structures and plans is by returning to the three-circle model (figure 8-1).

The Ownership Dimension

As the family business moves through the stages of ownership, the techniques for representing the owners' interests become more complex. In Controlling Owner companies, the voice of ownership is a vocal solo. There is no ambiguity about the controlling owner's right to represent the ownership point of view. That means that the structures of ownership are typically nonexistent or pro forma, such as the board of directors required for incorporation. Even in cases in which the board is taken seriously, as we will advocate below, its role in Controlling Owner companies is to

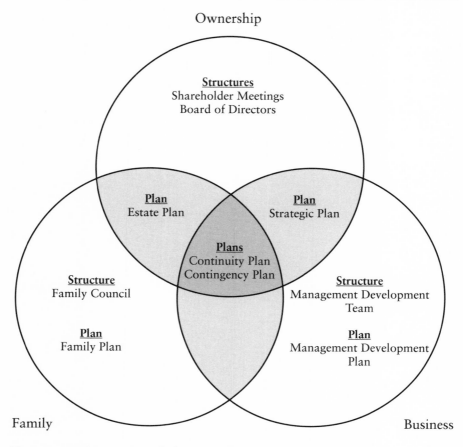

Figure 8-1 ■ *Structures and Plans in the Three-Circle Model*

provide strategic guidance, not to represent the interests of owners. The controlling owner does that for him or herself.

However, as soon as any shares of stock are passed to anyone else, the voice of ownership becomes a choir, and governance structures become more relevant. One of the most pervasive lessons we have learned is that, when the legitimate interests of ownership do not have a forum for expression, issues of control and return on investment will find a way to emerge in either the family or the operating business. When those issues do come to the surface in the "wrong" circle, they are almost always disruptive—and sometimes destructive. It is much better for the members of all three subsystems if owners have officially sanctioned opportunities to talk together and make their opinions known. The structures that provide that opportunity are shareholder meetings and boards of directors or advisers.

Shareholder Meetings

The shareholders' group is made up of all shareholders and only share-holders (not future shareholders, spouses of shareholders, or former share-holders). In pure Controlling Owner firms there is no group; in very large Cousin Consortiums, this group may easily include fifty or one hundred people; and in companies with public participation, there may be many thousands of shareholders. Whatever the number, taken together they own the company.

It is rare for shareholders in any corporation to meet more than once a year. When the shareholder group is very large, particularly if there is significant public participation in ownership, the meetings of family business shareholders are often not much different from any public corporation shareholders' meeting. They are usually informational. Management will explain what the company is doing and present the financial results for the previous year. Most important, the board of directors will be elected.

But in closely held family businesses moving from the Controlling Owner stage to Sibling Partnership and Cousin Consortiums, shareholder meetings can also be particularly important symbolic events. They are an excellent way to perpetuate a strong spirit of ownership, which is essential for keeping later generations psychologically and financially committed to the business. These meetings are an opportunity for family information sharing and relationship maintenance—in some extended families, the only opportunity for maintaining contact. They help family members who are small shareholders feel a valued part of the system. Large shareholders and family owner-managers do well to use these meetings to emphasize the importance of the contribution that all family investors bring to the company. At the same time, shareholder meetings subtly mark the boundary between family owners and other family members. Although this may be embarrassing at first, because distribution of shares is not often discussed in open family forums, clarifying individuals' actual ownership status can clear the air and diffuse potentially disruptive, taboo subjects. For example, siblings who learn at shareholder meetings that others have moved faster to implement tax-saving estate plans and gifting of shares to younger generations may be encouraged to be more proactive in the management of their own holdings. Shareholder meetings are also a good venue for ironing out the wrinkles in the internal market and facilitating the transfer of shares in accordance with family and individual needs.

On the other hand, shareholder meetings are poor vehicles for trying to manage the business or family dynamics. It is a sign that the family has not resolved core trust and delegation issues if the entire shareholder group is called upon to make policy or to debate business strategy. If shareholder meetings become the arena for debates over general family issues (such as resolving old disagreements about a deceased parent's estate plan, or responding to attacks on the family's role or reputation in the community) that are unrelated to stock ownership, it is also an indication that the needs for a *family* forum have not been met. Shareholders have the rights of ownership, without doubt. They deserve to have a procedure whereby their opinions can be heard. However, that procedure needs to include both shareholder meetings, where the broad issues of company vision can be discussed, and election to the board of directors, which should be designed as an effective task group. It is through the board that ownership interests are formed into policy and conveyed to top management. If the CEO is overly exposed to all shareholders, without the buffer of the board, it will almost certainly interfere with the efficient operation of the company.

Of course, in small companies and in many Sibling Partnerships, the shareholder group is very small. In that case, board meetings and shareholder meetings may involve essentially the same people. Still, separating the functions of the two groups is a desirable precedent to set. Some day the shareholder group will certainly expand if the company is a success. It is a good idea to clearly define the board as the policy-making structure for ownership interests from the very beginning.

Boards of Directors and Advisers

One of the real contributions that family business specialists have made to the field over the past decade has been encouraging owning families to create boards of directors. Ward, in particular, has made it a consistent theme in his writing.[1] We share the general endorsement of boards as a widely underutilized resource for family firms. But our model suggests that the importance and specific role of a board will depend on the developmental stage of the system, particularly on the ownership and business dimensions. It is important to consider when boards are particularly helpful, and in what form.[2]

The three fundamental purposes of a board of directors are (1) to consider and represent the owners' interests; (2) to formulate and monitor the long-term strategic agenda of the company; and (3) to be the primary adviser to the chief executive. In companies in which management is strictly professional, the CEO works for the board and is hired and supervised by it. When the CEO is also a key owner, as in most family businesses, the review function takes the form of honest feedback and, in some cases, monitoring the ability of senior management to implement the strategic plan of the company. For example, a board may review annual capital and operating budgets, examine a decision about whether to adopt a new line of business or drop an old one, review long-term contractual arrangements, consider major organizational restructuring, or offer counsel on any decisions that change the direction or emphasis of the business.

Family owner-managers often resist forming a board of directors and using it effectively. They are concerned about loss of autonomy and discretionary control. They worry about confidentiality and privacy. It is true that directors need to be carefully chosen and the rules of participation made explicit. But in fact, because the board serves at the pleasure of the shareholders, a controlling owner should not fear forming a board. Persistently disruptive or oppositional directors can be replaced. Owner-managers who see the board as a resource directly to themselves—as their best advisers, as they have no actual peers—come to rely on their boards and to look forward to their meetings eagerly. Time and time again we have seen the enormous advantage that a well-chosen and well-managed board can offer a family firm—sometimes making the difference between dissolution and survival.

Few Controlling Owner companies create working boards as long as they are in the Start-Up stage of business development. The founder is preoccupied with implementing his or her vision, not reflecting on it. Beyond the legal requirement, sometimes a board is foisted on a founder by otherwise-silent partners. These are basically Controlling Owner companies, but one or a few investors may have been given some minority shareholdings and therefore a seat as directors. The owner-manager's agenda in these cases is usually to minimize input from the board.

In Controlling Owner companies that do create real working boards, the owner typically wants them to focus on two of the three basic board functions. There is no need for the board to protect the interests of ownership. (In fact, although Controlling Owner companies are the most likely to have only family members on the board, they are the stage of ownership development where family directors are the least relevant.) Instead, the board needs to concentrate on advice and objective feedback to the controlling owner. As we discussed in chapter 1, the vulnerability of Controlling Owner businesses is the degree to which they have all their eggs in one basket. Few Start-Up firms can afford to hire top-level skilled professional managers to fill in all the gaps in the controlling owner's experience and talent. The board can help in that regard. A technically oriented CEO can be greatly aided by a strong financial point of view on the board; a company that will have to negotiate treacherous product liability or patent waters can benefit from someone with legal experience.

One of the problems faced by controlling owners who are interested in forming a board of outside directors is providing enough incentive to attract the kind of board members who can be truly helpful. There is rarely much status in sitting on the board of a Controlling Owner company, especially in the Start-Up stage. The company cannot afford to pay large director stipends. Usually the controlling owner is forced to rely on friends and business associates who will serve in response to a personal request. Only a small percentage of controlling owners are lucky enough to have the right friends. Those who do benefit greatly.

As helpful as boards can be in Controlling Owner and Start-Up companies, they become essential as the ownership group moves up to a Sibling Partnership or the company develops into the Expansion/Formalization stage. Now all three of the key board functions are operative. As soon as ownership is dispersed, representation issues arise. The most important dilemma faced by family businesses in forming boards is the optimum balance of family to nonfamily directors, and how the family directors should be chosen. We have learned that resolving these dilemmas most productively means keeping in mind the critical function of the board: to assist management in leading the company effectively and in accordance with the overarching goals of the owners. The board has important work to do, and it can only do that work efficiently if it includes the individuals who must be there, and no others. By the time the firm has reached the growth stage, the board should be made up primarily of outside directors. Family representation is important to convey and monitor compliance with the family's values, but it is not necessary that each twig on the family tree be present in the room. As was true for shareholder meetings, it is an indication of a problem in the level of family trust when owners feel that their interests are protected only if they have their own seat on the board. Two or three family representatives are optimal for a good working board. They are the links to other groups, which have more open membership, such as a family council (described below). A larger number of family members on the board is needed only if those individuals, because of their special expertise or experience, can contribute to the board's strategic, financial, or managerial oversight functions.

The same is true as the firm moves up the ownership developmental dimension to the Sibling Partnership and Cousin Consortium stages. Using the board as a structure for political representation of the various branches and factions in the family is a waste of potentially vital resources, which the business needs in order to succeed competitively. The family's dynamics and values are extremely important, but they should be debated and discussed until consensus is reached in the family council. Then those conclusions can be transmitted to the board through a small number of family directors.

The ideal nonfamily directors are experienced, independent *outsiders*—individuals who have no conflicts of interest with the business or the family. These individuals should have a strong track record of business achievements in areas useful to the company and should have skills that complement those of the owner-manager and each other. Directors may be leaders of companies that are developmentally a step ahead of the family business in terms of performance, size, or organizational complexity. The ideal director has the wisdom derived from having seen many of the dilemmas that senior management currently faces. Familiarity with the company's particular industry is desirable, but by no means indispensable. However, outside directors should be familiar with typical family business issues, such as succession and continuity, career development, and family dynamics. Finally, board members should be empathic with the owner-manager, enthusiastic about the future of the company, and supportive of the values and principles the family stands for.

Contrary to common practice, we generally believe that professional advisers, such as the company's lawyer, accountant, management consultant, or insurance agents should not be members of the board. Although their advice is important, they are also paid for their services, and having them on the board may create needless conflicts of interest. They appropriately work for the CEO, at his or her discretion, and their performance should be periodically reviewed by the CEO and the board. Companies are likely to be better served by maintaining these professionals on a fee-for-service arrangement—and most good professionals would prefer it this way.

Key managers in the company (be they family or not) also do not usually make good board members. This is not to imply that the views and opinions of these individuals are not important, just that their membership on the board is not necessary for their views to be heard and considered. Similarly, all kinds of "reward" appointments, including retired employees, old friends of the owner, and public officials are not appropriate choices for the board unless they are committed to providing significant service and have the ability to do so. Finally, it is also not a good idea to have important customers or suppliers on the board, as this will almost certainly create conflicts of interest.

Across all the ownership stages, the board assists in policy formation, helps the CEO think through complex decisions and develop long-term objectives, and monitors company performance. In the Controlling Owner stage of ownership development and the Start-Up stage of the business, the "input" functions of the board are central. Typical issues include: Is our product or service viable? When, and how, should we diversify? Do we have the right talent to run the operation at the lowest possible cost? How much risk can we take, and what are our sources of capital? What do we need to know in order to survive?

As ownership passes to a Sibling Partnership, the board agenda should respond to the sudden unlinking of the ownership and management dimensions. That is, in most Sibling Partnerships, there will be important family owners whose only connection to the company is through their shareholding, not through executive roles. For the first time the board must reflect a new relationship between owners and managers. This means working out new processes by which ownership interests can be conveyed to the executives and integrated into the company strategy, while at the same time protecting the ability of the owner-managers to run the company without undue interference. Boards have to make the final decisions on dividends, debt, and executive salaries. Whether the Sibling Partnership is a quasi-parent, first-among-equals, or democratic team type, these issues are potentially divisive. Without the buffering participation of a good-quality board, dominated (or at least strongly influenced) by competent outsiders, the pressure on the family relationships as the Sibling Partnership confronts these potentially divisive issues can easily become dysfunctional.

In addition, if the company is simultaneously moving into the Expansion/Formalization stage of business development, the board's technical expertise will be called upon to deal with many organizational design and product development questions. What are our targets for growth, and what volume of new products and services is required to sustain it? What organizational structure will work most efficiently now that we have established our place in the market? What do we need to know about new arenas where our growth strategy is leading us, such as new markets, internationalization, or diversification? How can we help the CEO decentralize and integrate a wider circle of senior professional management?

If there was a board in the Controlling Owner stage, the transition to a Sibling Partnership company and the Expansion/Formalization business stage will probably require a different mix of skills on the board. The appropriateness of each board member for the next phase should be reviewed by the controlling shareholders and the CEO. In most cases, a new stage means that some turnover of directors is called for. For that reason, we strongly advocate giving board members fixed terms from the beginning, with the expectation that only extraordinarily versatile individuals will be asked to stay on for a second or third term. This is also why an excess of family members can restrict the adaptability of the board, leaving too few slots to cover the changing requirements of the working board members.

Finally, the Cousin Consortium requires a further evolution in the nature of the board. The family representation system will have to be another step more formalized, with good rules to ensure equity and access across branches. Even more than in the Sibling Partnership, this is the time to consider entry requirements for family directors that go beyond election by a sector of the family. Many Cousin Consortium boards adopt criteria for family members who want to be directors: business experience, or participation in an educational experience about the company, or a minimum commitment of days per quarter to the business. It is important for the family to realize that family directors are not just watchdogs; they must contribute to the board's role of assisting these complex enterprises. Therefore representatives should be chosen according to their fit with the demands of the job, not just their seniority or status in the family.

Also, in Sibling Partnerships and even more so in Cousin Consortiums, management succession is an ongoing concern of the board. One of the board's key tasks is to define and implement its role in selecting candidates, overseeing their developmental progress, and making decisions about successors. This is an important collaborative effort of the board and the family council. Like most of these delicate policies, it is better hammered out before it is needed, when the issues can be dealt with as objective policy instead of ad hominem evaluations.

Finally, in the Cousin Consortium stage, there is likely to be more than one operating company and, as a result, more than one board of directors. Each of the operating companies in the larger enterprise needs a board with the particular mix of expertise that will most benefit that company in its industry and locale. Many Cousin Consortiums find it useful to have the boards of the operating companies dominated by outside directors, and to create a holding company whose shares represent the combined family equity. The holding company is the sole or primary shareholder of each of the operating companies, and the holding company board has a higher percentage of family members. This kind of system allows the family to spread the risk of new or less profitable ventures across the broad extended family, and also to share in the profitability of the established companies or divisions, without requiring complicated distributions of shares from a number of different entities.

Whether through one board or many, the family ownership group in the Cousin Consortium stage must continually address questions of finance and investment: What is the overall financial condition of the business? What return does shareholding offer to the owners and their families? How does it compare with alternative investments the family could make? What will the family's liquidity needs be in the future, particularly now that the number of nonemployed family members is growing so rapidly with each generation? Does our current dividend policy strike an optimal balance between the needs of the family and the business?

At whatever stage the ownership group decides to create a strong working board, it should be prepared to invest the effort necessary to do a thoughtful job. In our experience, this is a process that often takes months or even years to complete. It should not be rushed. Finding good candidates requires energizing the family's and the company's broadest network. There are many steps in the process, including identifying prospective candidates, investigating their backgrounds and experience, inviting them to meet the key managers or other board members, and a reasonable "getting to know you" period with the CEO and other key family executives. Aside from the issues of expertise and good fit, which we have already advocated, there should be an interpersonal rapport between family managers and prospective board members. It requires real insight and commitment for the owner-managers to anticipate their needs and initiate the formation of the board early enough, so that it is ready, functioning, and able to help the company through its developmental transitions.

As a final note, some companies prefer to form a board of advisers with outside directors, leaving the board of directors as a pro forma group of family members. A board of directors is a legal requirement of all corporations, and has specific powers. A board of advisers does not have the same legal status. However, both have the kind of authority that emanates from the experience and the wisdom of the advisers. This distinction of names is not nearly as important as the way a group is used. The advantages of a board of directors are: (1) they fulfill incorporation requirements (because you need a board of directors anyway, having only one functioning group reduces expensive duplication); (2) it may be easier to recruit the most highly talented members as directors instead of advisers; and (3) the board of directors may command more attention or respect in the environment (with banks, regulatory boards, political interests). The advantages of a board of advisers are: (1) some owner-managers may feel more comfortable with this structure; (2) some companies that are distribution dealers or franchisees may find that the parent firm is more accepting of this structure; and (3) the risk of director liability is reduced considerably.[3] Correspondingly, liability insurance premiums, which can be prohibitively expensive for a medium-sized family company, may be significantly diminished. Good legal advice can help a family choose the most appropriate structure.

Plans in the Ownership Dimension

In family businesses that form an active board of directors, part of its responsibility is to participate in the development of plans to guide the operation of the business. The board's role—and for that matter, the level of planning done in any of the sectors—will depend to a great extent on the developmental stage of the business and the style of its central leaders. In businesses with the most fully operational boards and most comprehensive reliance on planning, the board is involved in creating at least four important plans. First, in conjunction with the company's senior managers, the board formulates the *strategic plan*. This is standard business practice; Ward and others have written extensively about the strategic planning process in family companies.[4] In some companies, the board takes the lead in forming the strategic plan; in others, the board responds to strategic plans as developed by management and oversees their updating and implementation. In this process, as in all the planning done by the board, the board is guided by the overall direction of the family ownership group, formulated by the family council and conveyed to the board through joint members and the senior family/ownership leaders.

The board also works with senior management to create the *management development team,* which will be discussed in more detail below. In this case, the board usually takes more of a review role, relying on management to identify human resource needs and to evaluate potential inside candidates (both family and nonfamily) for each key position.

Finally, the board has an important role to play in the creation of two plans that draw input from structures in all three circles: the *continuity plan* and the *contingency plan.* Assuring continuity of leadership is one of the most important responsibilities of the board of directors, so the board will take a central part in the formulation and implementation of the continuity plan, or the overall blueprint for the succession process. The board's role follows the family's determination of the ownership structure that will be put in place for the next generation and its decisions about the rules and criteria that will govern family candidates for leadership. Then the board contributes its perspective on the realities of the medium- and long-term needs of the business.

The contingency plan is the part of the planning process that is most often neglected. Because families are reluctant to think about unexpected crises and because senior management is most often preoccupied with current operations, the board has the best chance of thinking clearly about the unthinkable. What will happen if key business leaders are suddenly unable to perform their functions? How prepared are we for unexpected, dramatic events in the economy, our facilities, or the ownership group? There is no need for overly specific scenarios; most crisis situations require a response that can be only partly anticipated. But the board can make sure that the system is prepared to take the legal and operational steps necessary to stabilize itself in the face of an emergency, and that the family and management have fallback options when the expected course of development is interrupted.

The Family Dimension

All families are organizational systems, but business-owning families in particular must give serious attention to their organizational needs. Throughout earlier chapters we have suggested that families need to communicate openly and talk about their future. Families need to discuss the separation of home and work obligations in the Young Business Family stage; they need to discuss the opportunities and rules for children who want to join the business in the Entering the Business stage; they need to monitor each other's opinions and reactions continuously in the Working Together stage; and they need to work out the objectives and timing of the events of Passing the Baton. Most families rely on celebrations, social events and holidays, and the telephone to work on these critical tasks—not the best ways to attempt such purposeful talking. According to this model, a better place is the family council.

The Family Council

A family council is a group who periodically come together to discuss issues arising from their family's involvement with a business. The fundamental purpose of a family council is to provide a forum in which family members can articulate their values, needs, and expectations vis-à-vis the company and develop policies that safeguard the long-term interests of the family.

There are at least four important reasons to set up a family council:

1. A family council provides an ideal setting for educating family members about the rights and responsibilities that come with business ownership and management.

2. A family council helps clarify the boundary between the family and the company, and gives family members who are not in the business or ownership circles a chance to be heard. This reduces the likelihood that family concerns will be inappropriately imported into business decisions and vice versa.

3. Experience shows that business families frequently rely on informal family gatherings, such as birthdays, Christmas, or Thanksgiving, to discuss pressing family business matters, usually with frustrating results. A family council provides an appropriate setting in which relatives can discuss their concerns without cluttering family events with business discussions.

4. A family council can provide the structure to help the family create a shared vision and a "code of understanding"—a family plan.

As in the ownership dimension, the usefulness and ideal composition of a family council depends on the developmental stage of the business family. At the beginning of the Young Business Family stage, the couple may belong to the family councils of their parents if they are in a successor generation, but they probably do not need a council of their own. The important conversations for their new marriage enterprise involve just the two of them. They may find it useful to set aside special times and places to talk about the core dilemmas of being a business couple—as they would for a family council—but having a special structure would be overkill.

However, this changes as their children approach adulthood and their nuclear family moves into the Entering the Business stage. Not only is there a whole set of issues to discuss regarding the younger generation's careers, the parents also are changing roles in the business environment and in relation to their own aging parents. At this time, in fact, if the parental generation has been using a family council of its own, the extended family is actually operating as a network of interlinked subfamilies, each with its own particular agenda and an interest in the common agenda of the family as a whole. Family councils can be tremendously helpful in providing opportunities for all these interlocking interests and goals to find their appropriate expression and for conflicts to be explored. Finally, in our view, family councils are extremely valuable in all Working Together and Passing the Baton business families, and in all Sibling Partnerships and Cousin Consortiums.

The composition of a family council typically changes as the family moves though different stages and planes. Because the family council is a structure of the family, not of the business or shareholders, it needs to honor the fact that all family members have a stake in issues of family identity—as current or future employees, current or future owners, or simply members of a family whose life is continuously affected by what happens in the business. The core membership of the family council is typically the owner-manager, his or her spouse, and their grown children and their spouses. In second- or third-generation companies, the council may also include siblings, cousins, and other relatives.

Some families choose to involve in-laws in the council as permanent members, whereas others prefer to include them only in certain council discussions. There are advantages and disadvantages to including in-laws in the family council. Having in-laws in the council may foster a spirit of openness in the family and encourage the in-laws to exert their influence directly, thus diminishing the likelihood that dysfunctional family triangles will develop. Many of the issues discussed in a family council, especially in the Entering the Business, Working Together, and Passing the Baton stages, have implications for the youngest generation. It is awkward to try to discuss those issues with one parent in the room and the other excluded. On the other hand, in some families the inclusion of in-laws as permanent members of the council may dampen the willingness of the blood relatives to confront their conflicts, rivalries, and disagreements. In larger families, the inclusion of in-laws may also greatly increase the size of the group, decreasing its effectiveness.

Treating the family in a formal, organizational way can feel a little strange at first in families that have a natural style that is very informal. One thing that helps a family council to work effectively is creating an agenda for each meeting and following it. In the first few meetings, the agenda helps people understand the purpose of the council; as the family council becomes an essential family routine over time, the agenda is necessary to enforce priorities and prevent council meetings from being overwhelmed with too many issues.

Some topics are recurring themes in most family councils at all stages. These issues concern the core values of the family and the family's relationship with the business: What are the central values of our family? How do we express these values? What do we do if someone feels a core value is being violated? How can these values be preserved and taught to future generations in the business and in the family? Sometimes these issues are best discussed in the abstract, with family members sharing their individual philosophies about the family and the business. Often, however, the underlying principles emerge as the family council discusses very specific dilemmas requiring decisions. For example, the family council may develop over time a set of positions on such issues as succession and continuity, liquidity, diversification, family perks, new venture support for family members, and the hiring and firing of relatives.

Many topics rise and fall in importance as the family moves through the family developmental dimension. In Young Business Family and Entering the Business families, the council will spend most of its time on educational and socialization issues for the younger generation, as well as resolving lingering ownership and career questions with parents and siblings. This may involve questions such as: Is the reward system in the business working to attract the right mix of family members into management and leadership roles? Will we encourage our children to work in the business? What qualifications should be set for family members who want to enter the business? How can we prepare future generations for the responsibilities of ownership?

Working Together family councils can play a critical role in resolving conflicts in the expanding family network. There is a seemingly endless list of policy questions to be resolved in the Working Together stage: How do the family's core values relate to the strategy and operation of the business? Should we develop a code of conduct for family members in the business? How will family members in the business relate to nonfamily managers and employees? How do we deal with the fact that members of the family may not benefit equally from the business? How do we help needy family members? What are the rights, privileges, responsibilities, and roles of family shareholders who do not work in the company? In addition to these business-related policies, the Working Together family council may be the key contact point for siblings and cousins who do not see each other in their family lives but want to stay connected to the family identity. In fact, one of the most important agenda items for family councils at this stage is organizing shared activities, rituals, vacations, and celebrations, in response to the question: How can we have fun together?

For the Passing the Baton family, the council is often dominated by issues around succession. The family council will be the starting point for the discussion of criteria for family leadership of the business in the future, beginning with a reconsideration of the basic question: Do we want to retain this business under family control in the next generation? What concentration of family ownership or family control is needed to ensure the vitality of the business? How do we respond if family members or branches want to liquidate their ownership? The family council is also a good place for the senior generation to discuss retirement and estate plans with the rest of the family. This will often lead to a more general discussion of the family's future: How can we convey our family history to future generations? What do we see as our family's role and reputation in our community? Do we have philanthropic or community service goals? How do we implement them?

Not all family council meetings have to be deadly serious and portentous. In fact, a good mix of important business and enjoyable "schmoozing" is important in keeping enthusiasm for the meetings high. One midwestern Working Together family council set aside a quarter of each meeting for a year to plan the house they were building on a mountain near Aspen, Colorado. Those conversations were not only lighthearted and full of teasing, they also were an opportunity for important issues to be worked on in a more sociable way, such as readying the senior generation for retirement, identifying the different priorities of the three generations who were present, and reassuring the seniors of their continuing emotional leadership in the eyes of all the family members. In a similar vein, many family councils work on conflict resolution better when it is attached to issues like the scheduling and cleanup rules for the family's beach house, instead of to competition for the inside track in an approaching business succession.

Many families interested in forming a family council are unsure how to go about it. There are some useful guidelines, which we have found lead to more successful family councils. In our experience, the councils that work best:

1. *Set up a timetable for meetings and stick to it.* Regular, predictable meeting dates, set well in advance, are the key to good attendance. The frequency of meetings should be determined by the number and urgency of the issues and the developmental stage of the family. Working Together and Passing the Baton family councils meet more frequently. Typically, family councils meet on a quarterly basis during the first year or two, as a backlog of issues and procedures is taken care of. They may meet two to four times per year after that.

2. *Pay attention to the process.* The development of a family council is an important event in the life of the family. Often, families are not used to getting together for discussions of this nature. It is therefore important to create a supportive atmosphere in which family members feel comfortable expressing their views and free to explore issues about which they

may not be very knowledgeable. The leaders should try to establish a "dumb questions are okay" norm from the start. It is also important to nurture the social and emotional ties among council members, some of whom may not have much contact on a day-to-day basis. Meetings can start or end with some time for family members to "catch up" with each other on what is going on in their lives. For instance, sharing information about new babies, job transitions, and health difficulties may serve to bring the group closer as a family.

3. *Establish clear leadership responsibilities in the group.* In general, one of the family leaders, probably in the senior generation at the start, should head the family council. However, it often clarifies the separation between the business and the family, and creates a more open atmosphere, if the company's leader is not the council chair.

4. *Run the meetings in a comfortable, but not excessively informal, style.* Meetings are best scheduled away from the business and the home, so that interruptions are kept to a minimum. Agendas are established with input from all council members and circulated in advance. It often works best to prioritize the agenda so that the easier issues are discussed first. It is important that family members learn to work together in the council and feel comfortable with each other before they address issues that are more emotionally loaded, such as estate planning. In a family council, "success breeds success"; if early meetings go well and the family finds them useful, there is a better chance that subsequent discussions about more difficult issues will also go well. It is especially important for the meeting leader or facilitator to make sure all members have adequate "air time" and follow some agreed-upon rules for respecting each other's rights to speak.

5. *Be flexible and creative in using different subgroup configurations.* It may be helpful to explore some issues in subgroups first (for instance, women and men, blood family and in-laws, first and second generation) and then to bring the subgroups together to learn about each other's experiences and perceptions. This discussion method often serves to heighten awareness of how people's feelings and perceptions are influenced by the positions they occupy in the family and in the business.

6. *Consider using professional facilitation, at least in the beginning.* Outside facilitators can help structure the meeting and encourage more

open communication. Facilitators can also support the educational function of the council by sharing management, family, and family business concepts. After the first several meetings or the first year, the council and the facilitator should reassess the professional's continuing role. Some families reach a point where they are ready to proceed on their own, whereas other family councils always use a facilitator. A third option is for the facilitator to rejoin the council periodically—for example, at one annual meeting—to help the group review its progress and work through issues that it could not resolve itself during the year.

The Family Plan

In serving its primary function as a forum for family discussion, the family council may be aided by organizing its tasks into an integrated family plan. Like the strategic plan on the business side, the family plan sets a family's sights on the future. To do so, however, we usually advocate beginning with a look back at the family's past. The four parts of most family plans include a family history, a vision of the future, a family mission statement, and an action plan.

Family History. Creating a family history from records and stories is one of the best early projects for a family council. It works beautifully to highlight the unique family identity and to remind senior family members of the legacy they represent. It is also the best tool for integrating and educating new family members and young offspring. Archival records, pictures, and artifacts are useful, as are videotaped interviews with senior members of the family.

Vision of the Future. The formal part of the family plan begins with "organized imagining." This process asks family members to step back from current roles and pressures and to look ahead five or ten years. It is useful for family members, individually and collectively, to dream about, and then discuss both how they would want the family and the business to look in the future, in the best of situations, and how they think they will look, given the realities facing the family and the firm.

Family Mission Statement. The family mission statement details the family's philosophy, including why the family is committed to maintaining the business. It includes the consensus values on ethics, community role, personal development, philanthropy, what makes up "the good life," and any other themes that have guided the family's vision of the future. In large families, once the family council has drafted a mission statement, it should be shared and discussed with other family members who are not members of the council.

Action Plan. The final step in the family plan is deciding on actions to bring it to life. This includes concrete steps to establish programs and activities for family members, including training (education about the business, leadership training, conflict resolution courses, seminars on family business issues), developing a code of conduct for the family, establishing processes for resolving disputes, consultation to resolve conflicts and to improve communication or counseling for family members who are experiencing more serious problems, and organized fun (vacations and outings). The most important action, and the one that facilitates all the others, is the family's investment in a vigorous, ongoing family council.

The Business Dimension

There is no need for us to argue that good management structures contribute to the successful operation of the business. However, it has often surprised us in our work with family firms to observe how reactively company management approaches the business's growth and continuity needs. As we discussed in chapter 3, business development requires anticipation of the human service needs of the next stage. The recruitment, selection, and training process that ensures the company's readiness to thrive in each successive stage takes months and years of preparation. It is often the case, however, that no structure in the firm is responsible for the necessary planning and training. If the business is large enough to have a full-service human resource department, it will probably be focused on entry selection, wages and salaries for employees, and benefits management. (And family firms often fall behind their publicly owned counterparts in their investment in human resource management.) Some companies are sophisticated enough to do a fine job of performance appraisal and feedback for their managers. Still, even those firms tend to ignore the strategic and anticipatory components of management development.

In family firms, when there is an interest in continuing to involve family members in senior management, it is even more essential to think developmentally about human resources needs. The complexity of special career pathing for family members, and the impact on all employees of differentiating between family and nonfamily managers' career expectations and ladders, requires focused attention. It is foolish to leave family readiness to meet the company's future leadership needs to chance.

Management development is a continuous process in any company, at least after the Start-Up stage. The career management of family members becomes particularly important in the Working Together and Passing the Baton stages of family development. In our experience, if the process is well handled in the Working Together stage, it can have a tremendously beneficial impact on the stress that both the family and the business experience as the Passing the Baton transition comes closer. If the criteria for evaluation of next-generation leaders are laid down as those potential successors are beginning their careers in the company, and a process is initiated to create a portfolio of experience and evaluations for each candidate, the relative importance of objectivity (over politics) will be enhanced. By the time selections have to be made, the choices may appear almost obvious to all stakeholders.

Forming a Management Development Team

This more proactive, developmental approach to management development requires a structure with the responsibility to guide it. We have seen family companies have great success with a management development team. This group is given the very specific responsibility for anticipating and planning the development of talent for key managerial roles in the future, with special attention to family members.

Besides the owner-manager, we recommend that the management development team be composed of the company's top human resources person and the top managers from some or all of the key divisions in the company. Sometimes one or more of the nonfamily directors from the board plays a role on the team, especially at the time it is considering a CEO succession. It should be kept a small working group (four to six members), with other managers invited to attend as needed to discuss particular issues. Unless a family successor has already been identified and is already in one of these key managerial positions, we recommend that potential candidates not be part of the group, because a key function of the plan is to discuss the career path and performance that would lead up to the choice of a successor. Of course, top management will already be meeting periodically with the successor in other contexts to talk about his or her progress in the company.

Regarding family managers, the team has to respond to an interesting dialectic. On one hand, it needs to be guided by the policies and goals of the owning family, as articulated by the family council. Decisions about the roles that must be reserved for family members, the access that members of different family branches should have to executive jobs, the criteria for company leadership that are most important to family members, and the timing of transitions are all legitimate decisions for the family to make. Even the basic family choice of ownership configuration (Controlling Owner, Sibling Partnership, or Cousin Consortium) will have an impact on the team's projections about available talent.

On the other hand, if the team is to do its work well, it cannot be captured by family politics. The team's yardstick must be its view of what the *business* needs. Once the family has made clear its basic philosophy, the team needs to be insulated from family members' attempts to influence the application of those rules to specific individuals. Owners should not lobby for certain high-visibility jobs to go to their offspring. Family senior managers should not be permitted to promote their own children unilaterally, especially if that action violates the agreed-upon review process. As soon as the team's assessments are controlled by a senior manager, the credibility of the whole process is destroyed.

Some families, especially in the Cousin Consortium stage, are so determined to protect the integrity of the process that they turn control of career management decisions for family managers completely over to a team from which family members are excluded. More commonly, the team is given a mandate to make objective decisions, but it serves as an advisory group to the senior owner-manager (either chair or CEO). Although the management development team provides critical data for the plan and serves as a sounding board for development ideas and policy, the owner-manager has the final word. When the actions of the family, the board, and the management development team are not in alignment, it is up to him or her to engage in a process of reconsideration, negotiation, and information sharing that leads to compromise and consensus. This issue is a perfect example of how each of the three circles has a role to play—distinct but interrelated—in creating the unique character of the business.

The Management Development Plan

The main purpose of the management development team is to create and implement a management development plan for the company. This plan is the team's projection of the company's executive staffing needs in the future, and the career paths of key family and nonfamily managers to fill those needs. In most cases, the investment of time in generating and updating the plan is not great; the payoff is.

The management development team begins its work by addressing a few core questions about the company: (1) Given our strategy for the future, in what areas do we expect to grow and shrink, how fast, and what will our management staffing needs be? How can we maintain flexibility to meet unexpected high- or low-growth conditions? (2) What business developmental stage are we currently in, and when do we expect that to change? (3) How is our environment changing, and what impact does that have on the career path, including experiences inside and outside the company, that would provide a successor with the greatest likelihood of success? (4) How can we integrate our performance appraisal and career management efforts?

As the team confronts these questions, preferably in consultation with the board of directors, it begins the specific work of creating a management development map of the company. This involves identifying the critical jobs in the company and the current ages and career aspirations of all the managers in those jobs. It then projects a timetable of when positions will or should be vacant in the future, and who will be in line to fill them. Most important, the plan specifies the learning path that identified management candidates, including next-generation family members, will follow to become prepared for roles in the forthcoming stages of the business. This includes the necessary experiences, the procedure for evaluating performance, and contingency plans.

Some owner-managers are skeptical of this planning process, because they feel that situations are likely to change and make the plan obsolete. This is a straw man. It is expected that important contingencies will change—some of them, over and over again. Key employees will leave unexpectedly. New opportunities, requiring an infusion of management talent, will suddenly appear. Performance appraisals will determine that some candidates exceed expectations and that others are disappointments.

It is important for leaders to realize that responding to these inevitable contingencies is much easier if a modifiable plan exists. In fact, improving the firm's ability to make the best strategic move when an unexpected change occurs in the management ranks is one of the most powerful reasons for proactively developing a plan in the first place.

In formulating the management development plan, the management team must balance the special need to develop family heirs in the business with the equally important business requirement to encourage and protect teamwork among all employees. On one hand, the plan must provide career paths for the potential successors, which permit hard-nosed assessment of their individual capabilities and ensure the readiness of those who are selected for senior executive roles. At the same time, the plan should support the essential nonfamily managers, providing clarity about their career options and highest attainable positions. The team can handle these dilemmas effectively only if the family and ownership leaders have been clear and consistent in their guiding policies. For example, the family council, the board, and the senior family managers must agree on whether or not nonfamily managers will be moved out of positions to permit successors-in-training to receive essential experience. Or, in the most common dilemma, the team needs guidance on whether or not it should demand of its nonfamily supervisors the same kind of objective assessment of and feedback on family member subordinates that they provide for nonfamily subordinates. Once the team has been given clear policies on these kinds of issues, it should then communicate this policy to all the managers and employees who are affected.

Finally, once a family firm begins this process, it will find that discussions about staffing, management development, and succession will raise other questions about its business strategy and operations. It is almost certain that the company's strategic plan will come under scrutiny, because projections of growth, mergers, acquisitions, and divestitures, new ventures, and geographic expansion form an essential foundation for projecting management needs. The human resource management system in general will also find itself in the spotlight, as the team looks at performance appraisal systems, compensation, benefit options, and supervision. It is tempting to feel that the development plan has to wait until all these core systems are revamped, but that is usually not necessary. Key managers might decide to meet more often to discuss these interrelated issues but should not stall on outlining the management development plan.

Coordinating Structures and Plans

We have described the structure that manages the family firm's development along each of the three dimensions in our model. It is useful to think of these structures according to the subsystem they serve, but in the end all of them will fail if there is inadequate coordination among them. There are three primary coordinating processes: integration through the oversight of the senior leader, integration through overlapping membership, and integration through structured direct communication among the groups. The senior family member–owner–manager, who sits in the center sector of the three-circle model, can be an effective coordinator. In some ways this is an extension of the hub-and-spokes communication model that is employed by so many founders in their new business ventures. In its most extreme form, one individual is the chair of the board, the CEO, and the chair of the family council. It can work, if the leader is a good communicator, is fair and objective in conveying information, and has the time to do the coordinating work. That is a lot to ask of any leader.

Along with or as an alternative to such an individual system, overlapping membership can spread the responsibility for coordination across a few more individuals. It is generally a good idea for the family directors on the board to be seen as officially responsible for representing the family council at board meetings, and in turn for keeping the council informed about the relevant portions of the board's activities. If these ambassadors do their job well, it relieves much of the pressure for excessive family representation on the board. Cross membership with the senior management group is a little more complicated. As we have already argued, senior managers in general are not good choices for the board; it is the CEO's job to be the link between those two groups. If there are family members in executive roles, they can be the communication link between the business and the family council. However, they need to be careful not to use the family council as a way to circumvent the management authority and communication channels, or to encourage family members to get inappropriately involved in business affairs. Once again, the senior leader is in the best position to monitor that information flow, keeping it adequate but not disruptive. If there are no family members in management, then the family council may ask for a company liaison to be chosen. This individual may make periodic reports to the council, or be available to join a council meeting when there is a particular piece of information that the council is interested in receiving (such as a description of a new company or facility that the business has acquired, or an explanation of a new public relations campaign).

Finally, in conjunction with overlapping membership, other regular information-sharing routines can be established. The family council can work out with the board of directors what kind of financial information will be shared in both directions. The board also needs to know how it will be made aware of family policy decisions that affect its own deliberations, on such issues as succession and retirement timetables, criteria for employment of family members, and the general philosophy regarding reinvestment versus dispersal of profits. It is better to work out policies about intergroup communication and then honor them religiously, instead of relying on ad hoc information sharing "when something comes up that the other group should know." The latter arrangement leaves too much to the discretion of the linking individuals. It can be too tempting to either emphasize or neglect specific issues because encouraging or discouraging open communication on that topic serves the agenda of the communicator. Information is power, in family businesses as anywhere else. Good coordination and communication are what can make each of these structures provide the maximum service to the business and to the family.

NOTES

1. Ward 1988b, 1991.

2. See also Danco and Jonovic 1981; Whisler 1988; Jonovic 1989; and Schwartz and Barnes 1991.

3. In recent years there has been a dramatic proliferation of lawsuits against directors. In an effort to reduce their exposure, many companies have turned their boards of directors into boards of advisers. However, the advantage may be illusory. Courts in some states have begun to treat the two entities alike with respect to the legal duties and responsibilities of members, the driving assumption being "If you behave like a board of directors, you *are* one."

4. Ward 1988a; Harris, Martinez, and Ward 1994.

5. Swartz, 1996.

9

Consulting with Family Businesses

SOME FAMILY BUSINESSES appear to sail along from year to year without ever getting caught in stormy weather. But most family business leaders have times when it feels as if they are continuously jumping from one difficult challenge to the next. Those moments often occur when the system is moving from one stage to another on one of the developmental dimensions, such as when ownership is distributed from a sole owner to a sibling group, or when a business undergoes a significant restructuring or a growth spurt. Even more demanding, however, are the occasional times when developmental changes occur in two or three arenas at the same time. These complicated shifts in the business and in the roles of key individuals in all three circles can confront family leaders with an overwhelming set of tasks—particularly because they are added to the ongoing responsibilities for managing the routine activities of the company. At these times, many owner-managers feel the need to call on outside experts for help.

The business world is filled with skilled professionals: general management consultants, financial planners, attorneys, bankers and trust officers, insurance brokers, and technical specialists for all aspects of operations. Similarly, when family conflict becomes unmanageable, or when some family members are experiencing stress reactions and other behavioral problems, there are many psychologists and family therapists who can help. Often, however, these professionals are put in a difficult position by their family business clients because the problems they are asked to help resolve cut across many fields and require concepts and experience outside their own. An estate planner may be at a loss to explain why a business-owning client resists or continuously delays acting on a beautifully crafted plan for the distribution of shares to her children. A business consultant is asked to design a change management project, then is told that no restructuring plan that unbalances the size of two sibling-headed divisions can be implemented, regardless of the business rationale. A family therapist tries to help a family understand why the entrepreneurial father seems increasingly depressed and disabled by alcohol just as his business is suddenly growing dramatically. Or an attorney watches a family drift toward destruction and costly litigation over what appears to be a very small dispute about the transfer of a few shares between cousins. These situations can be frustrating for both the adviser and the family; the specialist nature of our professional training does not serve us well in responding to these multifaceted developmental problems of family business.

In this chapter, we lay out some basic principles of intervention that we have found useful in applying our three-dimensional model to consulting work with family firms. We hope that our professional colleagues who do not specialize in family business will get some new ideas about the special challenges of advising these clients, and that family business owners will gain some understanding about what to expect from and how to use professional assistance.

In some ways, good consultation is good consultation, whether to a small venture or to a multinational corporation.[1] But we have found that the special demands of consultation with family companies arise from two characteristics of these businesses. The first is the complexity of the system. Most large businesses are complex, but family companies have their own special, complicated natures as a result of the interconnection of family and business concerns, the stresses of change and growth caused by so many overlapping life cycles, and the strategic and financial consequences of private ownership.[2] Consulting with family companies challenges the consultant's ability to hold the complex system in his or her mind, and to generate an understanding of the problems in current operations which takes into account the dynamics of all three dimensions. Each step in the consultation process must be considered in light of the ownership structure, the business situation, and the family dynamics.

Second, consultation often occurs in an emotional atmosphere of crisis. There may be resistance to addressing problems and hiring consultants in any business, but in family firms that reluctance is often exaggerated. Many family businesses stay closely held because they value their privacy very highly, and family members realize that focusing on business problems can probably not be done without illuminating personal and family issues as well. As a result, families often turn to outsiders only when they experience distress that has become truly unmanageable. When consultants do enter, emotions are usually running very high because developmental or externally caused stressors have been denied for too long. This means that consultants often have to help families repair damaged relationships and learn different ways of communicating before they can effectively plan actions to resolve business dilemmas. Fortunately, most families are extremely resilient and eager to restore harmony; family love and loyalty often outweigh hurts and rivalries. But sometimes relations are damaged irreparably—families may have lost the capacity to sit together and solve their business-related problems, or they may never have had that capacity to begin with. Either way, even to begin to assess the possibilities for progress, the consultant must have the experience and skill to work in highly charged emotional atmospheres.

These two characteristics affect the client's search for help, as well as the potential adviser's response. In hiring a family business consultant, the leaders of the client family often test their own strong norms of family and business privacy and self-sufficiency. Having decided to bring in an outsider, the real question becomes: How much will we have to change, and what will it cost (in emotional as well as financial terms)? Clients often must wrestle with their own temptation either to turn over all authority to the consultant, with a broad mandate to "fix it," or to turn over as little authority as possible, in the hopes that the consultation will not require radical change. After all, from the client's perspective there is a lot at stake. Resolution of conflicts and problems means more than achieving job satisfaction or increasing organizational efficiency. The future financial status of the entire family may be on the line. This heightened sense of vulnerability adds to the natural uncertainty about what will happen in the course of a consultation. Good consultants will discuss what they hope to see happen and will generate joint goals with the client, but no competent consultant can say definitively in advance what changes each family member will experience as a result of the work.

Consultants take different stances in doing their work, and the new client is in the difficult position of choosing an approach without knowing for sure if that choice is appropriate.[3] Some consultants operate as individual specialists, who provide focused consultation on a presumably well-bounded problem. These technical specialists may not have extensive experience consulting to family businesses. Typical problems addressed in this manner include tax and estate planning, business strategy, or, for counseling specialists, such family issues as marital discord among copreneurs. Many of the advisers who are already working with the company, such as the company attorney or tax accountant, would fit this category, although they do not normally call their work with the client "consultation," nor call themselves family business consultants. This can be the fastest and most efficient way to resolve a specific problem, and the total cost of the consultation may be low. But the disadvantages are that individual specialists may make assumptions in their approach that are incorrect in the family business environment. An intervention in one subsystem may have unintended consequences in another, which the consultant is not prepared to address. For example, the tax planner may not be aware that the strategy he is proposing contains assumptions that offend offspring who are not involved in the business. The planner may never meet these people, and the family will have to deal with the impact of the proposal after the technical design is done and the consultant is gone. This situation is actually less common than a decade ago. Increasingly, financial planners, attorneys, specialist business consultants, and family therapists are becoming aware that family businesses are uniquely complex clients, and they are training themselves and seeking collaborators to work in those settings.

A second type of consultant, which includes most of the individuals who actually call themselves family business consultants, are really individual generalists. These are professionals who, working alone, are trained to tackle most of the problematic issues that arise in family companies—succession planning, role conflicts, and communication in relationships. These consultants may have been educated in management, but they also have had training in group or family dynamics; or they may be clinically trained, with extensive practical experience in business settings. The consultant forms relationships with most if not all family members, as well as key nonfamily managers, and thus can understand the system in depth. The scope of the work is by definition comprehensive. Even so, the generalist may encounter some specialized issues that he or she is not specifically trained to handle; the trade-off here is for broad competence at the expense of advanced technical knowledge in some areas. Generalist family business consultants need to be realistic about their ability to "do it all"; competent generalists are comfortable with the boundaries on their expertise and clear about telling clients in the contracting phase that certain issues are beyond their scope of expertise.

This may lead to a need for the third type of consultant—actually a consulting team made up of a number of individuals with different specialties.[4] Team members are likely to assume specialized roles in the assessment and implementation phases of a consultation; that is, the family specialist will interview family members and work with the family council, and the business strategist will talk with business leaders and work on organizational changes. However, teams are very expensive. Consulting teams must also be extremely well managed to be effective. In addition, most family firms will already have professionals from many disciplines who do the company's work. It is unlikely that the owner-managers are interested in changing all of the advisers at one time. And the advisers already in place are often wary of outside consultants. Care needs to be taken to create and manage a good working relationship between these "standing" advisers and the project consultants, so that their efforts are complementary and not competitive.

Just as boards of directors and family councils have different purposes and structures depending on the developmental stages of ownership and the family, the most effective type of consultant may be related to the developmental stage of the business. Controlling Owner companies in the Start-Up stage would likely be overwhelmed by a team of external consultants engaged in a comprehensive, long-term project. They are most likely to use individual specialists, fully under the direction of the owner-manager and performing specific services at low cost. Sibling Partnerships and Cousin Consortiums, on the other hand, will almost always benefit from a family business generalist or a team skilled in group dynamics and family development, as well as in the business issues. Businesses in the Expansion/Formalization stage have the greatest need for expertise on business structure, finance, and organizational behavior. Those in the Maturity stage have the same needs, with a special emphasis on strategy. Whatever the most pressing problem that leads to the initiation of consultation work, they all require that the consultant consider the current developmental stage of the company, and the way structures, roles, and relationships are likely to change over time along each of the three developmental dimensions.

Phases of Consultation

Most consultation projects, whether with family companies or other businesses, include four phases:

1. *Contracting.* In which the client and the consultant first determine if they can forge a productive working relationship and, if so, agree on its terms.

2. *Assessment.* In which the consultant takes an in-depth look at the client system and reaches a preliminary understanding of the explicit and underlying issues.

3. *Planned Change/Implementation.* In which the client and consultant work together toward the client's change goals.

4. *Evaluation and Maintenance.* In which client and consultant evaluate the effectiveness of the project and try to find ways to institutionalize its benefits.

The boundaries between phases are often indistinct or, in fact, nonexistent. In some cases, two of these steps may be done as one. For example, in family businesses, assessment and implementation may be intertwined if the purpose of the consultation is the evaluation of successor candidates, or an estate plan review. Also, it is not uncommon to see a consultation project stop before reaching the fourth phase. Much depends on the clients' experience of the financial and emotional cost of the consultation, on the quality of the working relationship between the client and the consultant, on the client's capacity to do the work without outside help, and on a variety of unforeseen events (such as a death or business disruption) that can derail, redefine, or postpone a project.

In working with family businesses, the activities in all four phases will be shaped in important ways by the points of entry in each of the three circles, and by the developmental stage of each of the three subsystems. We have found the model a very useful guide in planning our interventions with a broad range of family companies.

Contracting

The overall task of the first phase is to determine the fit between the approach of the consultant and the client's needs, and to develop a clear and explicit, but flexible agreement about the work. Although it is easy to dismiss or rush through the contracting phase as just a formality, it is often the most important phase of the consultation process. Both consultants and clients can learn an enormous amount about the other in this stage, if they pay attention to details; it is at this phase that solid working relationships are forged.

It is also at this point that the fees are discussed. Typically, family business clients who do not regularly use outside consultants are surprised by the cost of engaging in such a project. Most consultants charge by the day, but some will charge by the hour; attorneys and other technical consultants may charge by the fraction of the hour. It is reasonable for the potential client to expect the consultant to estimate the number of days that will be required for at least the first few phases of the work, and a ballpark figure for the total cost. Observing how the client handles the discussion of cost, which part of the system will be paying for the work and who controls the budget for that area, and the family's willingness to commit money to the project provides the consultant with valuable information about the meaning of money in the family and the differing individual levels of investment in the consultation.

One consequence of the economics of professional life is that larger companies and those in later stages of development are more likely to have the resources to hire family business specialists. They also are more used to working with outside consultants. Although their problems may be just as disruptive, Start-Up companies and families in the Young Business Family and Entering the Business stages are often unable to bring in specialists, and have to rely on their financial and legal advisers. That puts special pressure on those advisers to be comfortable with at least the basics of a three-dimensional perspective.

The contracting phase typically consists of an initial phone contact and then one or more face-to-face meetings between the consultants and client leaders. Consultants always need to note which of the three circles makes the first contact; it is an important indicator of the dynamics among ownership, the family, and management in the overall system. It also provides the first data on the stages of business development. Was contact made by a controlling owner? If the company is a Sibling Partnership, which sibling made the contact—the leader in a first-among-equals system, the brother or sister who always gets assigned clerical tasks, or a nonfamily manager? How old are the key players, and which generation in a Working Together or Passing the Baton family seems to be the impetus for the work? Many times, the consultant will recommend to the clients that they discuss the project, and its costs, with other family and business members. This helps to deal with the politics of the consultants being seen as the hired gun of one individual, and diminishes the chance that other individuals will be surprised by the fees or the scope of the project once the consultant starts to work.

Most clients initiate the contracting discussions by identifying a relatively one-dimensional problem: a conflict between two siblings at work, for example, or an owner-manager who will not yield control to a chosen successor. To reasonably predict the work required, the consultant has the challenge of gathering enough information in a brief time to apply an initial developmental analysis to the client's identified problem in all three sectors—ownership, family, and business. For example, if an owner-manager asks for help in assessing the capabilities of her daughter as a potential successor, even a preliminary assessment will require data on such questions as: Is this a Controlling Owner company, or is the mother only one of a group of sibling or cousin owners? Is the family in the Entering the Business stage, so that the issue is whether or not to invest in developing the daughter, or is it a Passing the Baton situation, in which a decision and a transition are imminent? What stage of development is the business expecting for the near future, and what demands will that make on the daughter's generation of leadership? The consultant will also want to identify what structures and plans are currently in place, and the range and quality of the internal and external advisers. This preliminary assessment is necessary for the consultant to provide an accurate representation to the client of what the work is likely to entail.

Clients may be confused by this inquiry and resist it. It happens before there is a good relationship of trust. It violates family privacy norms. The consultant may be asking the very questions that the family members cannot ask each other: Who are the actual owners of the firm? How many members of the younger generation are interested in becoming executives in the company? Has the family already decided to keep the firm family controlled for another generation? It is one of the most demanding tests of the consultant's skill to broaden the perspective of the clients while still being responsive enough to their initial request for help.

It is always a dilemma for the consultant to decide how much to invest in a potential client before a contract is reached. On one hand, the more information the consultant can get, the more specifically the proposed work can be defined, and the more likely he or she is to get the contract. On the other hand, the consultant is often not getting paid for this work. This is especially true when the client is acting like a good consumer, and getting information and proposals from a number of consultants before picking one. Seasoned consultants can use their experience to shorten the precontract information gathering and make good guesses about what is going on in the family. But ultimately each opportunity requires the consultant to make a decision about how much to invest in selling the client, and when to say, "From this point on, if we continue, the project has started, and the clock is on."

The contracting phase, then, requires that the consultant learn enough about the potential client to say accurately and honestly whether he or she can help and what form that help might take. One key part of this task is the clarification of who is the client. Given the inherent interconnectedness of the three dimensions, this requires a balance between a view of the entire system as the ultimate client, and a circle-by-circle assessment of the key issues and players. The consultant must be clear on the source of the presenting problem: the family, the business, the ownership system, or an individual. Sometimes there is a very immediate, specific, and limited need for an intervention at one point—such as a financial analysis of the tax consequences of some shareholder or business change, or an immediate response to a family or business crisis. But beyond a crisis response or a technical analysis, it is almost always counterproductive to take on one sector of the system as the client without consideration of the others. Responding to an organizational restructuring request, for example, without taking into account the consequences for the family of shifts in the authority and span of control of family managers is not likely to succeed. Neither is any estate or succession planning effort that focuses exclusively on tax laws, business needs, or "objective" assessment of managerial talent. In fact, beginning to educate the family client precisely about the interdependent nature of the parts of the family business system—and determining their openness to a comprehensive approach—is one of the most important tasks of this contracting phase.

This conceptual approach needs to be tempered with cold reality, however. In many family business systems, the different circles are controlled by different individuals or groups, with quite different perspectives and agendas. Pre-engaging all of them into an authorization of the work is often not possible. This means that the consultant has to determine whether the degree of buy-in is sufficient to begin the work, with the intention of using the consultation process to educate and engage all of the key stakeholders as the work unfolds. Sometimes this works, most often when the authorizing leaders are senior enough or savvy enough to facilitate the access of the consultant to all parts of the system. Sometimes it is more difficult. For example, if a cousin group that is now in control of the business leadership roles asks for help in organizing themselves into an effective team, it may not be initially possible to gain authorization from the parental sibling group that still controls the ownership and family circles. In fact, there may be dynamics in that old Sibling Partnership that will systematically undermine and sabotage the consultant's efforts to create a viable Cousin Consortium—and the cousins themselves may be powerless to overcome them. The consultant needs to assess (even with minimal information) whether the project is viable. It may be that the most that can be accomplished is to help members of the system to whom the consultant does have access (in this case, the cousins) to learn as much as possible about the dynamics that shape and constrain their current situation.

The final dimension of the contracting task is the more intangible aspect: individuals can discuss the consultant's experience with a particular kind of problem and can agree on goals for the project, but what about the relationship? How can they tell if the other is trustworthy and if the working relationship will be successful? Our experience is that every interaction between client and consultant, from the very first phone call, is a good indication of the kind of interaction that will follow in the consultation. If the interaction is respectful, honest, and frank, the relationship is likely to develop on the same paths. If, however, the consultant experiences the client as manipulative, or the client experiences the consultant as overselling, then that experience is likely to persist in the relationship, even after specific questions and issues have been addressed. In the initial stages, it is up to each party to take its experience seriously and to determine if it is comfortable with proceeding.

Assessment

The tasks of this phase are to develop an in-depth understanding of the family business system and to craft a set of recommended approaches for accomplishing the desired changes. On the surface, the assessment phase appears to be a straightforward diagnostic, even a scientific, procedure. The consultant asks questions, the clients give answers, and the consultant in the end tells the client what the answers mean and suggests the appropriate "treatment." If this medical model works at all in organizational consulting, it doesn't work very often in family businesses. The powerful dynamics from all three subsystems, which have brought the system to its current developmental and operational condition, are not likely to be open to this kind of surgical cure by an outsider. Again, with the rare exception of very limited technical assistance, which does not require change in the underlying system dynamics, successful assessment requires careful understanding and management of the integrated family business system.

In assessment, the critical process is the development of a working alliance between consultant and client. In other words, the consultant engages the client as an active partner, not just a source, in the data gathering. The consultant continually refines the questions as more information is gathered about the client system and proposes options based on experience with similar situations. The client is guided to an increasingly clearer understanding of the dynamics that have created the current dilemmas, and the pathways to change. The specifics of this relationship, once again, will depend on the stages of family and ownership development. In Controlling Owner companies, for example, the focus is on the one-to-one alliance between the owner-manager and the consultant. However, it may be the most important aspect of the intervention for the consultant to make it clear that she or he expects to get input from a wide range of stakeholders, and to overcome the controlling owner's resistance. In this way, the process of the consultation also contributes to its content, helping prepare the controlling owner for a more collaborative approach in anticipation of the Sibling Partnership or the Working Together family toward which the system is moving.

Actually, the assessment of the client system should be well advanced by the time the contracting phase is completed. Now the consultant typically visits the family and the business and interviews key players. The number of interviews in each system will depend on the scope of the project, the access that the consultant was initially able to negotiate, the nature of the problem, and the developmental stage of the family and business. If the consultation is beginning with a focus on financial and ownership issues regarding a proposed buyout or restructuring, there may be a need for extensive review of records, estate plans, and financial performance data, as well as interviews with some key nonfamily executives. If the most pressing issues concern sibling conflict in a Sibling Partnership or among branches of a Cousin Consortium, the consultant may have conversations with a sample of family members to explore family history and dynamics in more depth. The consultant will typically interview all members of the nuclear family, as well as key nonfamily managers. The data gathering expands from there, as needed.

Even when access to one of the circles is easier, the consultant must be careful not to get trapped in one part of the system. One of the ways some family business consultants fail is by relying exclusively on the traditional data-gathering techniques of their parent discipline. Thus family psychologists, working on a problem that has been defined as a communication block between sibling managers, may rely only on interviews with family members and gather inadequate information on the business performance of various divisions or the views of key nonfamily managers. As a result, they cannot see that the problem reflects new constraints as a formerly profitable business unit moves from Expansion/Formalization to Maturity. Similarly, a consultant trained as a financial adviser may shortchange the gathering of family histories or investigation of interpersonal dynamics, even if the adviser understands conceptually the interdependence of all three circles. There are not many unconditional lessons from experience in this field, but one of them, which the three-dimensional model has taught us, is that certain data—a family history, a genogram, a three-circle "map," basic balance sheet and performance data, and ownership distribution—should be a part of the assessment phase in nearly every family business consultation.

Determining the developmental stage of each subsystem usually requires gathering some data about the past as well as the present. For example, has ownership always been concentrated in one family leader's hands? Has this family historically assumed that *all* the children would work in the company? Have women held important roles in the company in past generations? Have certain key events marked the transitions from one stage to another? Each piece of data suggests what additional information is needed to get the full picture. For example, if the first data on business performance show flattening profitability, the consultant might want to go further in looking at the rate of new product introduction, the amount of investment in research and development, and the overall competitive structure of the industry to see if the company is transitioning to Maturity. In another case, if siblings express concerns about the recent erratic or depressed behavior of the forty-four-year-old CEO, the consultant might ask more about other typical midlife transition issues, such as the departure of children from the family home or recent parental death.

At this point in the consultation process, if the consultant has been working closely with one or several members of the client family, it is common to ask for an extended meeting in order to summarize the assessment and recommendations for the client and to explore reactions to the plan. In this discussion, the consultant is not only looking for the client's agreement to proceed into the action phase, although this is part of his or her agenda; he or she is also gauging the family's reaction to the assessment. The family's reaction, positive or negative, will give the consultant several key pieces of information: How well have I captured the real dynamics of this family? How much do individuals in the family differ in their own explanations of the problem? How comfortable are family members in talking about their different perspectives? How hard or easy is it for the family to agree to proceed?

In many consultations, especially when the consultant's ability to engage in a truly collaborative process has been restricted from the beginning, this feedback session is as far as the work goes. Sometimes the consultant is faced with a real dilemma in preparing the feedback. Telling the family what it wants to hear may reduce anxiety but misrepresent the consultant's true analysis. Confronting them with the conclusions that the consultant has reached may be more challenging than the family can tolerate and may lead to the end of the project. In this way, the family business consultant is like any other professional adviser, who must find a way to be both effective and honest. The special demands on a family business consultant arise from the two characteristics discussed earlier— that the systems are so complex, psychologically and structurally; and that the work often occurs in a highly charged emotional atmosphere.

Planned Change/Implementation

The task of the implementation phase is to initiate a set of activities that will result in some desired changes in the family business system. The general principles of planned change apply in family companies: if change is to be successful, the system (members of the business or the family) must experience a need to change, key leaders must support the change, the change agent must establish clear timelines and open communication, and appropriate resources must be allocated to support change efforts.[5] In a family company, the interconnections among all the elements of the system, the varying stages of development in each dimension, and the resulting need to support the change effort in all three dimensions—family, business, and ownership—make the consultant's job a juggling act.

For example, the sixty-four-year-old founder of Kramer Construction announced his intention to sell his business to his son (aged thirty-eighty) three years ago, but in that period has not initiated any changes in his or his son's scope of responsibilities. Mr. Kramer Sr. is currently the controlling owner. He and his wife have decided to transfer the bulk of the stock to their son, with only a token number of nonvoting shares going to their daughter. At the suggestion of the family's longtime friend and attorney, who had been given responsibility for drafting the estate plan and buyout agreement, Mr. and Mrs. Kramer, their son, daughter-in-law, and daughter have met with a consultant to work out the succession plan and timetable. The consultant carried out a careful assessment of the company: a mature general residential construction firm, with plans (still not implemented) for a new venture in energy-efficient reconstruction for small businesses. The consultant then helped design a retirement plan for the father and an intensive training regime for the son. The family expected the focus of this effort to be in the workplace—specifically, on the work relationship between father and son. But the mother, daughter-in-law, and sister are all important players in this change process. In fact, the consultant knows that Mrs. Kramer Sr. feels that her son is rushing her husband out the door. Mrs. Kramer Jr. feels that her father-in-law is disrespectful of her husband and does not intend to retire at all. Meanwhile, the sister feels that she is being treated unfairly in her parents' estate, but she is not comfortable telling them so directly.

As a result of this assessment, the consultant had to gradually help the family see that establishing a family council and working on more open and honest communication might be just as important as the legal details of the estate plan. The consultant has kept the attorney involved as a colleague throughout the process. The attorney fully supports reconsideration and discussion of the estate plan to address the sister's concern about receiving fair treatment. The consultant has also initiated a strategy project involving the father and son and the board of directors, to implement the new venture idea and guide the company's transition to a combination of mature and start-up business units.

Work on multiple fronts, then, is the norm in family business consultations. Change efforts must account for the structural and emotional complexity of the family business system, and people's natural tendencies to fall back on familiar patterns in times of uncertainty. This resistance to change is powerful, but, in most cases, family members are not aware of the dynamic. In this case, for example, Mrs. Kramer Sr. may not want her husband pushed out of the business too fast, because she is uneasy about the change in their relationship that his presence at home will bring.

"He's used to being in control, and I'm used to running our home my way," she told the consultant. "After forty years of marriage, I don't want him looking over my shoulder telling me how to make a tuna fish sandwich." The daughter-in-law may worry that her husband will respond to his new work role by becoming more like his father, which would threaten their very different Young Business Family marriage. The daughter has always had a family role as parental protector and her father's favorite. She has a fine professional career and no interest in the business, but she doesn't want to lose her "specialness" as her brother and father become more intimately connected at work. Thus each family member, though consciously supporting the change effort, may unconsciously resist or even undermine it. The consultant must anticipate this and design a change process that helps individuals identify and overcome their own tendencies to resort to familiar behaviors.

A consultant might not stay as intensively involved with such a family throughout the whole implementation phase, unless the family or business continued to experience significant difficulty with the transition. In many cases, he or she would be most active in the first year, setting up a family council and helping the council, the board, and the owner-manager establish milestones for change. However, over the course of the second year, as the family learns to use the structures and take over the process, the consultant's role would shift from active change agent to adviser-on-call.

This is a common evolution in the implementation phase, with the exception that many families want the consultant to continue to facilitate the family council. Some families feel that outside facilitation helps keep the council process on track, and they feel more comfortable in the council with the reassurance that the consultant is there to keep difficult discussions from accelerating downhill.

Evaluation and Maintenance

Family business consulting is a very intense, personal relationship. Sometimes, if the work has gone well over an extended period of time, it is difficult for either the consultant or the client to initiate the end of the project and the consultant's departure. In the best of cases, the consultant will structure the conclusion of the work with a final stage, involving evaluation and ongoing support. The client and the consultant are both concerned with evaluating the success of the consultation project: Was the intervention helpful? Is the family or the business functioning better? Helping the family evaluate the change process can not only provide good data to the consultant and to the client, it can raise the family's appreciation of how much has been accomplished and build their confidence about carrying on without the consultant in the future. Although there are no concrete measures of success in family business interventions, a consultant can invite clients to consider their experience in several areas:

- Are family and business members clearer about their roles?

- Do individuals in the system understand and respect each other more?

- Does the family communicate better?

- Are individuals more satisfied with decision-making processes?

- Do individuals feel more secure about the future?

- Are all three circles better prepared to move to the next stage, with key issues resolved, and ready to address new challenges?

In addition to evaluation, usually both client and consultant recognize the important support that consultants can offer as the family business deals with the emotional and logistical implications of even a successful change effort. No change is without cost, and often individuals and organizations need time to adjust to new leadership, different communication patterns, and new norms for behavior. Some consultants prefer to arrange for a periodic "checkup," such as a special family council meeting every year to track some critical milestones and reflect on the year's progress. Other consultants prefer to make a clean break and refer the family and the business to other resources, as required, for follow-up work. One interesting way to stay in contact but move the relationship to new terms is for the consultant to involve the family in projects with other new clients who are at the same stage as the "graduated" family. Such family-to-family consultation can be a remarkable benefit to both sides and can provide additional rich learning for the consultant.

Interventions across Developmental Stages

Family businesses—*all* family businesses, regardless of how well they are managed and how strong the family—face significant challenges in the course of their life cycles. There are critical moments in many of the stages when assistance from an outside professional can be particularly helpful. In addition to our general lessons from experience consulting to family firms, we have reached some conclusions about the particular usefulness and risks of consultation in certain developmental stages.

Proactive Advising in the Early Developmental Stages

In the early stages of all three dimensions, control is consolidated in one person or a very small group. Especially in the Controlling Owner and Start-Up stages of ownership and business, the owner-manager may use consultation as a way to get peer responses. After all, there isn't anyone within the organization who shares the leader's role in these stages. An experienced consultant can act as a mentor, supportive challenger, and behind-the-scenes guide who can help build the owner-manager's confidence without undermining his or her public authority. These are the family firms that are least likely to have effective nonfamily boards of directors. It may be very complicated for the young owner-manager in the second or later generation to rely frequently on a parent for counsel. Even if the intergenerational relationship is a very good one, the process of taking charge and changing direction, even slightly, benefits from an outside voice of feedback and support. For all these reasons, a one-on-one relationship with a valued adviser can be a great resource for the leadership of the firm at this stage.

For these kinds of consultative relationships, special care needs to be taken in the selection of the consultant. Unless the company has an unusual need for special skills—such as advice on raising funds in risky high-tech ventures, or a particular technical problem inherited by the owner-manager from the previous generation—a generalist is most likely to have the broad perspective useful at this stage. Most important is individual rapport between the owner-manager and the consultant. If an atmosphere of trust and friendliness does not develop quickly in the interaction, the owner-manager should probably try out some other candidates.

Family Interaction Advising

In Sibling Partnerships, and when families have reached the Working Together stage, the problems that emerge are most often related to family dynamics and the relationships among relatives. These challenges lead to the most intricate consultative interventions. In the first case, the dynamics are mostly intragenerational, among brothers and sisters. In the second case, the issues are intergenerational, between parents and offspring. In addition, the sibling and parenting dilemmas frequently stimulate issues in the marital relationships that add to the mix. All of these family dynamics affect business operations at critical times, often in the growth stage. These may be the situations in which a family is least likely to bring in a consultant but in which good-quality help can make the greatest difference.

It is most important in these cases to use a consultant who is knowledgeable and sophisticated about family dynamics. Many sibling partners or mid-career owner-managers at these times feel a strong tendency to rely on traditional legal and financial advice, because the family issues may appear so threatening and painful. However, although there are clearly important decisions to be made about technical issues such as estate planning, ownership rights, growth capital, and buy-sell agreements, they are unlikely to be effectively implemented if family conflict blocks the way. In the Sibling Partnership–Working Together–Expansion/Formalization business, for example, a family business consultant can help the owners simultaneously address the business opportunities for diversification and expansion, and the family's plans for preparing the next generation from all family branches for leadership.

These are also the stages of business development at which a family council and an effective board become essential for most firms. A consultant with organizational and facilitation expertise can be a real help in getting a council started. Many consultants are equipped to help design a board and even locate potential candidates for membership. (However, as we stated in chapter 8, the consultant does not usually belong as a member of the board. He or she is a professional adviser, like the legal and financial advisers.)

One of the most important determinants of successful consultation at these stages is the ability to gain the trust of all the key players, and to convey a style of evenhandedness and reliability. It is not easy for a consultant to work equally effectively with two or three generations, both genders, and a wide range of personality styles, but that is often what is required. Flexibility and clear respect for all the different stakeholders in the system are critical criteria for a consultant who has the best chance to steer the family and the firm through these complex waters.

Finally, this is one of those times when consultants need to have a firm grip on the limits of their expertise. Some families need more than awareness of family dynamics; they need family therapy. Defining the boundary between family-focused family business consulting and family therapy is one of the most difficult, and important, challenges of this work. When the family begins to trust a consultant who is sensitive to interpersonal issues and has a working familiarity with psychological concepts, it can be very seductive for the consultant. The family expresses its needs and asks for help. The consultant can experience a strong impulse to push deeply into therapy-like interventions, exploring powerful intrapersonal and interpersonal dynamics. But there are many dangers on that path. Besides the obvious issue of appropriate training and credentials, the consultant rarely has the access or time to act as a therapist for the family. Recommending appropriate therapy (some families respond better to the word "counseling") or actually making a referral are better options. In some cases, the family may accept a referral with the explicit agreement that there will be some follow-up sharing of information between the therapist and the consultant. This is in keeping with the multidisciplinary team concept, although it must be handled carefully in light of the special nature of therapy and the ethical and professional constraints on therapists. With or without follow-up, the fact that the consultant has helped the family identify problems in the family system and respond to them will alter the nature of the consultation, in many cases making it possible to move ahead on other consultation tasks.

Advising the Complex System

In Cousin Consortium companies, the consultative process comes closest to the style you would find in nonfamily companies. In the Cousin Consortium–Working Together–Mature firm, for example, the greatest needs will be for policies and procedures that are not person-specific. These organizations rely less on individual entrepreneurship and more on organizational design and smooth operations for their success. In these cases, there is probably a need for a variety of consultants. Many technical specialties can contribute to the vitality of the firm: human resources planning, marketing, mergers and acquisitions, public financing, government relations, and international operations, for example. The functional divisions may be so well defined that for some technical projects the advisers do not *need* to interact, or even be aware of each other (although we feel it almost always enhances the quality of service). In other cases, a team approach is much better, especially when there is still a reliance on one operating company, run by a highly integrated management group. Businesses of this size are also more likely to be able to afford a consulting team approach.

This greater reliance on separate technical experts does not mean that the family business generalist is irrelevant, however. This is still family enterprise. Cousins are usually a little more distanced from the intensity of family dynamics that siblings and parents and children experience, but they are not strangers. In fact, helping families understand how Cousin Consortiums differ from Sibling Partnerships may be the most important task in helping the firm reach stable owner-manager relationships for the future. The issues of management opportunity and development for family members, succession planning, corporate values and culture, dividends, and buy-sell arrangements require sensitive handling of extended family dynamics. Focusing on the Cousin Consortium family's vision for the future, and translating that vision into policies, is often facilitated by good consultation.

The key consideration for selecting advisers in these stages is the mix of skills, and the management of the team effort. It may be hard for owners who have been well served by a family attorney or tax accountant for many years to think about bringing in a specialist on applications to family firms. However, as companies move through growth and maturity, they need the advantage of up-to-date knowledge and varied experience more than ever. In addition, families who have worked together smoothly through the Entering and Working Together phases, and through Controlling Owner and Sibling Partnership forms, may find themselves suddenly unable to understand or manage the interaction among cousins. Bringing in a family business specialist, even for a short-term educationally focused session, may be enough to keep the diaspora of the cousin group invested and committed to the family legacy. Family leaders need to find ways to make use of new specialists without jeopardizing the security and ease that come from working with the loyal close advisory group.

Succession

Succession planning is undoubtedly the issue that most often motivates family business owners to work with consultants. It has been talked about and written about so much, both in the professional and the popular press, that the stigma against calling for help seems to have diminished. In fact, many firms who are experiencing problems in family conflict or problematic leadership may label their trouble as "succession planning" in order to feel free enough to seek assistance. This makes the contract-setting phase especially important in the Passing the Baton stage, since these are the most likely cases for a poor self-diagnosis by the client.

Contingency planning for unexpected successions is an issue in every type of family business, but there are also some special considerations about consultation on planned succession in the Passing the Baton combinations. First, in our experience, successful intervention with family firms in the Passing the Baton stage requires broadening the focus from "leader substitution." The best writing in the field takes the position that continuity is a process, not an event. It follows that the best advisers help manage the process, not just schedule the event. It is for that reason that we have focused our attention on the *continuity* process—the preparation in all three circles for a transition to an envisioned future—more than on the succession task.

Second, there are succession specialists, but clients need to be careful. The fact that the market finds it easiest to ask for this service means that it is also the easiest specialty for service providers to declare and compete in. Not all succession advisers are real family business consultants. The key task in finding a consultant to help with continuity planning is to look for broad understanding of all three circles.

This chapter returns us to the lessons from our own experiences with family firms, which followed from the Kurt Lewin quote: the theory informs the practice, and practical experience shapes the theory. Family businesses are unbelievably complex enterprises; their success represents a remarkable accomplishment by their members. The nature of good-quality service to these systems is inherently interdisciplinary. It is important for professionals not to be trapped in the law of the hammer: "When your only tool is a hammer, every problem looks like a nail." Clients deserve a network of available advisers who have pooled their experiences and learned from them, building theories that allow each of them to make educated guesses that go beyond their personal experience. In that way, the instruments in our toolboxes can become as varied and complex as the family firms we serve.

NOTES

1. Block 1981; Schein 1988; Bellman 1990.
2. Lane 1989; McCollom 1990; Vago 1995.
3. Hilburt-Davis and Senturia 1995.
4. Swartz 1989.
5. Beckhard 1969; Zaltman and Duncan 1976; Kanter 1983; Bennis, Benne, and Chin 1985.

Conclusion

Lessons from the Life Cycles

THE BASIC GOALS of family business owners are not mysterious. They want their businesses to be profitable, providing a good standard of living for their family members and appreciating in value. They want their families to be comfortable, loving, and nurturing for all their members, and especially, most often, for their children. But many business families fear that the accomplishment of one of those goals will come at the expense of the other. They worry that family conflict, indifference, or unprofessionalism will undermine the ability of the business to thrive, undoing financial support for the family and eroding the legacy and the institution they have worked so hard to build. At the same time, they are concerned that the pressure of the business will create tension, jealousy, or resentments that will split apart the family and make the company's success meaningless. Underneath all the problems that family businesses bring to professionals—succession planning, intergenerational and intragenerational relationships, governance dilemmas, dividends and inheritance, career planning—there is a common desire. They want the business and the family to be mutually supportive, not destructive, capitalizing on each other's strengths, and more successful together than either could be alone.

The model that we have presented in this book is the best tool that we have been able to develop over the past twenty years to help families satisfy that desire. In some ways it is complicated, with as many contingencies and variations as there are family business stories. Without being uselessly reductionist, there is no way to create a very simple model to describe such maddeningly complex and elegant organizations. But in another way the model is based on a few simple ideas about systems and development. We can summarize its core concepts as two lessons from experience, which we have learned from the family businesses themselves—those that are approaching their goals, as well as others that are struggling to triumph over their fears.

Lesson 1: Treat the Business Like a Business, the Family Like a Family, and Ownership with Respect

There is one reason that the three-circle idea is so appealing to family business owners and the professionals who work with them. It helps untie knots. When a CEO in a Sibling Partnership gets a request from his nonemployee sister, asking for a job for her troubled twenty-year-old child, the dilemma may feel unresolvable. Saying "yes" violates company policy and angers the managers and coworkers in the division that is unlucky enough to be assigned the nephew. Saying "no" disappoints a sister who is also a coowner and whose support is needed for much more important challenges facing the company.

The best chance for a win-win resolution of such dilemmas is to recognize that the conflicting alternatives come from different circles of the system, only one of which is appropriate for the particular problem. The problem is in the family circle: a drifting, unemployed nephew and a single-parent sister who is worried about him. The proposed solution is in the business circle: a job for which the candidate is not qualified and which may have a negative impact on the company's performance. In the actual case from which this example was taken, the CEO realized that the appropriate response to a family need is through the family. The sister objected at first, but he held firm that a job in the company was the easy, but wrong, solution. Acting like a brother, not a CEO, he talked with his sister about her concerns, spent some weekend time with his nephew, discovered that the problems were more serious than his sister had realized, and helped the young man get the professional help he needed.

Not all such situations work out. And some problems actually do exist in two or three circles at the same time. But even in those cases, sorting out the *parts* of the issue that come from ownership, business, or family can be the first step toward action. We use the perspective of this model to try to see beneath individual behavior and personality, into the deep structure of the family business system. This puts people's actions into context. We have found that, as a result, our own understanding of what is happening and why has been greatly enhanced—and this is the kind of understanding that can be shared with the family members themselves.

As for all basic lessons, however, this one has its limits. The value of separating the circles is greatest for those who are immersed in the complexities of a dilemma and need help in sorting out all the contributing factors. But it is equally important to remember that focusing on one subsystem at a time is just a diagnostic aid; in the end, this is a model of an integrated, multidimensional system. The complications of family businesses and their unique strengths are two sides of the same coin. You cannot successfully resolve problems in family businesses by deciding to look only at the business, or the family, or the shareholders. Perhaps the fuller version of this lesson is: Treat the business like a *family* business, owned and run by people who are much more than business associates to each other; treat the family like a *business* family, involving relatives who have chosen to bring their careers and financial lives into the family domain; and treat owners *with the respect they have earned* by investing not just their assets but their personal identity and the future of their children in the success of the enterprise.

One of the oldest stories in the field still speaks eloquently to families about the need to attend to both the whole and the parts of family businesses. It concerns a remarkably successful family business in the eastern United States, run by a dynamic, visionary founder. The business had grown to include several large stores, which had received national acclaim for their profitability, customer service, and innovative management. The founder had three sons working with him in the business: two who were conscientious and competent, and the youngest, who was charismatic and affable, but who had trouble dedicating himself to steady work. When he was around, he was everybody's favorite guy, but he wasn't around very often.

When the father finally discovered the poor work record of his youngest son, he was at first ambivalent about how to respond. The nonfamily supervisor was clear that, if the young man were not the owner's son, he would have been fired months earlier. But the father also knew that he had not been on top of the situation and that his increasingly busy schedule meant that he had not spent nearly as much time with his youngest son as he had with the older two. In the end, the father asked his son to join him for an important conversation, which (as the story is always told) took place in the jacuzzi at the father's home. The son was very excited, expecting that this was finally the day when he would be promoted to the same level as his brothers and take his place as one of the family leaders.

The father began by saying that owning a family business meant that he had to wear many different hats. "Let me start by putting on my CEO hat," he said. "Sir, your supervisor has told me about your unsatisfactory performance over the past year, despite his warnings. I'm sorry, but you're fired." The young man was stunned, and nearly slipped below the water level. His father said, "Wait. Now I have to put on my father hat." After a brief pause, he continued in his most sympathetic voice, "Son, I'm so sorry to hear that you just lost your job. What can I do to help?"

As the story concludes, both men were able to talk as father and son in a way that they had not for several years. The son acknowledged that he wanted to be successful like his brothers but did not know how, and that he felt that he needed more of the kind of mentoring that his older siblings had received. Together they worked out a plan for the son to return to school for an MBA. After graduating, he worked in another company for several years, accumulating some great experience and an impressive résumé. In the end he did return to the family company as a successful member of the Sibling Partnership. The father concluded, "I didn't understand why at the time, but something told me I had to respond to my son in two ways, as a businessman and as a father, each with a very different message." We couldn't say it any better.

Lesson 2: Keep in Mind the Inevitable, Constant Nature of Developmental Change

Like the weather in the Midwest, if you don't like the way things are in a family business at the moment, just wait—it will soon be completely different. In trying to get a handle on how family businesses work, it is very easy to become locked into a "snapshot" perspective. The dynamics are so complex that it seems a conceptual triumph to freeze all the balls in the air at the same time and really come to understand how the system works. Unfortunately, the freezing is an illusion. The system is constantly evolving in all three dimensions, even when it seems calm on the surface.

The *ownership structure* changes least often, but most dramatically. We have emphasized that it is often not the identity of individual owners that is important, but the structure of the ownership group that determines so much about the operation of the family business system. The distinctions between Controlling Owner, Sibling Partnership, and Cousin Consortium companies are not only consequences of the serendipity of pro-creation and estate plans. They are choices, made in pursuit of individual and collective dreams. Nearly all of the other dynamics we have presented in this book—among family members, managers, and shareholders—follow from the stage of ownership development, and change when the ownership structure changes.

The *family* changes continuously, as every family member ages year by year. Still, the rhythm of individual and family development also resolves into a sequence of stages that are distinctive and have meaning for business families. We have made extensive use of Levinson's adult development concepts because they seem to work so well in helping to explain this pattern of stability and transition in families. The lesson that we have learned is that it is rarely adequate to talk about "the business family" without taking into account its developmental stage. The differences be-tween Young Business Family, Entering the Business, Working Together, and Passing the Baton families have important consequences for the busi-ness as well as the family, because they influence what is on the minds of the key family members, and what is closest to their hearts.

Finally, the *business* changes erratically, along a course that is devel-opmental only in the broadest sense. In this dimension, it is not so much the sequence of stages that is critical, but the recognition that business size and complexity make a difference. For example, it is easy to see that Start-Up companies are different in some ways from all others, resulting from the level of effort (some might say obsession) that is required in the Start-Up stage. As we began to pay more attention to this dimension, we were also impressed by the subtle but powerful impact of the distinction between Expansion/Formalization companies and those that have reached Maturity. The demands of growth and the consequences of more complex structures provide both opportunities and challenges that can dominate the family and the ownership group. The leveling off of expansion can also have a profound effect on financial decisions and career opportunities for involved family members.

All things considered, this recognition of development is the core lesson of our model. We have found it a useful analytic tool. We are also realistic about its limitations, and we look forward to learning more about its applicability. After all, like an artist's sketch, a model does not capture reality, it only suggests it. Nevertheless, paying attention to stages can help increase business families' proactive control over important parts of their lives. There is one great advantage of a developmental model, if it is rooted in experience and broadly valid. Developmental perspectives give us not only an understanding of the past, but also a glimpse of the future. Once owners, or family members, or managers find their current place along a developmental dimension, they know a bit more about what lies ahead. Controlling owners can anticipate the predictable consequences of all their succession options, before the moment of transition is upon them. Executives in Expansion/Formalization companies can begin far in advance to prepare for the needs of Maturity, and put the wheels in motion for their business's renewal. And family members, who already know that their children are growing up and that they are growing older, can benefit from having some light thrown on the experiences of many other business families who have traveled the same road before. Thoughtful family business members do not need a developmental model to tell them that things are always changing but rather to illuminate the likely consequences of these inevitable changes throughout their complex, interconnected systems. As a result, they may be able to improve the chances that their family business will continue to sustain them and the people they love, from generation to generation.

References

Adams, B. 1968. *Kinship in an urban setting*. Chicago: Markham Press.

Adizes, I. 1979. Organizational passages: Diagnosing and treating lifecycle problems of organizations. *Organizational Dynamics* 8 (1): 2–25.

Aldous, J. 1978. *Family careers: Developmental change in families*. New York: John Wiley and Sons.

———. 1990. Family development and the life course: Two perspectives on family change. *Journal of Marriage and the Family* 52: 571–83.

Aldrich, H.E., and R. Waldinger. 1990. "Ethnicity and entrepreneurship." *Annual Review of Sociology* 16: 111–35.

Aristotle. 1992 edition. "The ownership of property" in *The politics*. London: Penguin: 112–19.

Arthur Andersen and Company. 1995. *American family business survey*.

Auwers, L. 1978. "Fathers, sons, and wealth in colonial Windsor, Connecticut." *Journal of Family History* 3 (2): 136–49.

Ayers, G.R. 1990. Rough family justice: Equity in family business succession planning. *Family Business Review* III (1): 3–22.

Bank, S., and M.D. Kahn. 1982. *The sibling bond*. New York: Basic Books.

Barnes, L.B. 1988. Incongruent hierarchies: Daughters and younger sons as company CEOs. *Family Business Review* I (1): 9–21.

Barnes, L.B., and S.A. Hershon. 1976. Transferring power in the family business. *Harvard Business Review* 54 (4): 105–14.

Barnett, F., and S. Barnett. 1988. *Working together: Entrepreneurial couples*. Belmont, Calif.: Ten Speed Press.

Barry, B. 1975. The development of organization structure in the family firm. *Journal of General Management* 3 (1): 42–60.

Bayus, B.L. 1994. Are product life cycles really getting shorter? *Journal of Product Innovation Management* 11 (4): 300–08.

Beckhard, R. 1969. *Organization development: Strategies and models*. Reading, Mass.: Addison-Wesley.

Beckhard, R., and W.G. Dyer, Jr. 1983. Managing continuity in the family-owned business. *Organizational Dynamics* 12 (1): 5–12.

Bedford, V.H. 1989. Sibling research in historical perspective: The discovery of a forgotten relationship. *American Behavioral Scientist* 33 (1): 6–18.

Beehr, T.A. 1986. The process of retirement: A review and recommendations for future investigation. *Personnel Psychology* 39: 31–5.

Bellman, G.M. 1990. *The consultant's calling.* San Francisco: Jossey-Bass.

Bennis, W.G., K.D. Benne, and R. Chin, eds. 1985. *The planning of change.* 4th ed. New York: Holt, Rinehart and Winston.

Bennis, W.G. and H. Shepard. 1956. A theory of group development. *Human Relations* 9: 415–37.

Benson, B., E.T. Crego, and R.H. Drucker. 1990. *Your family business: A success guide for growth and survival.* Homewood, Ill.: Dow Jones-Irwin.

Berenbeim, R.E. 1984. How business families manage the transition from owner to professional management. The Conference Board. Reprinted in 1990 in *Family Business Review* III (1): 69–110.

Berle, A.A., and G.C. Means. 1932. *The modern corporation and private property.* New York: Macmillan.

Bird, B.J. 1989. *Entrepreneurial Behavior.* Glenview, Ill.: Scott, Foresman.

Birley, S., and I.C. MacMillan, eds. 1995. *International entrepreneurship.* New York: Routledge.

Block, P. 1981. *Flawless consulting.* San Diego: University Associates.

Blood, R.O., and D.M. Wolfe. 1960. *Husbands and wives: The dynamics of married living.* Glencoe, Ill.: The Free Press.

Bolman, L., and T. Deal. 1984. *Modern approaches to understanding and managing organizations.* San Francisco: Jossey-Bass.

Bossard, J.H.S., and E.S. Boll. 1960. *The sociology of child development.* 3rd ed. New York: Harper and Row.

Bowen, D.D., and R.D. Hisrich. 1986. The female entrepreneur: A career development perspective. *Academy of Management Review* 11 (2): 393–407.

Bowen, M. (attributed). 1972. Toward the differentiation of self in one's own family. In *Family interaction,* edited by J.L. Framo. New York: Springer.

Brockhaus, R.H., Sr., and P.S. Horwitz. 1986. The psychology of the entrepreneur. In *The art and science of entrepreneurship,* edited by D. Sexton and R. Smilor. Cambridge, Mass.: Ballinger.

Brodsky, M.A. 1993. Successful female corporate managers and entrepreneurs: Similarities and differences. *Group and organization management* 18 (3): 366–78.

Brown, F.H. 1991. *Reweaving the family tapestry: A multigenerational approach to families.* New York: Norton.

Bruno, A.V., and T.T. Tyebjee. 1982. The environment for entrepreneurship. In *Encyclopedia of entrepreneurship*, edited by C.A. Kent, D.L. Sexton, and K.H. Vesper. Englewood Cliffs, N.J.: Prentice-Hall.

Calder, G.H. 1961. The peculiar problems of family businesses. *Business Horizons* 4 (3): 93–102.

Carlock, R.S. 1994. A classroom discussion with James R. Cargill. *Family Business Review* VII (3): 297–307.

Carroll, R. 1988. Siblings and the family business. In *Siblings in therapy: Life span and clinical issues*, edited by M.D. Kahn and K.G. Lewis. New York: Norton.

Carter, E., and M. McGoldrick, eds. 1988. *The changing family life cycle: A framework for family therapy*. New York: Gardner Press.

Cates, J.N., and M.B. Sussman. 1982. Family systems and inheritance. *Marriage and Family Review* 5 (3): 1–24.

Centers, R., B.H. Raven, and A. Rodrigues. 1971. Conjugal power structure: A re-examination. *American Sociological Review* 36 (2): 264–78.

Chandler, A. 1962. *Strategy and structure*. Cambridge, Mass.: MIT Press.

Chau, T.T. 1991. "Approaches to succession in East Asian business organizations." *Family Business Review* IV (4): 161–89.

Christensen, C.R., and B. Scott. 1964. Review of course activities. Working paper. IMEDE, Lausanne, Switzerland.

Churchill, N., and V. Lewis. 1983. The five stages of small business growth. *Harvard Business Review* (May–June): 30–51.

Cicirelli, V.G. 1985. Sibling relationships throughout the life cycle. In *The handbook of family psychology and therapy*, edited by L. L'Abate. Homewood, Ill.: Dorsey Press.

Clignet, R. 1995. Efficiency, reciprocity, and ascriptive equality: The three major strategies governing the selection of heirs in America. *Social Science Quarterly* 76 (2): 274–93.

Cohn, M. 1990. *Passing the torch: Transfer strategies for your family business*. Blue Ridge Summit, Penn.: Liberty Hall Press.

Collin, S., and L. Bengtsson. 1991. Diversification and corporate governance. Paper presented at the annual meeting of the Academy of Management, Dallas, August.

Combrinck-Graham, L. 1985. A developmental model for family systems. *Family Process* 24 (2): 139–51.

Connidis, I.A., and L.D. Campbell. 1995. Closeness, confiding, and contact among siblings in middle and late adulthood. *Journal of Family Issues* 16 (6): 722–45.

Copland, A. 1995. Deconstructing the lone genius myth: Toward a contextual view of creativity. *Journal of Humanistic Psychology* 35 (3): 69–112.

Covin, J., and D. Slevin. 1990. New venture strategic posture, structure, and performance: An industry life cycle analysis. *Journal of Business Venturing* 5: 123–35.

Cramton, C.D. 1993. Is rugged individualism the whole story? Public and private accounts of a firm's founding. *Family Business Review* VI (3): 233–61.

Cushman, J.W. 1986. "The Khaw group: Chinese business in early twentieth-century Penang." *Journal of Southeast Asian Studies* XVII (1): 58–79.

———. 1991. *Family and state: The formation of a Sino-Thai tin-mining dynasty.* Singapore: Oxford University Press.

Daily, C.M., and M.J. Dollinger. 1992. An empirical examination of ownership structure in family and professionally managed firms. *Family Business Review* V (2): 117–36.

Danco, L.A. 1975. *Beyond survival: A business owner's guide for success.* Cleveland: University Press.

Danco, L.A., and D.J. Jonovic. 1981. *Outside directors in the family-owned business.* Cleveland: University Press.

Davis, J., and R. Tagiuri. 1989. The influence of life stage on father-son work relationships in family companies. *Family Business Review* II (1): 47–74.

Deutsch, M. 1977. *The resolution of conflict: Constructive and destructive processes.* New Haven: Yale University Press.

DiMaggio, P., and W. Powell. 1983. The iron cage revisited: Institutional isomorphism and collective rationality in organizational fields. *American Sociological Review* 48: 147–60.

Dodge, H., and J. Robbins. 1992. An empirical investigation of the organizational life cycle model for small business development and survival. *Journal of Vocational Behavior* 36: 258–73.

Donckles, R., and E. Fröhlich. 1991. Are family businesses really different? European experiences from STRATOS. *Family Business Review* IV (2): 149–60.

Donnelly, R. 1964. The family business. *Harvard Business Review* 42: 93–105.

Dreux, D.R. 1990. Financing family business: Alternatives to selling out or going public. *Family Business Review* III (3): 225–43. Amended 1992, *Family Business Review* V (1): 111–12.

Dumas, C. 1989. Understanding of father-daughter and father-son dyads in family-owned businesses. *Family Business Review* II (1): 31–46.

———. 1990. Preparing the new CEO: Managing the father-daughter succession process in family businesses. *Family Business Review* III (2): 169–81.

Dunn, J., and R. Plomin. 1990. *Separate lives: Why siblings are so different.* New York: Basic Books.

Duvall, E.M. 1957. *Family development.* Chicago: J. B. Lippincott Company.

———. 1977. *Marriage and family development.* 5th ed. Philadelphia, J. B. Lippincott.

Duvall, E.M., and R.L. Hill. 1948. *Report of the committee on the dynamics of family interaction.* Washington, D.C.: National Conference on Family Life.

Dyer, W.G., Jr. 1986. *Cultural change in family firms: Anticipating and managing business and family transitions.* San Francisco: Jossey-Bass.

———. 1989. Integrating professional management into a family owned business. *Family Business Review* II (3): 221–35.

———. 1992. *The entrepreneurial experience.* San Francisco: Jossey-Bass.

Elder, G.H., Jr. 1987. Families and lives: Some developments in life-course studies. *Journal of Family History* 12 (1–3): 179–99.

Engels, F. 1942. *The origin of the family, private property, and the state (1884).* New York: International Publishers.

Engels, F., and K. Marx. 1848. *Communist Manifesto.*

Erikson, E.H. 1963. *Childhood and society.* 2nd ed. New York: Norton.

———. 1980. *Identity and the life cycle.* New York: Norton.

Flamholtz, E. 1986. *How to make the transition from an entrepreneurship to a professionally managed firm.* San Francisco: Jossey-Bass.

Francis, A. 1980. Families, firms, and finance capital: The development of U.K. industrial firms with particular reference to their ownership and control. *Sociology* 14 (1): 1–27.

Friedman, S.D. 1991. Sibling relationships and intergenerational succession in family firms. *Family Business Review* IV (1): 3–20.

Furstenberg, F.F., Jr. 1979. Recycling the family: Perspectives for researching a neglected family form. *Marriage and Family Review* 2: 12–22.

Furstenberg, F.F., Jr., and G.B. Spanier. 1984. *Recycling the family: Remarriage after divorce.* Beverly Hills: Sage.

Gallo, M.A., and J. Sveen. 1991. Internationalizing the family business: Facilitating and restraining factors. *Family Business Review* IV (2): 181–90.

Gersick, C. 1988. Time and transition in work teams: Toward a new model of group development. *Academy of Management Journal* 31 (1): 9–41.

———. 1991. Revolutionary change theories: A multilevel exploration of the punctuated equilibrium paradigm. *Academy of Management Review* 16 (1): 10–36.

Gersick, K. 1992. Ethnicity and organizational forms: An interview with William Ouchi. *Family Business Review* V (4): 417–36.

———. 1996. Equal isn't always fair. *Family Business* 7 (2): 44–9.

Gibbon, A., and P. Hadekel. 1990. *Steinberg: The breakup of a family empire.* Toronto: Macmillan of Canada.

Gilligan, C. 1982. *In a different voice.* Cambridge, Mass.: Harvard University Press.

Gillis-Donovan, J., and C. Moynihan-Bradt. 1990. The power of invisible women in the family business. *Family Business Review* III (2): 153–67.

Glick, P.C. 1947. The family cycle. *American Sociological Review* 12: 164–74.

———. 1955. The life cycle of the family. *Marriage and Family Living* V: 3–9.

———. 1977. Updating the family life cycle. *Journal of Marriage and the Family* 39: 5–13.

Gould, R. 1978. *Transformations: Growth and change in adult life.* New York: Simon and Schuster.

Greenhaus, J. 1987. *Career management.* Hinsdale, Ill.: The Dryden Press.

Greiner, L. 1972. Evolution and revolution as organizations grow. *Harvard Business Review* (July–August): 37–46.

Handler, W.C. 1994. Succession in family business: A review of the research. *Family Business Review* VII (2): 133–74.

Handler, W.C., and K.C. Kram. 1988. Succession in family firms: The problem of resistance. *Family Business Review* I (4): 361–81.

Hannan, M.T., and J. Freeman. 1977. The population ecology of organizations. *American Journal of Sociology* 82: 929–64.

Hareven, T.K. 1978. *Transitions: The family and the life course in historical perspective.* New York: Academic Press.

Harris, D., J.I. Martinez, and J.L. Ward. 1994. Is strategy different for the family-owned business? *Family Business Review* VII (2): 159–74.

Harvey, M., and R.G. Evans. 1994. Family business and multiple levels of conflict. *Family Business Review* VII (4): 331–48.

———. 1995. Forgotten sources of capital for the family-owned business. *Family Business Review* VIII (3): 159–76.

Havighurst, R.J. 1966. *Developmental tasks and education.* New York: David McKay.

Heer, D.M. 1963. The measurement and bases of family power: An overview. *Marriage and Family Living,* 25: 133–39.

Hetherington, E.M., D. Reiss, and R. Plomin, eds. 1994. *Separate social worlds of siblings: The impact of nonshared environment on development.* Hillsdale, N.J.: Lawrence Erlbaum.

Hilburt-Davis, J., and P. Senturia. 1995. Using the process/content framework: Guidelines for the content expert. *Family Business Review* VIII (3): 189–99.

Hines, P.M., N. Garcia-Preto, M. McGoldrick, R. Almeida, and S. Weltman.

1992. Intergenerational relationships across cultures. *Families in Society: The Journal of Contemporary Human Services* 23: 323–38.

Hofferth, S.L. 1985. Updating children's life course. *Journal of Marriage and the Family* 47 (1): 93–115.

Hoffmire, J.S., J.H. Willis, and R.J. Gilbert. 1992. Practice note: Questions and answers regarding ESOPs for family businesses. *Family Business Review* V (2): 173–80.

Hollander, J.L. 1973. *Making vocational choices.* Englewood Cliffs, N.J.: Prentice-Hall.

Hollander, B.S. 1990. Hail to the chiefs. *Family Business* 1 (3): 40–3.

Hollander, B.S., and N.S. Elman. 1988. Family-owned business: An emerging field of inquiry. *Family Business Review* I (2): 145–64.

Hsu, P.S.C. 1984. The influence of family structure and values on business organizations in Oriental cultures: A comparison of China and Japan. In *Proceedings of the Academy of International Business*, June, 754–68.

Hunt, L.A. 1992. *The family romance of the French Revolution.* Berkeley: University of California Press.

Jaffe, D. 1990. *Working with the ones you love: Conflict resolution and problem-solving strategies for a successful family business.* Berkeley: Conari Press.

Johnson, S.C. 1988. *The essence of a family business.* Indianapolis: Curtis.

———. 1990. Why we'll never go public. *Family Business* 1 (4): 16–21.

Jonovic, D.J. 1989. Outside review in a wider context: An alternative to the classic board. *Family Business Review* II (2): 125–40.

Judge, D.S. 1995. American legacies and the variable life histories of women and men. *Human Nature* 6 (4): 291–323.

Kadis, L.B., and R. McClendon. 1991. A relationship perspective on the couple-owned business. *Family Business Review* IV (4): 413–24.

Kanter, R.M. 1983. *The change masters.* New York: Simon and Schuster.

Kasl, S.V. 1980. The impact of retirement. In *Current concerns in occupational stress,* edited by C.L. Cooper and R. Payne. New York: John Wiley and Sons.

Katz, D., and R.L. Kahn. 1978. *The social psychology of organizations.* New York: John Wiley and Sons.

Kaye, K. 1985. Toward a developmental psychology of the family. In *Handbook of family psychology and therapy,* edited by L. L'Abate. Volume I. Homewood, Ill.: Dorsey.

———. 1991. Penetrating the cycle of sustained conflict. *Family Business Review* IV (1): 21–44.

Kepner, E. 1983. The family and the firm: A coevolutionary perspective. *Organizational Dynamics* 12 (1): 57–70.

Kets de Vries, M. 1985. The dark side of entrepreneurship. *Harvard Business Review* 63 (6): 160–67.

Kimberly, J. 1979. Issues in the creation of organizations: Initiation, innovation and institutionalization. *Academy of Management Journal* 22 (3): 437–57.

Kimberly, J., R.H. Miles, and Associates. 1980. *The organizational lifecycle*. San Francisco: Jossey-Bass.

Kotter, J., V. Faux, and C. McArthur. 1978. *Self-assessment and career development*. Englewood Cliffs, N.J.: Prentice-Hall.

Lamb, M., and B. Sutton-Smith, eds. 1982. *Sibling relationships: Their nature and significance across the life span*. Hillsdale, N.J.: Lawrence Erlbaum.

Lane, S.H. 1989. An organizational development / team-building approach to consultation with family businesses. *Family Business Review* II (1): 5–16.

Lank, A.G. 1991. Challenging times for European family enterprises. *Family Business Review* IV (2): 121–25.

Lansberg, I. 1983. Managing human resources in family firms: The problem of institutional overlap. *Organizational Dynamics* 12 (1): 39–46.

———. 1985. Family firms that survived their founders. Paper presented at the annual meeting of the Academy of Management, San Diego.

———. 1988. The succession conspiracy. *Family Business Review* I (2): 119–43.

———. 1991. On retirement: A conversation with Daniel Levinson. *Family Business Review* IV (1): 59–73.

———. 1994. A lesson in humility from the Greek gods. *Family Business* V (1): 9–10.

———. Forthcoming. *Succession and continuity in family firms*. Boston: Harvard Business School Press.

Lansberg, I., and E. Perrow. 1990. Understanding and working with leading family businesses in Latin America. *Family Business Review* III (3): 127–48.

Larner, R.J. 1966. Ownership and control in the largest non-financial corporations, 1929 and 1963. *American Economics Review* 56: 777–87.

LeMasters, E.E. 1957. Parenthood as crisis. *Marriage and Family Living* 19: 352–55.

Levi, L.D., H. Stierlin, and R.J. Savard. 1972. Fathers and sons: The interlocking crises of integrity and identity. *Psychiatry* 35 (1): 48–56.

Levine, J.H. 1972. The sphere of influence. *American Sociological Review* 37: 14–27.

Levinson, D.J. 1978. *Seasons of a man's life*. New York: Basic Books.

———. 1986. A conception of adult development. *American Psychologist* 41 (1): 3–13.

———. 1996. *Seasons of a woman's life*. New York: Knopf.

Levinson, D.J., and W. Gooden. 1985. The life cycle. In *Comprehensive textbook of psychiatry,* 4th ed., edited by H.I. Kaplan and B.J. Sadock. Baltimore: Williams and Wilkins.

Levinson, H. 1971. Conflicts that plague family business. *Harvard Business Review* (March–April): 90–8.

Lewin, K. 1951. Problems of research in social psychology (1943–44). In *Field theory in social science,* edited by D. Cartwright. New York: Harper and Row.

Lippitt, G.L., and W.H. Schmidt. 1967. Crises in a developing organization. *Harvard Business Review* (November–December): 102–12.

Loscocco, K.A., and K.T. Leicht. 1993. Gender, work-family linkages, and economic success among small business owners. *Journal of Marriage and the Family* 55 (4): 875–87.

McCollom, M. 1990. Problems and prospects in clinical research on family firms. *Family Business Review* III (3): 245–62.

———. 1992. The ownership trust and succession paralysis in the family business. *Family Business Review* V (2): 145–60.

———. 1995. Reevaluating group development: A critique of the familiar models. In *Groups in context: A new perspective on group dynamics,* edited by J. Gillette and M. McCollom. Lanham, Md.: University Press of America.

McGivern, C. 1989. The dynamics of management succession: A model of chief executive succession in the small family firm. *Family Business Review* II (3): 401–11.

McGoldrick, M., and R. Gerson. 1985. *Genograms in family assessment.* New York: Norton.

McGoldrick, M., and J.G. Troast, Jr. 1993. Ethnicity, families, and family business: Implications for practitioners. *Family Business Review* VI (3): 283–300.

Mangelsdorf, M.E. 1994. Start-up funding: Consider the sources. *Inc.* 16 (8): 32.

Marcus, G.E. 1980. Law in the development of dynastic families among American business elites: The domestication of capital and the capitalization of family. *Law and Society Review* 14 (4): 859–903.

Marshack, K.J. 1993. Copreneurial couples: A literature review on boundaries and transactions among copreneurs. *Family Business Review* VI (4): 355–69.

Massachusetts Mutual Life Insurance Company. 1994. *1994 Research findings: A telephone survey of 1002 family business owners.*

Mattessich, P., and R. Hill. 1987. Life cycle and family development. In *Handbook of marriage and the family,* edited by M.B. Sussman and S.K. Steinmetz. New York: Plenum.

Matthews, S.H., P.J. Delaney, and M.E. Adamek. 1989. Male kinship ties: Bonds between adult brothers. *American Behavioral Scientist* 33 (1): 58–69.

Menchik, P.L. 1980. Primogeniture, equal sharing, and the U.S. distribution of wealth. *The Quarterly Journal of Economics* XCIV (2): 299–316.

Millar, F.E., and L.E. Rogers. 1988. Power dynamics in marital relationships. In *Perspectives on marital interaction*, edited by P. Noller and M.A. Fitzpatrick. Philadelphia: Multilingual Matters Ltd.

Miller, D., and P.H. Friesen. 1984. A longitudinal study of the corporate lifecycle. *Management Science* 30 (1): 1161–1183.

Mintzberg, H., and J. Waters. 1982. Tracking strategy in an entrepreneurial firm. *Academy of Management Journal* 25 (3): 465–99.

Minuchin, S. 1974. *Families and family therapy.* Cambridge, Mass.: Harvard University Press.

Minuchin, S., B. Montalvo, B.G. Guerney, Jr., B.L. Rosman, and F. Schumer. 1967. *Families of the slums.* New York: Basic Books.

Mitchell, B.A. 1994. Family structures and leaving the nest: A social resource perspective. *Sociological Perspectives* 37 (4): 651–71.

Murdock, M., and C.W. Murdock. 1991. A legal perspective on shareholder relationships in family businesses: The scope of fiduciary duties. *Family Business Review* IV (3): 287–301.

Muson, H. 1995. How to keep the Campbell kids happy. *Family Business* 6 (1): 48–52.

Nelton, S. 1986. *In love and in business: How entrepreneurial couples are changing the rules of business and marriage.* New York: Wiley.

Nock, S.L. 1988. The family and hierarchy. *Journal of Marriage and the Family* 50 (November): 957–66.

Olson, P.D. 1987. Entrepreneurship and management. *Journal of Small Business Management* 25 (3): 7–12.

O'Rand, A.M., and M.L. Krecker. 1990. Concepts of the life cycle: Their history, meanings, and uses in the social sciences. *Annual Review of Sociology* 16: 241–62.

Osherson, S. 1980. *Holding on or letting go: Men and career change at midlife.* New York: Free Press.

Panglaykim, J., and I. Palmer. 1970. Study of entrepreneurship in developing countries: The development of one Chinese concern in Indonesia. *Journal of Southeast Asian Studies* I (1): 85–95.

Pfeffer, J., and G.R. Salancik. 1978. *The external control of organizations.* New York: Harper and Row.

Piaget, J. 1963. *The origins of intelligence in children.* New York: Norton.

Plato. 1970 edition. *The laws,* edited by T.J. Saunders. London: Penguin.

———. 1987 edition. *The republic,* edited by H. Lee. New York: Penguin.

Ponthieu, L.D., and H.C. Caudill. 1993. Who's the boss? Responsibility and decision making in copreneurial ventures. *Family Business Review* VI (1): 3–17.

Pope Leo XIII. 1940. Rerum novarum (encyclical on the condition of the workingmen: May 15, 1891). In *Social wellsprings: Fourteen epochal documents by Pope Leo XIII,* edited by J. Husslein. Milwaukee: Bruce Publishing Company.

Poza, E.J. 1989. *Smart growth: Critical choices for business continuity and prosperity.* San Francisco: Jossey-Bass.

Reich, R.B. 1987. Entrepreneurship reconsidered: The team as hero. *Harvard Business Review* (May–June): 77–83.

Rosenberg, G.S., and D.F. Anspach. 1973. Sibling solidarity in the working class. *Journal of Marriage and the Family* 35: 108–13.

Saluter, A.F. 1994. *Marital status and living arrangements: March 1994.* U.S. Department of Commerce, Bureau of the Census, Washington, D.C.

Schachter, F.F. 1982. Sibling deidentification and split-parent identification: A family tetrad. In *Sibling relationships: Their nature and significance across the lifespan,* edited by M.E. Lamb and B. Sutton-Smith. Hillsdale, N.J.: Lawrence Erlbaum.

Schein, E.H. 1983. The role of the founder in creating organizational culture. *Organizational Dynamics* 12 (1): 13–28.

———. 1988. *Process consultation: Its role in organizational development.* Reading, Mass.: Addison-Wesley.

———. 1992. *Organizational culture and leadership.* San Francisco: Jossey-Bass.

Schwartz, M.A., and L.B. Barnes. 1991. Outside boards and family business: Another look. *Family Business Review* IV (3): 269–85.

Scott, M., and R. Bruce. 1987. Five stages of growth in small business. *Long-Range Planning* 20 (3): 45–52.

Scott, W.R. 1992. *Organizations: Rational, natural, and open systems.* 3rd ed. Englewood Cliffs, N.J.: Prentice-Hall.

Sharfman, M.P., B. Gray, and A. Yan. 1991. The context of interorganizational collaboration in the garment industry: An institutional perspective. *Journal of Applied Behavioral Science* 27 (2): 181–208.

Shapero, A., and L. Sokol. 1982. The social dimensions of entrepreneurship. In *Encyclopedia of entrepreneurship,* edited by C.A. Kent, D.L. Sexton, and K.H. Vesper. Englewood Cliffs, N.J.: Prentice-Hall.

Simonton, D.K. 1983. Intergenerational transfer of individual differences in hereditary monarchs: Genetic, role-modeling, cohort, or sociocultural effects? *Journal of Personality and Social Psychology* 44 (2): 354–64.

Sonnenfeld, J.A. 1988. *The hero's farewell: What happens when CEOs retire.* New York: Oxford University Press.

Sonnenfeld, J.A., and P.L. Spence. 1989. The parting patriarch of a family firm. *Family Business Review* II (4): 355–75.

Sorokin, P.A., C.C. Zimmerman, and C.J. Galpin. 1931. *A systematic source book in rural sociology, II.* Minneapolis: University of Minnesota Press.

Spanier, G.G., and P.C. Glick. 1980. The life cycle of American families: An expanded analysis. *Journal of Family History* 5: 97–111.

Steinmetz, L. 1969. Critical stages of small business growth: When they occur and how to survive them. *Business Horizons* (February): 29.

Stevenson, H.H., and W.A. Sahlman. 1987. Entrepreneurship: A process, not a person. Working paper, Harvard Business School, Cambridge, Mass.

Stevenson, H.H., M.J. Roberts, and H.I. Grousbeck. 1994. *New business ventures and the entrepreneur.* 4th ed. Burr Ridge, Ill.: Irwin.

Stevenson, L.A. 1986. Against all odds: The entrepreneurship of women. *Journal of Small Business Management* 24: 30–6.

Swartz, J. 1996. Toward a model of justice in ownership succession: An exploratory study of the intergenerational transfer of family business ownership. Ph.D. diss., California School of Professional Psychology, Los Angeles.

Swartz, S. 1989. The challenges of multidisciplinary consulting to family-owned businesses. *Family Business Review* II (4): 329–39.

Tagiuri, R., and J.A. Davis. 1982. Bivalent attributes of the family firm. Working paper, Harvard Business School, Cambridge, Mass. Reprinted 1996, *Family Business Review* IX (2):199–208.

Thornton, A., T.L. Orbuch, and W.G. Axinn. 1995. Parent-child relationships during the transition to adulthood. *Journal of Family Issues* 16 (5): 538–64.

Thornton, A., L. Young-De Marco, and F. Goldscheider. 1993. Leaving the parental nest: The experience of a young White cohort in the 1980s. *Journal of Marriage and the Family* 55: 216–29.

Timmons, J.A. 1989. *The entrepreneurial mind.* Andover, Mass.: Brick House Publishing.

———. 1994. *New venture creation.* 4th ed. Burr Ridge, Ill.: Irwin.

Torbert, W. 1974. Pre-bureaucratic and post-bureaucratic stages of organization development. *Interpersonal Development* 5: 1–25.

Vaillant, G. 1977. *Adaptation to life.* Boston: Little, Brown.

Vago, M. 1995. Why fish must learn to see the water they swim in. *Family Business Review* VIII (4): 313–25.

Van de Ven, A.H., and G. Walker. 1984. The dynamics of interorganizational coordination. *Administrative Science Quarterly* 29: 5598–621.

Vance, S.C. 1983. *Corporate leadership: Boards, directors, and strategy.* New York: McGraw-Hill.

Vancil, R.F. 1987. *Passing the baton: Managing the process of CEO succession.* Boston: Harvard Business School Press.

Walsh, F. 1994. Healthy family functioning: Conceptual and research developments. *Family Business Review* VII (2): 175–98.

Ward, J.L. 1987. *Keeping the family business healthy.* San Francisco: Jossey-Bass.

———. 1988a. The special role of strategic planning for family businesses. *Family Business Review* I (2): 105–17.

———. 1988b. The active board with outside directors and the family firm. *Family Business Review* I (3): 223–29.

———. 1991. *Creating effective boards for private enterprises: Meeting the challenges of continuity and competition.* San Francisco: Jossey-Bass.

Ward, J.L., and C.E. Aronoff. 1994. How family affects strategy. *Small Business Forum* (Fall): 85–90.

Weiser, J., F. Brody, and M. Quarry. 1988. Family business and employee ownership. *Family Business Review* I (1): 23–35.

Whisler, T.L. 1988. The role of the board in the threshold firm. *Family Business Review* I (3): 309–21.

Whiteside, M.F., and F.H. Brown. 1991. Drawbacks of a dual systems approach to family firms: Can we expand our thinking? *Family Business Review* IV (4): 383–95.

Wicker, A.W., and K.A. Burley. 1991. Close coupling in work-family relationships: Making and implementing decisions in a new family business and at home. *Human Relations* 44 (1): 77–92.

Wong, S. 1985. The Chinese family firm: A model. *British Journal of Sociology* 36 (1): 58–72.

Zaleznik, A., and M.F.R. Kets de Vries. 1975. *Power and the corporate mind.* Boston: Houghton Mifflin.

Zaltman, G., and R. Duncan. 1976. *Strategies for planned change.* New York: John Wiley and Sons.

Zeitlin, M. 1976. Corporate ownership and control: The large corporation and the capitalist class. *American Journal of Sociology* 79 (5): 1073–119.

Index

ABOUT THE AUTHORS

JOHN A. DAVIS is the president of the Owner Managed Business Institute in Santa Barbara. Formerly, he was a member of the faculty at the University of Southern California. Dr. Davis has organized family business executive programs at several leading business schools, and consults to many family businesses worldwide on the topics of working with relatives, strategic and succession planning, and professionalizing the family business.

Dr. Davis's research interests include family work relationships and family business governance. He is on the editorial board of *Family Business Review,* contributes to *Family Business* magazine, and is currently writing a book on the best practices of successful family companies.

KELIN E. GERSICK is a cofounder and senior partner of Lansberg, Gersick and Associates, a consulting and research firm in New Haven, Connecticut, specializing in family enterprise and family philanthropy. He has taught at Harvard and Yale, and is currently a professor of organizational psychology at the California School of Professional Psychology and a senior faculty associate of the Owner Managed Business Institute.

Dr. Gersick's research and consulting work with family firms focuses on the interplay among family dynamics and business governance and management. He has written on family business, family foundations, parenting, and adult development. He is a former co-editor-in-chief of *Family Business Review* and a contributor to *Family Business* magazine.

MARION MCCOLLOM HAMPTON is an associate professor of organizational behavior at the Boston University School of Management and a senior faculty associate at the Owner Managed Business Institute. Her research interests include organizational culture, family business, group dynamics, and intergroup relations. Dr. McCollom Hampton has published articles in a variety of journals, and is the coeditor of *Groups in Context: A New Perspective on Group Dynamics* and the coauthor of *The Physician-Manager Alliance*.

IVAN LANSBERG is an organizational psychologist in New Haven, Connecticut, and a cofounder and senior partner of Lansberg, Gersick and Associates. He is also a senior faculty associate at the Owner Managed Business Institute. Dr. Lansberg was a member of the organizational psychology faculty at the Yale School of Organization and Management for seven years, and a research fellow at Yale's Institute for Social and Policy Studies. Prior to his affiliation with Yale, he taught at the Columbia University Graduate School of Business.

Dr. Lansberg has lectured at many international family business centers. He is the founder and former editor-in-chief of *Family Business Review* and the author of *Succession and Continuity in Family Firms*, forthcoming from HBS Press. Currently, he writes a column for *Family Business* magazine and conducts research in such areas as leadership succession and family business continuity.